B67 PHI

QMW

D0551850

Philosophy and the Natural Environment

ROYAL INSTITUTE OF PHILOSOPHY SUPPLEMENT: 36

WITHDRAWN
FROM STOCK
QMUL LIBRARY

DATE DUE FOR RETURN

NEW ACCESSION

CANCELLED

22 NOV 1994 10AM

12 DEC 1994

23 MAR 1995

21 JAN 2000

16 JAN 2002

Published by the Press Syndicate of the University of Cambridge
The Pitt Building, Trumpington Street, Cambridge, CB2 1RP
40 West 20th Street, New York, NY 10011-4211, USA
10 Stamford Road, Oakleigh, Melbourne 3166, Australia

© The Royal Institute of Philosophy and the contributors 1994

*A catalogue record for this book is available
from the British Library*

Library of Congress Cataloguing in Publication Data

Philosophy and the natural environment/edited by Robin Attfield and
   Andrew Belsey
      p. cm.—(Royal Institute of Philosophy supplement: 36)
      "Deriving from the Royal Institute of Philosophy conference,
   1993."
      Includes bibliographical references and index.
      ISBN 0–521–46903–1 (pbk.)
      1. Environmental ethics— Congresses. 2. Philosophy of nature—
   Congresses. I. Attfield, Robin. II. Belsey, Andrew.
   III. Series
   GE42.P48 1994
   179'.1—dc20   94–10025
                                                                CIP

ISBN 0–521–46903–1 (paperback)

Origination by Michael Heath Ltd, Reigate, Surrey
Printed in Great Britain by the University Press, Cambridge

Contents

Contents

QMW LIBRARY
(MILE END)

Preface

The Royal Institute of Philosophy Conference, on 'Philosophy and the Natural Environment', was held at the University of Wales in Cardiff from 20 to 22 July 1993. We are grateful to the Royal Institute of Philosophy for allowing us the privilege of organising its Conference, which attracted 150 participants, 30 from outside the United Kingdom. The success of the Conference was due in no small part to the co-operative efforts of many individuals and organisations, and we wish to place on record our thanks to the officers of the Royal Institute of Philosophy, for their advice; the City of Cardiff, for hosting a reception in Cardiff Castle; the British Council, for entertaining the overseas participants; the staff of the University of Wales, Cardiff, especially the Conference Office, for the professionalism of their organisation; our colleagues and students in Philosophy, for their supererogatory assistance; the speakers, for agreeing to write papers and for writing them on time; and all the participants, for providing the stimulating discussions, both formal and informal, without which there would have been no Conference.

Frederick Ferré was prevented by family circumstances from attending the Conference and reading his paper in person, but he kindly contributed to the discussion by sending an overview of the other papers, which is reprinted here, in addition to his main paper. One of the papers read at the Conference, Ruth Chadwick's 'Global Bioethics: Geneticism, Environmentalism and Population', is not printed here, at Professor Chadwick's request.

In preparing this volume for publication we are grateful to the contributors, who revised their papers speedily and then responded tolerantly to all sorts of demands and queries from the Editors. We must also express very many thanks to Tricia Latham and Elisabeth Palser for preparing much of the manuscript, and to our research assistants Ginny Philp and Robin Wackerbarth for checking it. Without them it would not have been possible to publish the Conference papers in this volume. Needless to say, any editing faults it has are the responsibility of the editors.

Robin Attfield and Andrew Belsey
Cardiff, January 1994

Notes on Contributors

Robin Attfield is Professor of Philosophy at the University of Wales, Cardiff

Andrew Belsey is Lecturer in Philosophy at the University of Wales, Cardiff

Stephen Clark is Professor of Philosophy at the University of Liverpool and Joint Editor of the *Journal of Applied Philosophy*

Roger Crisp is Fellow of St Anne's College, Oxford

Nigel Dower is Senior Lecturer in Philosophy and in Politics and International Relations, and Director of the Centre for Philosophy, Technology and Society, University of Aberdeen

Robert Elliot is Senior Lecturer in Philosophy, University of New England, Armidale, NSW

Frederick Ferré is Research Professor of Philosophy at the University of Georgia and Editor of *Research in Philosophy and Technology*

Tim Hayward is Lecturer in Philosophy at the University of Glamorgan

Alan Holland is Lecturer in Philosophy at the University of Lancaster and Editor of *Environmental Values*

Dale Jamieson is Professor of Philosophy at the University of Colorado at Boulder

Keekok Lee is Senior Lecturer in Philosophy and Director of the Centre for Environmental Ethics, University of Manchester

Peter List is Professor of Philosophy at Oregon State University, Corvallis

Ruth McNally is a researcher at the University of the West of England, Bristol, and a Director of Bio-Information (International) Ltd

Mary Midgley is a writer and broadcaster on philosophical issues, and a former Senior Lecturer in Philosophy at the University of Newcastle upon Tyne

Holmes Rolston III is Professor of Philosophy, Colorado State University, Fort Collins, and President of the International Society for Environmental Ethics

Peter Wheale is Principal Lecturer at the European Business School, and a Director of Bio-Information (International) Ltd

Introduction

ROBIN ATTFIELD AND ANDREW BELSEY

The philosophy of nature is at least as old as the presocratics, but has undergone comparative neglect in philosophical circles this century until recently, at least in English-speaking lands. The philosophy of science concentrates on scientific concepts and methods and the interpretation of scientific theories, rather than on the concept of nature itself, while, with significant exceptions (e.g., Hepburn, 1984), aesthetics focuses on the experience of art rather than on that of nature. Meanwhile moral, political and social philosophy has focused on the social environment, but the natural environment has often been lost to view. Indeed it has been argued, with some cogency, that mainstream Western metaphysics, epistemology and ethics have historically been inhospitable to conservation, to environmentalism and to their values (see Hargrove, 1989; Attfield, 1994a).

All this, however, is beginning to change, in Britain as well as overseas. Environmental ethicists have for some years now been arguing for revisions of ethical theory; the Society for Applied Philosophy held its 1986 Annual Conference on environmental and animal welfare themes; and a series of public seminars of that Society on environmental values continues to be held at the University of Lancaster, where the journal *Environmental Values* is also edited. Yet the 1993 Cardiff Conference of the Royal Institute of Philosophy was the first large philosophical gathering in Britain held to consider the themes of nature, the natural environment, and related issues of value, ethics and society. In view of the greater impact of environmental philosophy in recent years in the USA and Australia, it was fitting that several of the speakers came from those countries, including the keynote speaker (and President of the International Society for Environmental Ethics), Holmes Rolston III.

Rolston, already well-known for his championing of objective value in the natural world, fascinated his audience with an audio-visual presentation which argued for the presence of valuing and thus of value throughout the organic realm. This undertaking was accomplished (as in Rolston's paper here) by presenting an opposing point of view, and progressively undermining it. Rolston also well defended (and here defends) viewing ecosystems as real entities and not just epiphenomenal aggregates, in that they shape the existence and the behaviour of their members; more precariously he ascribes to them and to the Earth a distinctive kind of value, systemic value, which is neither intrinsic nor instrumental, and which makes these other kinds of value possible. His main conclusion, however, is that there can be value without subjective valuers, and that such value is possessed by all organic beings, processes and systems.

Some of Rolston's questioners clearly considered his account of valuing an over-extended and attenuated one, and suggested that the intrinsic value of natural creatures is not dependent on activities of valuation or self-defence or value-generation on their part; while others such as Frederick Ferré (see his 'Highlights and Connections') were not convinced that species and ecosystems are units either of valuation or of independent value. Even if natural selection is more careful with species than with individual organisms, the reply could be made to Rolston that this does not imply that species themselves have intrinsic value, or that a 'biocentrism that focuses on individuals' (p. 22) is mistaken. But this would in no way undermine the possibility of value without subjective valuers, a theme debated further by Attfield, Elliot and Ferré.

Robert Elliot defends a subjectivist view of meta-ethics as adequate to underpin a normative belief in the intrinsic value of nature. Further, the properties which confer this value are nature's otherness, its aesthetic value, and its evolutionary, non-purposive origins. In meta-ethics, Elliot attempts to disabuse objectivists of the belief that subjectivism makes values contingent on the existence and views of human valuers; here he shows that actual valuations made in our world could apply to worlds empty of valuers, but does not show how there could be values even if no valuers had ever existed or valued.

In his conclusion he reports himself as having suggested that 'non-anthropocentric meta-ethics . . . is not possible' (p. 42); but this is a stronger conclusion than any for which a case is presented. Salient arguments are earlier furnished for the consistency of his account of value-adding properties with certain claims of restoration ecologists; further arguments, however, would be needed to convince those reluctant to grant that aesthetic value is a kind of intrinsic value, or that the non-purposive is valuable as such, or indeed intrinsically superior to the purposive.

Robin Attfield also discusses the metaphysics and ethics of ecological restoration, rejecting the view of Eric Katz that restorations are artefacts and that restoring nature is impossible, and maintaining that an area with the same flourishing creatures has the same intrinsic (as opposed to aesthetic) value whatever its origins. If so, the intrinsic value of a wilderness does not principally consist in its wildness. The possibility of enhancing an area's value could imply an obligation to do so, but only when ecosystems are sufficiently understood to facilitate success.

Commenting on the recent Rolston/Callicott debate about wilderness, Attfield grants that a pure wilderness cannot be managed, but argues that rehabilitating a wilderness (e.g., through returning lost species) is sometimes desirable, and at the same time that nature can retain its value when transplanted into cultural settings such as parks, gardens and city streets. Against Rolston he argues that sustainable development need not be an anthropocentric policy and with Callicott that it can be ecologically benign, as well as satisfying human needs; thus 'there is in general a stronger obligation to support and implement sustainable development than there is to enhance the value of natural areas' (p. 55). Humanity has the role of making nature sustainably habitable, as well as of rehabilitating it. To this metaphysical conclusion, Attfield adds his support for a Rolston-like meta-ethics, as defended elsewhere (and in Rolston's paper). Attfield's belief in the possibility of value in the absence 'of all valuers actual and possible' was to provoke astonished dissent from Ferré (p. 231).

Meanwhile Ferré's main paper seeks to reconcile the objections to individualism of the Organicism which he finds in Deep Ecology with the Personalism which he finds Deep Ecologists to presuppose despite themselves. To accomplish this, he advocates the rejection of All-or-Nothing attitudes and the adoption of Personalistic Organicism, incorporating a Whiteheadian value-theory recognizing degrees of value, plus a matching ontology; in support, he argues for degrees of subjectivity throughout the organic realm, and for the heightened presence of key characteristics of non-human organisms in the lives of persons.

Personalistic Organicism provides a way out of otherwise intractable problems such as the mind-body relation and the nature of the value-theories of deep ecologists; and recognizes 'perspectival anthropocentrism', since 'we have no choice but to think as humans'. Relatedly Ferré proceeds to assert an account of intrinsic value which ties it conceptually to experiencing valuers; most aspects of Personalistic Organicism, however, seem not to depend on acceptance of this account.

In the cause of elucidating what makes one world better than another, Roger Crisp makes some valuable distinctions among goods, incorporating a sense of intrinsic value which makes a thing's intrinsic value independent of external contingencies (including the enjoyment of experiencing subjects). What is less clear is that beauty, his example of this, is intrinsically valuable, i.e., valuable even if never appreciated, as well as being good as an end and good objectively; even if beauty lacked intrinsic value, it could still be a value which supplies some of the point of the development of people's faculties for aesthetic appreciation. For Crisp, moral values too, such as justice, have a value independent of their impact on individual welfare; but the thought-experiment introduced to attest this (p. 82) proved controversial at the Conference.

While rejecting a general obligation to maximise value, Crisp recognizes that maximising value always supplies a reason for action, except where nothing could motivate this. Crisp now adduces a further thought-experiment to show that in the present state of the world aesthetic value (and therewith, claims Crisp, the philosophical stance of deep ecology) is standardly trumped by welfare values, since the relief of suffering supplies a stronger reason, though in fact the links between the projects of development and of environmental conservation mean that both sets of values can usually be promoted simultaneously. He adds that such efforts have a self-interested pay-off, and thus his motivation condition is satisfied.

Horrified at technological proposals for 'terraforming' Mars (and making it habitable like Earth), Keekok Lee constructs a quite different concept of intrinsic value applicable to abiotic nature. Lee's intrinsic value applies to whatever satisfies the No-Teleology Thesis (existing for itself), the Autonomy Thesis (not depending on humanity for origination or survival) and the Asymmetry Thesis (depended on by humanity but independent of it). Since Mars satisfies these theses, it befits us to treat it with awe and humility, and as bearing intrinsic value.

Lee recognizes that she is committed to there being value in 'the existence of any material entity which is independent of human design and effort' (p. 99). (If purists resist calling this 'intrinsic value' it can be called 'human-independent value' instead.) But she replies that the contrary view stems from strong anthropocentrism, the stance which makes humans both the source and the locus of value, or else from 'biocentric chauvinism', for which abiotic nature is valueless unless it has value for biotic nature, and which defines value in terms of living interests. To avoid such arbitrariness we should respect intrinsic value in Lee's sense, and reject the terraforming of Mars. Doubts could be felt, however, about whether this rejection should stand if considerable value (in the ordinary, reason-giving, sense, relating perhaps to the flourishing of life) were to conflict with intrinsic values (in Lee's sense).

Anthropocentrism is also targeted by Mary Midgley, who, however, acknowledges that people have no choice but to be specially interested in themselves and those close to them (Ferré's perspectival anthropocentrism). Midgley's criticism is focused on the kind of Enlightenment belief in human centrality expressed in Kant's view of man as 'titular lord of nature' and nature's 'ultimate end', and, despite the erosion of this belief on the part of numerous intellectual developments of the last two hundred years, on the Strong Anthropic Principle that 'The Universe must have those properties which allow life to develop within it at some stage in its history' (p. 107).

This principle makes the central business of the universe the production of man the physicist, whose observation of quantum events makes the universe at last fully and properly real (p. 108); but this, Midgley argues, is not science, but a piece of wild metaphysics, motivated by fear of cosmic insignificance. While everyone needs a background framework giving life a meaning, there is no need for the kind of anthropocentrism which amounts to 'human chauvinism' or 'exclusive humanism', particularly when (as Crisp also maintained) the measures needed to save humanity and to save the rest of the biosphere are, for practical purposes, the same. Humanism of the exclusive kind (effectively the new religion of 'anthropolatry') is indefensible; and philosophers need to work hard to forge and explain less egoistic and less individualistic alternatives.

Stephen Clark suggests that only religious commitment, transcending the petty limits of our time and space, can allow us to tackle our social and environmental problems. Religion is often blamed for the crisis, but the supposed 'Christian axiom' of Lynn White that 'nature has no reason for existence save to serve man' bears little relation to the Bible or the Koran, or again to medieval Christianity. Nor should blame be directed at the Enlightenment, with its deprecation of waste and concern for posterity, or even at Descartes, who actually attacked individualism; the problems stem at least as much from 'the ordinary need of people to make a better life' (p. 119).

Nor do we need a *new* religion, Clark continues. Romantic myths of a lost world of harmony with nature do not solve ecological needs, any more than an objectivism which defines the real world as what does not matter. Rather we need a real appreciation of the world's Otherness and our dependence on it, as in sacramental theism, as opposed to folk Christianity. Sacramental theism teaches that we do not own the world, but enjoy its fruits as a gift on condition of leaving as good for others, and also that the one true religion is to do justice and love mercy and walk humbly with the one God. This 'global religion' is present alike in Judaism, Islam and Christianity; this, Clark considers, if anywhere, is where hope of confronting the crisis is to be found. (Others, however, may find hope in a Stoicism which yokes cosmic piety and Enlightenment values.)

Tim Hayward, in any case, seeks to rehabilitate Kant, with regard to the widespread charge (of John Passmore (1980), Christina Hoff (1983) and others) that he denies moral standing to non-rational beings. The charge is sometimes that Kant subscribes to the 'patient-agent parity thesis': only creatures which can do wrong can be wronged. But this charge reduces to the 'no direct duties thesis'. Where this means that Kant denies non-rational beings rights-bearing status, it is accurate but beside the point, since the critics mostly deny this too. Alternatively this could mean the denial that direct duties are owed to such beings for their own sake; that their good sometimes generates a duty to pursue that good. Some ethicists who accept this view allow that whether obligations are generated depends not just on having moral standing but also on having moral significance; but where non-rational creatures are concerned, Kant could endorse such moral standing but resist particular claims about moral significance on a basis of our lack of knowledge of the creature's good. On the same basis Kant could resist the alternative view of ethicists such as Paul Taylor that creatures with a good of their own have (equal) moral worth which entitles them (one and all) to respect. Unless Kant is wrong about knowledge, his position remains secure, and does not involve denying moral consideration.

Hayward's diagnosis of the problem concerns the issue of moral standing or considerability being conflated with other issues such as Kant's denial of rights for non-rational creatures and his not treating their good as the reason for duties in their regard. He therefore proposes a refined terminology: 'bare considerability' to mean ability to be taken into consideration, even if only instrumentally or incidentally; 'vested considerability' to mean having some specific significance; and 'moral standing' to mean capacity to bear rights. (But it could be replied to Hayward that both 'bare' and 'vested considerability', which would now apply to the instruments of moral action, would be too weak to cover beings which must morally be taken into consideration for their own sake, and 'moral standing' (Hayward's proposed sense) would be too strong for this role. So Kenneth Goodpaster's concept of moral considerability would have to be reinvented.) Finally Hayward suggests (optimistically?) that Kant is correct in his belief that the imperatives of human dignity are incompatible with inhumanity to animals and with irresponsible treatment of the environment; this may involve the kinds of anthropocentrism favoured by Midgley or Elliott, but not the 'human chauvinism' which Midgley rejects.

Nigel Dower points out that the very concept of the environment itself is worth careful attention. From David Cooper he derives the thought that the environment can be understood as a field of significance, in which a person or animal might (or might not) feel 'at home'. Yet the environment can also be a system of causes and effects, ecological as well as causal, and there must be an environment in this sense if there are fields of significance. Indeed Cooper is criticised for rubbishing talk of saving the global environment, when what is amiss is not the concept of environment embodied in such talk but (often) the implicit normative principles; and also for presupposing the very causal-system sense of 'environment' which he rejects. Dower now elaborates a whole battery of distinctions, which serve to indicate how the concepts of fields of significance and of causal systems interrelate and overlap; and proceeds to argue that there is a widespread mismatch between fields of significance (environments with which people identify) and the global environment, which is being allowed to deteriorate and to disrupt perceived environments.

For Dower, then, the challenge is to render the global environment into a field of significance, not through homogenised attitudes to the planet but through diverse adjustments in perceptions and life-styles, sufficient to allow the common environmental base to be sustained. For fields of significance can be meaningful without being good, and offer possibilities to human beings for their modification. Indeed the single concept of having an environment involves both there being a surrounding objective causal system and having a field of significant possibilities. Such is the duality of the concept of the environment that one can change one's environment either through physical modification or through changed perceptions. One's environment may also, he claims, have a moral character, something relevant to concern for the state of the objective physical environment. Thus a recognition of environments as fields of significance, far from leading us to reject the global for the local environment, can prompt a reconceptualising of concern for the shared environment and of its significance for individuals.

In 'Chaos and Order, Environment and Anarchy', Andrew Belsey first stresses the presocratic concept of cosmos, which is both an ordered and intelligible universe and a value-laden, beautiful one. Despite Plato's attempts in *Timaeus* to reintroduce the supernatural, his cosmos too is regular and free of supernatural intrusions, as indeed, according to Vlastos, must be the universe

7

which is presupposed by natural science. This cosmos is recognizably the environment, in the widest possible sense. Belsey, like Dower, here contests Cooper's rejection of any environmentalism based on a concept of the global environment. While sharing Cooper's scepticism about religious reverence, Belsey argues that Cooper's concept of environment is self-undermining and also impractical; for the problems concern the shared, global environment, and local resistance alone cannot tackle them. Nothing less than at least a planetary outlook will suffice—for these purposes or, perhaps, for giving meaning to life.

Now Plato sought to derive an ordered political philosophy from his understanding of nature; but the very imposition of order shows, as anarchists have pointed out, that it is not natural at all. Anarchists such as Herbert Read have their own account of the natural, one more congenial to ecologists, by which if everything follows its own nature, all is well, but disaster ensues if a species departs from its nature. Here there is common ground between the anarchists and the presocratics, with their understanding of nature as balance and as harmony; without any attempt to discover the 'Mind' of 'Nature', awareness of laws of nature (such as those of entropy and of evolution) and of the facts about continuing ecological disruption shows how life can be lived in accordance with nature's balance. Thus the anarchist recapitulation of presocratic cosmology can be of ecological value, even if the issue of how to relate anarchist approaches (of local autonomy and democracy) to global problems is unresolved. Solving the problems involves both transforming society and 'a proper appreciation of the cosmos'; and thus 'liberatory cosmology' (p. 167).

Alan Holland examines the viability of what he calls the 'social scientific approach' to sustainable development, i.e., the approach of David Pearce and his fellow-authors of *Blueprint for a Green Economy* (Pearce *et al.*, 1989). These authors call for capital (capital wealth or productive potential) to remain constant over time, either in the form of overall capital (including human-made capital) or of natural capital. But the first alternative (overall capital) does not debar irreversible developments, despite the authors' belief to the contrary; and the second (natural capital, the approach preferred by the authors), if interpreted as concerning constant physical stock, prohibits using non-renewable resources, and, if interpreted rather as concerning the economic value of natural assets being held constant, reintroduces technological means of raising that value, and thus licences, for example, destroying a wilderness to increase productive potential. Justifications of all this in the name of justice to future people fail to capture what environmentalists have in mind. Besides, it can be shown that several of the criteria associated with considerations internal to theories of justice (non-substitutability, uncertainty, irreversibility, resilience) do not favour preserving all natural capital.

Holland suggests that, despite their disavowals of a 'values-in-nature' view, something of this kind is to be ascribed to the authors of *Blueprint for a Green Economy* to account for their tenacious defence of natural capital. Similarly the appeal to loss aversion as a ground for protecting natural capital indicates an evaluative commitment to preference utilitarianism in general and to this particular aversion (as opposed to others) in particular: further signs of undisclosed values on their parts. After making some parallel criticisms of Bryan Norton's position, Holland suggests that what the social scientific approach omits is the importance of maintaining the integrity of ecosystems, and thus 'enough of the historically particular forms of association and their historically particular components' (p. 178).

Hence physical stock is what should be valued and preserved; indeed the claim that the actual natural world as we know it is good is eminently defensible, and no defence of the environment is secure without it. (Here, it may be remarked, is natural piety of the kind commended by Clark; yet, even if vindicated, it hardly demands the preservation of physical stock in general. 'Enough' preservation of the actual world could well be consistent with many life-enhancing uses even of non-renewable resources, even if anthropocentric *Blueprints* present inadequate values and thus inadequately grounded policies.)

Peter List draws attention to the dearth of philosophical treatments of the ethics of ecological protest. He proceeds to argue, in the light of actual cases of ecological civil disobedience in America, that standard philosophical accounts of the justification of such protests are inadequate. His first example concerns non-violent obstruction of the logging of an old-growth forest. While the protesters are seeking moral and legal recognition of non-human species and the importance of the integrity of ecosystems, accounts of justifications of civil disobedience such as that of John Rawls disallow disobedience which is not focused on the basic principles of justice as selected by rational humans in the hypothetical original position. Unlike Elliot, List does not attempt the heroic task of bringing ecological goods within Rawls's system; rather he concludes that such anthropocentric theories are fundamentally inadequate at coping with ecological values and their social implications. (This being so, nothing less than a new social and political philosophy will be needed.)

List goes on to cite the defences of protesters who ram drift-net fishing boats in the Pacific, appealing by way of justification to the moral implications of laws of ecology. When these defences are juxtaposed with Carl Cohen's account of civil disobedience, again they appear to fail. Cohen's account recognizes both utilitarian justifications (but these are not in question) or appeals to higher law; but appeals to higher law fail for lack of public verification of the alleged laws and the lack of a tribunal which could validate them. The candidate higher laws cited by List all fall short on these criteria; but, as he maintains, this degree of precision and security cannot plausibly be required, as the moral case for such action is quite intelligible without it. Instead of coming up with well-attested ecological laws of nature, ecology can supply 'general ethical principles that are verified by common sense and ecological application in particular instances', which are also '"first-order ethical principles" that humans violate at their peril and at the risk of damage to non-human life and natural systems' (p. 197). Sooner than wait for unrestricted ethical knowledge, List may be implying, the ethics of protest requires recognition of an equivalent of the Precautionary Principle increasingly recognized in Europe in the ethics of policy, which authorises action to avert irreversible ecological damage in advance of full evidence and the knowledge which it might bring. Conscientious protest at ecological injustice could then be acknowledged as such.

Dale Jamieson too draws attention to philosophers' tendency to tackle old problems and neglect current ones. Treating it as established that there are international obligations, he addresses issues surrounding global environmental justice. One such issue could concern expanding the beneficiaries of justice to natural entities, but this is not what people usually have in mind. (If so, should not philosophers seek to make it more prominent?) On another sense of 'global environmental justice', 'environmental' serves as a constraint, for example, on international redistribution; the issue here is whether global justice can permissibly be pursued only in an ecologically sensitive manner. But more often 'global environmental justice' concerns the international (re)distribution of the environment, conceived as a commodity, or of the related costs and benefits. Compensation for past exploitation would be an example; and 'big picture' theories of justice, like Rawls's, are of at least apparent relevance. But the very aims of ecological benefits support that conditionality whose advocates were so embattled with those of sovereignty at the 1992 Rio de Janeiro Conference. Unconditional transfers seem not to be in the interests of donors or, sometimes, of the recipients, and certainly not of nature or of populations in Third World countries.

Jamieson regards these problems as a reason against regarding the environment as a commodity to be distributed in accordance with international justice; other problems concern how some environmental 'commodities' like the ozone shield have benefits which cannot be distributed, and how some are irreplaceable and beyond compensation. (Yet arguably there are parallel problems with health provision, which do not erode international obligations in matters of health care.) Lastly Jamieson suggests that the obligations of global environmental justice do not all attach to governments; some belong to non-governmental organisations, scientists or individual consumers. (The condition, one that Jamieson would accept, must surely be that the responsibilities of governments and international agencies like the IMF are in no way reduced by this recognition.) Jamieson adds that the environment cannot be regarded solely as a commodity, as it surrounds and nurtures every one of us; but, as Dower shows, these facts do not reduce international duties with regard to the common global environment, on which all local environments depend.

Ruth McNally and Peter Wheale break new ground in a different way. Bioethics, they suggest, is engaged in a socio-technical process in which modernity, as characterised by Anthony Giddens, is being transformed into a new post-modern and possibly not wholly dystopian order. While their main example of a challenge to the institutions of modernity concerns genetic engineering and the associated discourse, they are clearly committed to the view that one of the transforming factors is located in environmental bioethics as well as medical bioethics. For the reflexive process in which society responds to systems of knowledge and to challenges to these systems is fostered by diminished trust that the institutions of modernity can cope with current environmental problems, as well as the problems arising from genetic engineering. So environmental concern, and the associated discourse of environmental bioethics, is represented as one of the harbingers of a new dispensation.

While there is some evidence to the contrary, for example in the recent decision of the British government to go ahead with the THORP reprocessing unit at Sellafield, there is evidence in favour of their thesis too, such as the frequent genuflections of this and other governments to the goal of sustainable development and the discourse of the Brundtland Report of the World Commission on Environment and Development (1987). Environmental philosophy too, then, could be contributing, however indirectly, to the emergence of a new world.

The final paper embodies Frederick Ferré's overview of the

Conference. Ferré elegantly warns against premature resort to bipolar oppositions in the philosophy of nature, commending instead epistemological holism, a metaphysics in which (*pace* Rolston) the natural and the artificial are not contradictory categories, and a value theory which reconciles subjectivism and objectivism.

In this theory, value is located wherever there are organisms, and yet there are no values without valuers; for all organisms are themselves valuers (a theme reminiscent of Rolston's stance, for all that Ferré criticises Rolston here for resort to binary opposition). But if (it might be replied) values always supply reasons for action, there is no need to detect the presence of valuers or valuation before recognizing the presence of value, however cogent the argument may be for the actual occurrence (or at least the potentiality) of valuing throughout the organic realm. Given his own valuation-related sense of 'value', Ferré's blend of objectivism and subjectivism has some cogency, but it has no tendency to undermine the objectivist case that the well-being of creatures is of value (in the reason-giving sense) independently of the activities of valuers, even if some of these creatures turn out to be incapable of subjectivity and of valuation. To maintain otherwise is a premature (albeit sophisticated) resort to a binary opposition, presenting all entities as either valuing or (intrinsically) valueless.

While these papers will have served a purpose insofar as they variously further the debates (to borrow Rolston's title) on the value in nature and the nature of value, on environmental ethics and also on the very concept of the environment, they also bring forcefully to light the need for further work on political and social philosophy, on aesthetics and also on ontology, of a kind which takes these debates seriously.

Value in Nature and the Nature of Value

HOLMES ROLSTON III

I offer myself as a nature guide, exploring for values. Many before us have got lost and we must look the world over. The unexamined life is not worth living; life in an unexamined world is not worthy living either. We miss too much of value.

Valuable Humans

Let us start from well-mapped ground: humans are able to value. Descartes's *cogito* is as well an indubitable *valeo*. I cannot doubt that I value. Humans are able to value nature instrumentally, to value their own experiential states both intrinsically and instrumentally. Objective natural things and events may contribute to these subjective interest satisfactions, a tree supplies firewood, a sunny day makes a picnic possible.

Taking the first step on our journey into non-human nature, some travellers notice that we must take along this indubitable valuing self; afterwards, along the way, finding these selves always present, they deny any value outside our own minds. Wilhelm Windelband insists: 'Value . . . is never found in the object itself as a property. It consists in a relation to an appreciating mind . . . . Take away will and feeling and there is no such thing as value' (Windelband, 1921, p. 215). Bryan Norton concludes: 'Moralists among environmental ethicists have erred in looking for a value in living things that is *independent* of human valuing. They have therefore forgotten a most elementary point about valuing anything. Valuing always occurs from the viewpoint of a conscious valuer . . . . Only the humans are valuing agents' (Norton, 1991, p. 251).

Taking an interest in an object gives humans a value-ability. Additionally to valuing nature instrumentally, humans can sometimes value nature intrinsically. When we value a giant sequoia tree, our valuing stops in the tree itself, without further contributory reference. What then is going on? Philosophical travellers, after taking a look at the tree, will want to take a look at their language. 'Intrinsic' means without instrumental reference, but that

13

leaves unsettled whether the value is located in the tree independently, autonomously intrinsic, or placed on the tree upon our arrival. We cannot just take it as elementary that there is no such thing as non-human value. Is this intrinsic value discovered or conferred? There is excitement in the beholder; but what is valued is what is beheld.

If the value-ability of humans is the source of this valued excitement, then value is anthropogenic even though it is not anthropocentric (Callicott, 1984; 1986). Tourists in Yosemite do not value the sequoias as timber but as natural classics, for their age, strength, size, beauty, resilience and majesty. This viewing constitutes the trees' value, which is not present independent of the human valuing. Value thus requires subjectivity to coagulate it in the world. But the value so coagulated, it will be claimed, is placed objectively on the tree. Such value is not self-regarding, or even human-regarding, merely, though it is human-generated. It is not centred on human well-being. That 'n is valuable' does mean that a human, H, takes an interest in n, a natural object, but it need not mean 'n satisfies H's desire', since H may take an interest in the trees for what they are in themselves, and not merely to satisfy H's desires. Meanwhile, there is no value until consciousness comes on scene.

Visiting the Grand Canyon, we intrinsically value the rock strata with their colour bands. Visiting Kentucky, we value Mammoth Cave, with its stalactites. Taking any interest whatever constitutes value *ipso facto*. An otherwise valueless object can thus come to have intrinsic value. As travellers we will wonder what was here before, what will remain after. The obvious answer is that there will be whatever properties these trees, canyons, and caves have. Even Descartes found himself unable to doubt the existence of external nature, and no philosopher who doubts that the world exists bothers to take a trip through it.

What account do we give when, excited by a sense of deep time at the Grand Canyon, we realize that humans have rarely been there? At that point, we may wish to give a dispositional twist to value. To say that n is valuable means that n is able to be valued, if and when human valuers, Hs, come along, but n has these properties whether or not humans arrive. Faced with trilobite fossils, we conclude that the trilobites were potentially intrinsically valuable. By this account there is no actual value ownership autonomous to the valued and valuable trees, canyons, trilobites; there is a value ignition when humans arrive. Intrinsic value in the realized sense emerges relationally with the appearance of the subject-generator.

Despite the language of value conferral, if we try to take the term *intrinsic* seriously, this cannot refer to anything the object gains, to something *within* ('intra') the present tree or the past trilobite, for the human subject does not really place anything on or in the natural object. We have only a 'truncated sense' of *intrinsic* (Callicott, 1986, p. 143). The *attributes* under consideration are objectively there before humans come, but the *attribution* of value is subjective. The object causally affects the subject, who is excited by the incoming data and translates this as value, after which the object, the tree, appears as having value, rather like it appears to have green colour. But nothing is really added *intrinsically*; everything in the object remains what it was before. Despite the language that humans are the *source* of value which they *locate* in the natural object, no value is really located there at all.

The term *intrinsic*, even when truncated, is misleading. What is meant is better specified by the term *extrinsic*, the *ex* indicating the external, anthropogenic ignition of the value, which is not *in*, *intrinsic*, internal to the nonsentient organism, even though this value, once generated, is apparently conferred on the organism. In the *H-n* encounter, value is conferred by H on n, and that is really an extrinsic value for n, since it comes to n from H, and likewise it is an extrinsic value for H, since it is conferred from H to n. Neither H nor n, standing alone, have such value.

We humans carry the lamp that lights up value, although we require the fuel that nature provides. Actual value is an event in our consciousness, though natural items while still in the dark of value have potential intrinsic value. Man is the measure of things, said Protagoras. Humans are the measurers, the valuers of things, even when we measure what they are in themselves.

Valuable Animals

A mother free-tail bat, a mammal like ourselves, can, using sonar, wend her way out of Bracken Cave, in Texas, in total darkness, catch 500–1000 insects each hour on the wing, and return to find and nurse her own young. That gives evidence of bat-valuing; she values the insects and the pup. Now, it seems absurd to say that there are no valuers until humans arrive. Animals do not make humans the measure of things at all. There is no better evidence of non-human values and valuers than spontaneous wildlife, born free and on its own. Animals hunt and howl, find shelter, seek out their habitats and mates, care for their young, flee from threats, grow hungry, thirsty, hot, tired, excited, sleepy. They suffer injury and lick their wounds. Here we are quite convinced that value is non-anthropogenic, to say nothing of anthropocentric.

These wild animals defend their own lives because they have a good of their own. There is somebody there behind the fur or feathers. Our gaze is returned by an animal that itself has a concerned outlook. Here is value right before our eyes, right behind those eyes. Animals are value-able, able to value things in their world. But we may still want to say that value exists only where a subject has an object of interest. David Prall writes: 'The being liked or disliked of the object is its value . . . . Some sort of a subject is always requisite to there being value at all' (Prall, 1921, p. 227). So at least the higher animals can value too, because they are experiencing subjects and can take an interest in things.

Do animals value anything intrinsically? We may not think that animals have the capacity, earlier claimed for humans, of conferring intrinsic value on anything else. Mostly they seek their own basic needs, food and shelter, and care for their young. But then why not say that an animal values its own life for what it is in itself, intrinsically, without further contributory reference? Else we have an animal world replete with instrumental values and devoid of intrinsic values, everything valuing the resources it needs, nothing valuing itself. That is implausible. Animals maintain a valued self-identity as they cope through the world. Valuing is intrinsic to animal life.

Valuable Organisms

Outdoors it is difficult to get out of sight of plants. It is also difficult for philosophers to 'see' plants philosophically. Few are botanists. Also, it is easy to overlook the insects. Even fewer philosophers are entomologists.

A plant is not a subject, but neither is it an inanimate object, like a stone. Plants, quite alive, are unified entities of the botanical though not of the zoological kind, that is, they are not unitary organisms highly integrated with centred neural control, but they are modular organisms, with a meristem that can repeatedly and indefinitely produce new vegetative modules, additional stem nodes and leaves when there is available space and resources, as well as new reproductive modules, fruits and seeds.

Plants make themselves; they repair injuries; they move water, nutrients, and photosynthate from cell to cell; they store sugars; they make tannin and other toxins and regulate their levels in defence against grazers; they make nectars and emit pheromones to influence the behaviour of pollinating insects and the responses of other plants; they emit allelopathic agents to suppress invaders; they make thorns, trap insects. They can reject genetically incompatible grafts.

A plant, like any other organism, sentient or not, is a spontaneous, self-maintaining system, sustaining and reproducing itself, executing its program, making a way through the world, checking against performance by means of responsive capacities with which to measure success. Something more than physical causes, even when less than sentience, is operating; there is *information* superintending the causes; without it the organism would collapse into a sand heap. The information is used to preserve the plant identity.

All this cargo is carried by the DNA, essentially a *linguistic* molecule. The genetic set is really a *propositional* set—to choose a provocative term—recalling how the Latin *propositum* is an assertion, a set task, a theme, a plan, a proposal, a project, as well as a cognitive statement. These molecules are set to drive the movement from genotypic potential to phenotypic expression. Given a chance, these molecules seek organic self-expression. An organism, unlike an inert rock, claims the environment as source and sink, from which to abstract energy and materials and into which to excrete them. It 'takes advantage' of its environment.

We pass to value when we recognize that the genetic set is a *normative set*; it distinguishes between what *is* and what *ought to be*. The organism is an axiological system, though not a moral system. So the tree grows, reproduces, repairs its wounds, and resists death. The physical state that the organism defends is a valued state. A life is defended for what it is in itself, without necessary further contributory reference. Every organism has a *good-of-its-kind*; it defends its own kind as a *good kind*. In this sense, the genome is a set of conservation molecules.

Does not that mean that the plant is valuable (able to value) itself? If not, we will have to ask, as an open question: Well, the plant has a good of its own, but is there anything of value to it?[1] Possibly, even though plants have a good of their own, they are not able to value because they are not able to feel anything. Nothing matters to a plant. Hence, says Peter Singer, 'there is nothing to be taken into account' (Singer, 1976, p. 154). There is plant good, but not plant value. There is no valuer evaluating anything. Plants can do things that interest us, but the plants are not interested in what they are doing. They do not have any options among which they are choosing. They have only their merely functional goods.

[1] Robin Attfield remarks that 'even if trees have needs and a good of their own, they may still have no value of their own' (Attfield, 1981, p. 35).

But, though things do not matter *to* plants, things matter *for* them. We ask, of a failing plant: What's the matter *with* that plant? If it is lacking sunshine and soil nutrients, and we arrange for these, we say: The tree is benefiting from the sunshine and the soil nutrients; and *benefit* is—everywhere else we encounter it—a value word. Can we ask, as an open question: The tree is benefiting from the sun and the nutrients, but are those valuable to it? That hardly seems coherent. 'This tree was injured when the elk rubbed its velvet off its antlers, and the tannin secreted there is killing the invading bacteria. But is this valuable to the tree?' Botanists say that the tree is irritable in the biological sense.

Or if trees cannot be irritated, you no doubt think that bees can, even though you may not know what to think about bees as subject valuers. Objectively, it is difficult to dissociate the idea of value from natural selection. Biologists regularly speak of the 'survival value' of plant activities: thorns have survival value. Bees sting and do their waggle dance. These survival traits, though picked out by natural selection, are innate (= intrinsic) in the organism, that is, stored in its genes and expressed in structure and behaviour.

But, it will be protested, careful philosophers will put this kind of 'value' in scare quotes. This is not really value at all, because there is no felt experience choosing from alternatives, no preferences being exercised. This so-called value is not a value, really, not one of interest to philosophers because it is not a value with interest in itself. Meanwhile we humans value many things about which we have no options (photosynthesis and protein), or even no knowledge (perhaps vitamin B_1 or the cytochrome-c molecules). What are we to say of all these functional 'values'? Do they become of real value only upon their discovery, and even then have only instrumental value?

Why is the organism not valuing what it is making resources of?—not consciously, but we do not want to presume that there is only conscious value or valuing. That is what we are debating, not assuming. A valuer is an entity able to defend value. Insentient organisms are the *holders* of value, although not the *beholders* of value. Some value is already present in nonsentient organisms, normative valuative systems, prior to the emergence of further dimensions of value with sentience. Otherwise we have to ask, as an open question: Well, the bee is making use of the nectar, but is the honey valuable to the bee? My mind is not subtle enough to use words with such precision. The bee's defending its own life for what it is in itself is just as much fact of the matter as is its using its stinger or making honey to do so.

No, these are observations of value in nature with just as much certainty as they are biological facts. We are misled to think that all the value of the tree, instrumental or intrinsic, must be subjectively conferred, like the greenness, a secondary quality, or even a tertiary one. A simpler, less anthropically based, more biocentric theory holds that some values, instrumental and intrinsic, are objectively there, discovered not generated by the valuer. Trees may not be coloured without a perceiver, but they exist *per se*; and only if their existence is dynamically defended. That is not an analogue of colour at all. Trees do appear to be green, and perhaps we do not want to call the electromagnetic waves actually there 'greenness'. Trees also photosynthesise with or without humans watching them. Even those who think that all the tree's intrinsic value has to be conferred by humans still think that matters can be better or worse for the tree, and this amounts to saying that the tree on its own has its goods and harms. Norton and Windelband, unable to forget their experiential omnipresence as valuers, have forgotten elementary biology.

Some worry that we here commit the naturalistic fallacy. We find what biologically is in nature and conclude that something valuable is there, something which we may say we ought to protect. But does it not rather seem that the facts here are value facts, when we are describing what benefits the tree? Such value is pretty much fact of the matter. If we refuse to recognize such values being objectively there, have we committed some fallacy? Rather, the danger is the other way round. We commit the subjectivist fallacy if we think all values lie in subjective experience, and, worse still, the anthropocentrist fallacy if we think all values lie in human options and preferences.

Valuable Species

On our travels we may see endangered species. If so, we will value them. But are we seeing, and valuing, species? Or just that trumpeter swan, this grizzly bear, that we were lucky enough to see? That is partly a scientific and partly a philosophical problem. I have seen, and valued, swans and bears in Yellowstone over four decades. But not the same individuals, rather bear replaced by bear replaced by bear, swan-swan-swan.

Certainly humans are able to value species both by instrumental use and by conferring intrinsic value on them. But can a species be value-able all by itself, able to value at the species-level? A species has no self. There is no analogue to the nervous hookups or circulatory flows that characterize the organism. But now we must ask whether singular somatic identity conserved is the only process that is valuable. A species is another level of biological identity reasserted genetically over time. Identity need not attach solely to the centred or modular organism; it can persist as a discrete pattern over time.

The life that the organismic individual has is something passing through the individual as much as something it intrinsically possesses. The genetic set, in which is coded the *telos*, is as evidently the property of the species as of the individual through which it passes. Value is something dynamic to the specific form of life. The species *is* a bigger event than the individual with its interests or sentience. Events can be good for the well-being of the species, considered collectively, although they are harmful if considered as distributed to individuals. When a wolf is tearing up an elk, the individual elk is in distress, but *Cervus canadensis* is in no distress. The species is being improved, shown by the fact that wolves will subsequently find elk harder to catch. If the predators are removed, and the carrying capacity is exceeded, wildlife managers may have to benefit a species by culling its member individuals.

Even the individuals that escape external demise die of old age; and their deaths, always to the disadvantage of individuals, are a necessity for the species. A finite life span makes room for those replacements that enable development, allowing the population to improve in fitness or to adapt to a shifting environment. The surplus of young, with most born to perish prematurely, is disadvantageous to such individuals, but advantageous to the species. Without the 'flawed' reproduction that incorporates mutation and permits variation, without selection of the more fit few, and death of the less fit, which harms most individuals, the species would soon be extinct in a changing environment. The individual is a receptacle of the form, and the receptacles are broken while the form survives, but the form cannot otherwise survive.

Reproduction is typically assumed to be a need of individuals, but since any particular individual can flourish somatically without reproducing at all, indeed may be put through duress and risk or spend much energy reproducing, by another logic we can interpret reproduction as the species staying in place by its replacements. In this sense a female grizzly does not bear cubs to be healthy herself. Rather, her cubs are *Ursus arctos*, threatened by nonbeing, recreating itself by continuous performance. A female animal does not have mammary glands nor a male testicles because the function of these is to preserve its own life; these organs are defending the line of life bigger than the somatic individual. The locus of the value that is defended over generations is as much in the form of life, since the individuals are genetically impelled to sacrifice themselves in the interests of reproducing their kind.

An insistent individualist can claim that species-level phenomena (vitality in a population, danger to a species, reproduction of a life form, tracking a changing environment) are only epiphenomena, byproducts of aggregated individuals in their interrelationships. But our more comprehensive account, interpreting the species itself as a kind of individual, historic lineage over time, is just as plausible. Biologists have often and understandably focused on individual organisms, and some recent trends interpret biological processes from the perspective of genes. But a consideration of species reminds us that many events can be interpreted at this level too. Properly understood, the story at the microscopic genetic level reflects the story at the ecosystemic specific level, with the individual a macroscopic mid-level between. The genome is a kind of map coding the species; the individual is an instance incarnating it.

Much of what we earlier said about individual organisms as nonmoral normative systems can be resaid, *mutatis mutandis*, of species. The single, organismic-directed course is part of a bigger picture in which a species too runs a telic course through the environment, using individuals resourcefully to maintain its course over much longer periods of time. The species line is the *vital* living system, the whole, of which individual organisms are the essential parts. The species defends a particular form of life, pursuing a pathway through the world, resisting death (extinction), by regeneration maintaining a normative identity over time. It is as logical to say that the individual is the species' way of propagating itself as to say that the embryo or egg is the individual's way of propagating itself. The value resides in the dynamic form; the individual inherits this, exemplifies it, and passes it on. If so, what prevents value existing at that level? The appropriate survival unit is the appropriate location of valuing.

Even a species is a kind of valuer. Species as historical lines have a defended biological identity, though they do not have any subjective experience. Species are quite real; that there really is a bear-bear-bear sequence is about as certain as anything we believe about the empirical world. Species are lively and full of life, they are processes, they are wholes, they have a kind of unity and integrity. The species line too is value-able, able to conserve a biological identity. Indeed it is more real, more value-able than the individual, necessary though individuals are for the continuance of this lineage.

We said earlier that natural selection picks out whatever traits an organism has that are valuable to it, relative to its survival. But if we ask what is the essence of this value, it is not the somatic sur-vival of the organismic individual; this value ability is the ability to reproduce. That locates value-ability innate or intrinsic within the organism, but it just as much locates the value-ability as the capaci-ty to re-produce a next generation, and a next generation posi-tioned to produce a next generation after that. Any biocentrism that focuses on individuals has got to argue away the fact that nat-ural selection is rather careless with individuals; the test to which it puts them is whether they can pass on the historical lineage.

Valuable Ecosystems

Exploring, we will see different ecosystems: an oak-hickory forest, a tall grass prairie. At least we see trees and grasses. But do we see ecosystems? Maybe we immerse ourselves in them, for an ecosys-tem is not so much an object in the focus of vision as an enveloping community, a place in space, a process in time, a set of vital rela-tionships. This can mean that philosophers have difficulty seeing, and valuing, ecosystems. Yet, really, the ecosystem is the funda-mental unit of development and survival.

Humans can value whatever they wish in nature. This can include ecosystems. 'A thing is right,' concluded Aldo Leopold, 'when it tends to preserve the integrity, stability, and beauty of the biotic community. It is wrong when it tends otherwise' (Leopold, 1966, p. 240). Leopold wanted a 'land ethic'. So humans can value ecosystem communities intrinsically—for what they are in them-selves—as well as instrumentally. But can ecosystems be valuable all by themselves?

Actually, there is a deeper worry again, partly scientific and part-ly philosophical. Perhaps ecosystems do not exist—or exist in too loose a way to be valuers. They are nothing but aggregations of their more real members, like a forest is (some say) nothing more than a collection of trees. Even a human will have trouble valuing what does not really exist. We can value collections, as of stamps, but this is just the aggregated value of individual stamps. Still, an ecosystem, if it exists, is rather different. Nothing in the stamp col-lection is alive; the collection is neither self-generating nor self-maintaining. Neither stamp nor collection is valuable on its own. But perhaps ecosystems are both valuable to humans and, if they exist, value-able as systems in themselves.

We need ecology to discover what biotic community means as an organisational mode. Then we can reflect philosophically to dis-cover the values there. Ecosystems can seem little more than stochastic processes. A sea-shore, a tundra, is a loose collection of externally related parts. Much of the environment is not organic at all (rain, groundwater, rocks, nonbiotic soil particles, air). Some is dead and decaying debris (fallen trees, scat, humus). These things have no organized needs; the collection of them is a jumble. The fortuitous interplay between organisms is simply a matter of the distribution and abundance of organisms, how they get dispersed, birth rates and death rates, population densities, moisture regimes, parasitism and predation, checks and balances. There is really not enough centred process to call community.

An ecosystem has no brain, no genome, no skin, no self-identification, no *telos*, no unified program. It does not defend itself against injury or death. It is not irritable. The parts (foxes, sedges) are more complex than the wholes (forests, grasslands). So it can begin to seem as if an ecosystem is too low a level of organisation to be the direct focus of concern. Ecosystems do not and cannot care; they have no interests about which they or we can care.

But this is to misunderstand ecosystems, to make a category mistake. To fault *communities* as though they ought to be organismic *individuals* is to look at one level for what is appropriate at another. One should look for a matrix of interconnections between centres, for creative stimulus and open-ended potential. Everything will be connected to many other things, sometimes by obligate associations, more often by partial and pliable dependencies; and, among other components, there will be no significant interactions. There will be shunts and criss-crossing pathways, cybernetic subsystems and feedback loops. One looks for selection pressures and adaptive fit, not for irritability or repair of injury, for speciation and life support, not for resisting death. We must think more systemically, and less organismically.

An ecosystem generates a spontaneous order that envelops and produces the richness, beauty, integrity and dynamic stability of the component parts. Though these organized interdependencies are loose in comparison with the tight connections within an organism, all these metabolisms are as vitally linked as are liver and heart. The equilibrating ecosystem is not merely push-pull forces. It is an equilibrating of values.

We do not want in an undiscriminating way to extrapolate criteria of value from organism to biotic community, any more than from person to animal or from animal to plant. Rather, we want to discriminate the criteria appropriate to this level. The selective forces in ecosystems at once transcend and produce the lives of individual plants and animals. Evolutionary ecosystems over geological time have increased the numbers of species on Earth from zero to five million or more. R. H. Whittaker found that on continental scales and for most groups 'increase of species diversity . . . is a self-augmenting evolutionary process without any evident limit'. There is a tendency toward what he called 'species packing' (Whittaker, 1972, p. 214).

Superimposed on this, the quality of individual lives in the upper trophic rungs of ecological pyramids has risen. One-celled organisms evolved into many-celled, highly integrated organisms. Photosynthesis evolved and came to support locomotion—swimming, walking, running, flight. Stimulus-response mechanisms became complex instructive acts. Warm-blooded animals followed cold-blooded ones. Neural complexity, conditioned behaviour, and learning emerged. Sentience appeared—sight, smell, hearing, taste, pleasure, pain. Brains evolved, coupled with hands. Consciousness and self-consciousness arose. Persons appeared with intense concentrated unity. The products are valuable, able to be valued by these humans; but why not say that the process is what is really value-able, able to produce these values?

Ecosystems are selective systems, as surely as organisms are selective systems. The system selects over the long ranges for individuality, for diversity, for adapted fitness, for quantity and quality of life. Organisms defend only their own selves or kinds, but the system spins a bigger story. Organisms defend their continuing survival; ecosystems promote new arrivals. Species increase their kinds, but ecosystems increase kinds, and increase the integration of kinds. The system is a kind of field with characteristics as vital for life as any property contained within particular organisms. The ecosystem is the depth source of individual and species alike.

In the current debate among biologists about the levels at which selection takes place—individual organisms, populations, species, genes—the recent tendency to move selective pressures down to the genetic level forgets that a gene is always emplaced in an organism that is emplaced in an ecosystem. The molecular configurations of DNA are what they are because they record the story of a particular form of life in the macroscopic, historical ecosystem. What is generated arises from molecular mutations, but what survives is selected for adaptive fit in an ecosystem. We cannot make sense of biomolecular life without understanding ecosystemic life, the one level as vital as the other.

Philosophers, sometimes encouraged by biologists, may think ecosystems are just epiphenomenal aggregations. This is a confusion. Any level is real if there is significant downward causation. Thus the atom is real because that pattern shapes the behaviour of electrons; the cell because that pattern shapes the behaviour of amino acids; the organism because that pattern co-ordinates the behaviour of hearts and lungs; the community because the niche shapes the morphology and behaviour of the foxes within it. Being real requires an organisation that shapes the existence and the behaviour of members or parts.

Axiologically, in the more comprehensive levels, the terms 'instrumental' and 'intrinsic' do not work very well. Ecosystems have 'systemic value'. But if we want to know what is value-able, able to create value, why not say that it is the productivity of such ecosystems, bringing into existence these phenomena that, when we arrive, the human consciousness is also able to value? What is incredible is not the existence of ecosystems. What is really incredible is that we humans, arriving late on the evolutionary scene, ourselves products of it, bring all the value into the world, when and as we turn our attention to our sources. That claim has too much subjective bias. It values a late product of the system, psychological life, and subordinates everything else to this. It mistakes a fruit for the whole plant, the last chapter for the whole story.

All value does not end in either human or non-human intrinsic value, to which everything else is contributory. Values are intrinsic, instrumental, and systemic, and all three are interwoven, no one with priority over the others in significance, although systemic value is foundational. Each locus of intrinsic value gets folded into instrumental value by the system, and vice versa. There are no intrinsic values, nor instrumental ones either, without the encompassing systemic creativity. It would be foolish to value the golden eggs and disvalue the goose that lays them. It would be a mistake to value the goose only instrumentally. A goose that lays golden eggs is systemically valuable. How much more so is an ecosystem that generates myriads of species, or even, as we next see, an Earth that produces billions of species, ourselves included.

Valuable Earth

I promised to explore the whole world; so let's get the planet in focus. Viewing Earthrise, Edgar Mitchell, was entranced: 'Suddenly from behind the rim of the moon, in long-slow motion moments of immense majesty, there emerges a sparkling blue and white jewel, a light, delicate sky-blue sphere laced with slowly swirling veils of white, rising gradually like a small pearl in a thick sea of black mystery. It takes more than a moment to fully realize this is Earth . . . home' (Kelley, 1988, at photographs 42–45). Michael Collins was Earthstruck: 'When I travelled to the moon, it wasn't my proximity to that battered rockpile I remember so vividly, but rather what I saw when I looked back at my fragile home—a glistening, inviting beacon, delicate blue and white, a tiny outpost suspended in the black infinity. Earth is to be treasured and nurtured, something precious that *must* endure' (Gallant, 1980, p. 6).

Pearls are, a philosopher might object, valuable only when humans come around. But this mysterious Earth-pearl, a biologist will reply, is a home long before we humans come. This is the only biosphere, the only planet with an ecology. Earth may not be the only planet where anything is valuable—able to be valued by humans intrinsically or instrumentally—but it is the only place able to produce vitality before humans come. The view from space symbolizes all this.

Earlier the challenge was to evaluate persons, animals, plants, species, ecosystems; but environmental valuing is not over until we have risen to the planetary level. Earth is really the relevant survival unit. But valuing the whole Earth is unfamiliar and needs philosophical analysis. We may seem to be going to extremes. Earth is, after all, just earth. The belief that dirt could have intrinsic value is sometimes taken as a *reductio ad absurdum* in environmental philosophy. Dirt is not the sort of thing that has value by itself. Put like that, we agree. An isolated clod defends no intrinsic value and it is difficult to say that it has much value in itself. But that is not the end of the matter, because a clod of dirt is integrated into an ecosystem; earth is a part, Earth the whole. Dirt is product and process in a systemic nature. We should try to get the global picture, and switch from a lump of dirt to the Earth system in which it has been created.

Earth is, some will insist, a big rockpile like the moon, only one on which the rocks are watered and illuminated in such way that they support life. So maybe it is really the life we value and not the Earth, except as instrumental to life. We do not have duties to rocks, air, ocean, dirt, or Earth; we have duties to people, or living things. We must not confuse duties to the home with duties to the inhabitants. We do not praise so much the dirt as what is in the dirt, not earth so much as what is on Earth. But this is not a systemic view of what is going on. We need some systematic account of the valuable Earth we now behold, before we beheld it, not just some value that is generated in the eye of the beholder. Finding that value will generate a global sense of obligation.

The evolution of rocks into dirt into fauna and flora is one of the great surprises of natural history, one of the rarest events in the astronomical universe. Earth is all dirt, we humans too arise up from the humus, and we find revealed what dirt can do when it is self-organizing under suitable conditions. This is pretty spectacular dirt. Really, the story is little short of a series of 'miracles', wondrous, fortuitous events, unfolding of potential; and when Earth's most complex product, *Homo sapiens*, becomes intelligent enough to reflect over this cosmic wonderland, everyone is left stuttering about the mixtures of accident and necessity out of which we have evolved. For some the black mystery will be numinous and signal transcendence; for some the mystery may be impenetrable. Perhaps we do not have to have all the cosmological answers. Nobody has much doubt that this is a precious place, a pearl in a sea of black mystery.

The elemental chemicals of life—carbon, oxygen, hydrogen, nitrogen—are common enough throughout the universe. They are made in the stars. But life, rare elsewhere, is common on Earth, and the explanation lies in the ordinary elements in an extraordinary setting, the super-special circumstances in which these common chemicals find themselves arranged on Earth, that is, in the self-organizing system. On an everyday scale, earth, dirt, seems to be passive, inert, an unsuitable object of moral concern. But on a global scale?

The scale changes nothing, a critic may protest, the changes are only quantitative. Earth is no doubt precious as life support, but it is not precious in itself. There is nobody there in a planet. There is not even the objective vitality of an organism, or the genetic transmission of a species line. Earth is not even an ecosystem, strictly speaking; it is a loose collection of myriads of ecosystems. So we must be talking loosely, perhaps poetically or romantically, of valuing Earth. Earth is a mere thing, a big thing, a special thing for those who happen to live on it, but still a thing, and not appropriate as an object of intrinsic or systemic valuation. We can, if we insist on being anthropocentrists, say that it is all valueless except as our human resource.

But we will not be valuing Earth objectively until we appreciate this marvellous natural history. This really is a superb planet, the most valuable entity of all, because it is the entity able to produce all the Earthbound values. At this scale of vision, if we ask what is principally to be valued, the value of life arising as a creative process on Earth seems a better description and a more comprehensive category.

Perhaps you think that species are unreal. Perhaps you still insist that ecosystems are unreal, only aggregations, but how about Earth? Will you say that Earth too, being a higher level entity, is unreal? Only an aggregation, and not a systemic whole? There is no such thing as a biosphere? Surely, Earth has some rather clear boundaries, does it not? Will you say that this is a planet where nothing matters? Nothing matters to Earth, perhaps, but everything matters on Earth, for Earth.

Do not humans sometimes value Earth's life-supporting systems because they are valuable, and not always the other way round? Is this value just a matter of late-coming human interests? Or is Earth not historically a remarkable, valuable place, a place able to produce value prior to the human arrival, and even now valuable antecedently to the human uses of it? It seems parochial to say that our part alone in the drama establishes all its worth. The production of value over the millenia of natural history is not something subjective that goes on in the human mind. In that sense, a valuable Earth is not the *reductio ad absurdum* of valuing dirt. It is not even locating the most valuable thing in the world; it is locating the ultimate value of the world itself. The creativity within the natural system we inherit, and the values this generates, are the ground of our being, not just the ground under our feet. Earth could be the ultimate object of duty, short of God, if God exists.

Valuable Nature

William James, toward the beginning of our century, starkly portrayed the utterly valueless world, transfigured as a gift of the human coming:

> Conceive yourself, if possible, suddenly stripped of all the emotion with which your world now inspires you, and try to imagine it *as it exists*, purely by itself, without your favorable or unfavorable, hopeful or apprehensive comment. It will be almost impossible for you to realize such a condition of negativity and deadness. No one portion of the universe would then have importance beyond another; and the whole collection of its things and series of its events would be without significance, character, expression, or perspective. Whatever of value, interest, or meaning our respective worlds may appear endued with are thus pure gifts of the spectator's mind. (James, 1925, p. 150)

At the end of this century, this is not what the astronauts think at all. They do not see Earth as negativity and deadness, nor do they think that this portion of the universe has no significance beyond any other part, except by gift of our spectating minds. They did not say that the world was valuable only because they took along an indubitable self into space and projected value onto Earth.

They rather see that human life arises in a spectacular place, in a nature of whose creative patterns they are part.

According to the old paradigm, so long dominant that to some it now seems elementary, there is no value without an experiencing valuer, just as there are no thoughts without a thinker, no percepts without a perceiver, no deeds without a doer, no targets without an aimer. Valuing is felt preferring by human choosers. Possibly, extending this paradigm, sentient animals may also value. But plants cannot value; they have no options and make no choices. *A fortiori*, Earth and nature cannot be bona fide valuers. One can always hang on to the claim that value, like a tickle or remorse, must be felt to be there. Its *esse* is *percipi*. Nonsensed value is nonsense. It is only beings with 'insides' to them that have value.

But the problem with the 'no value without a valuer' axiom is that it is too individualistic; it looks for some centre of value located in a subjective self. And we nowhere wish to deny that such valuers are sufficient for value. But that is not the whole account of value in a more holistic, systemic, ecological, global account. Perhaps there can be no doing science without a scientist, no religion without a believer, no tickle without somebody tickled. But there can be law without a lawgiver, history without a historian; there is biology without biologists, physics without physicists, creativity without creators, story without story-tellers, achievement without achievers—and value without valuers. A sentient valuer is not necessary for value. Another way is for there to be a value-generating system able to generate value. If you like, that is another meaning of value-er; any x is a valuer if x is value-able, able to produce values.

It is true that humans are the only evaluators who can reflect about what is going on at this global scale, who can deliberate about what they ought to do conserving it. When humans do this, they must set up the scales; and humans are the measurers of things. Animals, organisms, species, ecosystems, Earth, cannot teach us how to do this evaluating. But they can display what it is that is to be valued. The axiological scales we construct do not constitute the value, any more than the scientific scales we erect create what we thereby measure.

Humans are not so much lighting up value in a merely potentially valuable world, as they are psychologically joining ongoing planetary natural history in which there is value wherever there is positive creativity. While such creativity can be present in subjects with their interests and preferences, it can also be present objectively in living organisms with their lives defended, and in species that defend an identity over time, and in systems that are self-organizing and that project storied achievements. The valuing subject in an otherwise valueless world is an insufficient premise for the experienced conclusions of those who value natural history.

Conversion to a biological and geological view seems truer to world experience and more logically compelling. This too is a perspective, but ecologically better informed; we know our place on a home planet. From this more objective viewpoint, there is something subjective, something philosophically naive, and even something hazardous in a time of ecological crisis, about living in a reference frame where one species takes itself as absolute and values everything else in nature relative to its potential to produce value for itself. Such philosophers live in an unexamined world, and, in result, they and those they guide live unworthy lives, because they cannot see their valuable world.

Ecology and the Ethics of Environmental Restoration

ROBERT ELLIOT

Some people think that nature has intrinsic value, that it has value in itself quite apart from its present and future economic, intellectual, recreational and aesthetic uses. Some people think that nature's intrinsic value grounds an obligation to preserve it and to minimise human interference with it. I agree. It is important, however, to try to say exactly why nature has intrinsic value, to go beyond merely stating some idiosyncratic attitude and to provide some justification of that attitude with which others might engage. Presumably there are properties that wild nature exemplifies in virtue of which it is intrinsically valued. Only when these are indicated is rational debate as to whether wild nature has intrinsic value possible. Only when these are indicated is it possible to begin to persuade dissenters to change their views. Indeed, unless one can at least begin to say what these properties are it is not clear that the attitude could have any meaningful content. While it is perhaps possible to value something without immediately understanding what it is about the thing that makes it valuable, the failure to come up with any candidate value-adding property after some reflection suggests that the initial value-judgment is vacuous.

Williams puts the problem as follows:

> there are serious questions of how human answers can represent to us the value of things that are valued for reasons that go beyond human interests. Our approach to these issues cannot and should not be narrowly anthropocentric. But what is it that we move to when we move from the narrowly anthropocentric, and by what ethical route do we get there? (Williams, 1992, p. 61)

Here I shall try to answer Williams's questions, using a suggestion that he himself makes but does not unambiguously endorse. In doing this I shall draw on some views, concerning the value of alleged restorations of wild nature, for which I have elsewhere argued (see Elliot, 1982; 1983; 1989; 1992; 1994). And I shall take account of criticisms of those views implicit in the writings of some so-called restoration ecologists. First it is helpful to sharpen Williams's questions.

Robert Elliot

Meta-ethics or Normative Ethics

Williams's questions have to do with substantiating certain norma-tive claims made by environmentalists rather than with meta-ethi-cal questions. Many would disagree, urging that to move to an other than narrowly anthropocentric position requires the devel-opment and defence of a certain kind of meta-ethical theory according to which intrinsic value is 'part of the fabric of the world' (Mackie, 1978, p. 23), that in the most literal sense values are 'discovered' not conferred (Rolston, this volume, p. 19). But Williams rejects such views (see Williams, 1985). For Williams, to move to an other than narrowly anthropocentric position is to adopt certain normative principles which give recognition to the value of nature independently of the uses to which nature might be put and of the human interests that it might serve. That is the answer to the first question, which is really a question about the coherence of a particular project. The answer to the second ques-tion involves supplying some motivation for the normative princi-ples in question; it involves an attempt to convey exactly what it is that those who see value in nature are responding to.

Perhaps I should say why there is no inconsistency between a subjectivist meta-ethics and the non-anthropocentric normative claims in question. It is consistent both to endorse the view that values reduce to the attitudes or preferences of humans, arguably subject to correction in ideal conditions, and to urge that the con-tent of such values includes states of affairs in which human inter-ests and human states of mind are not affected or do not feature (Routley and Routley, 1980; Elliot, 1985; Lewis, 1989). The atti-tudes and preferences in question necessarily reflect our human perspective but they do not take as their objects only states of affairs in which we feature. Rolston signals the distinction with a contrast between 'anthropogenic values' and 'anthropocentric val-ues' (Rolston, this volume, p. 14). He seems to think that a rejec-tion of both is required if we are to move to a sufficiently robust environmental ethic. But it is difficult to understand why this would have to be so. There is no type of evaluation that I can think of which might be made by an environmentalist and which cannot be supported by a subjectivist meta-ethics.

Consider an example that Rolston uses to question the adequacy of anthropogenic theories of value. Once there were trilobites. An environmentalist might want to say that, when alive, they had intrinsic value. But no humans were then around to value them. Still, I, here and now, might have a certain attitude towards them. A consideration of their properties, including their property of exhibiting biological organisation and complexity, inclines me to value them, to attribute to them intrinsic value. They do not have to directly causally impact on me in order to have intrinsic value, even though their having intrinsic value is dependent on my regarding them in a certain, positive way. Maybe the point is even clearer if we envisage a future state of affairs rather like that past state of affairs, since even indirect causal impacts on me by the putatively intrinsically valuable state are impossible. So, I contemplate a future state in which there is no human life, indeed no sentient life and so no conscious states whatsoever, but in which there is still considerable biotic diversity. Now I think that such a future state possesses intrinsic value, which is, on the subjectivist view, just to say that I have a certain type of positive attitude towards it. And even after I am dead it will be the case that at this time I have that attitude. Moreover it is the attitude that I have now that determines whether or not the future state has intrinsic value. In both examples it is my present attitudes and preferences which underpin the attributions of intrinsic value. So, whatever Rolston thinks of the meta-ethics, he cannot condemn it because it too much restricts environmentalist evaluations.

Rolston and others (for example, Attfield and Crisp, in this volume) no doubt feel a lingering insecurity because of the contingency of the value judgments which subjectivist views imply. They are troubled by the thought that the attitudes and preferences on which the value judgments are based have no more secure a foundation than the social, cultural and biological influences which have shaped the psychologies of those making the judgments; the judgments are not endorsed and somehow rendered objective by God, by the Cosmos or by Nature. Contingency, however, is something we have no choice but to live with (see Elliot, 1992, pp. 141–145; D'Agostino, 1993). Perhaps those who pine for objectivity are troubled by the thought that the subjectivism I have sketched implies that had the relevant valuer not existed, nothing then would have had any value. But this thought is flawed. As a matter of fact I do exist. As a matter of fact I value both the trilobites and the future state of biotic complexity. Their having value is in one sense dependent on my valuing them but it does not follow that had I not existed they would have had no value. The reason is that my evaluations are not limited to past, present and future states of the actual world but to the whole array of possible worlds (see Elliot, 1985, pp. 107–114). So, from my unavoidably human perspective in the actual world I can, and do, judge that wild nature has intrinsic value in those worlds from which I and my species, indeed any sentient species, are completely absent. A subjectivist theory of value can accommodate any environmentalist evaluation.

We need to distinguish, then, between the meta-ethical view that intrinsic value, and other moral properties, do not in effect reduce to human attitudes and preferences and the normative view that human interests necessarily feature in those states of affairs judged to possess intrinsic value. The former view may be rejected without committing one to the latter view. Once this is recognised, the philosopher seeking to defend environmentalist claims can disengage from the dubious project of elaborating and justifying a non-subjectivist theory of value. There is a more crucial task to be addressed; namely to delineate what it is in nature that we, from 'our ineliminable human perspective' (Williams, 1992, p. 68) have the capacity to comprehend, to respond to and to value.

The Political Dimension

There must be something which environmentalists see in nature which is the basis of their claims that it has intrinsic value, that it should be respected, that it should be preserved for its own sake, and so on. The project of articulating this something has philosophical interest but, more importantly, it is politically vital (see Williams, 1992, p. 68). There are two reasons for this, one obviously practical and the other a little more theoretical. The practical reason is that the more people there are who share the value response to wild nature, the more political clout environmentalism is likely to have and the more people there are likely to be willing to adjust their lifestyles and make the 'sacrifices' taking environmental values seriously requires. Obviously there is an instrumental basis for supporting environmentalist policies, having to do with such things as valuing present and future human recreational, aesthetic and scientific opportunities and, more pressingly, guaranteeing the continuation of conditions necessary for a tolerable life for humans. These concerns for human interests might spill over into a concern for the interests of at least higher order nonhuman animals. Nevertheless the appeal to the intrinsic value of nature gives an additional edge to environmentalism.

The more theoretical reason has to do with political liberalism. John Rawls, for instance, represents a theory of liberal justice as determining the basic structure of a social arrangement within which citizens are free to pursue their own, perhaps various, conceptions of the good. The liberal state is to assume a position of neutrality between competing conceptions of the good, favouring no particular conception of the good above others. Now Rawls does think that there are certain primary goods—goods which we may presume every citizen will count as worth having irrespective of the contours of his or her particular conception of the good. These include such things as 'rights and liberties, powers and opportunities, income and wealth . . . health and vigor, intelligence and imagination' (Rawls, 1971, p. 62). The liberal state may permissibly work towards an essentially egalitarian distribution of these goods, except where inequalities improve the position of the worst off, and towards their maximisation. Beyond this, it cannot permissibly dictate particular uses or expenditures of these goods. In particular, it might not be permissible for the liberal state to allocate resources to protect and preserve the natural environment or to rehabilitate and restore damaged or despoiled nature. To do so may be to favour a particular conception of the good, or view of what has intrinsic value, above some other. But it needs to be stressed that many aspects of environmentalist policy, namely those which aim to promote certain shared human interests, will be defensible in terms of liberal justice.

If it could be argued successfully that nature as such fell within the scope of a principle of justice then the tension between those demands of environmentalism which focus on the intrinsic value of the nonhuman world and the requirements of liberal neutrality would be somewhat eased. There may be some movement in this direction through the inclusion of higher order animals within the scope of justice (see Elliot, 1984). The extension of justice or rights beyond the human domain, however, takes us only so far; certainly no further than creatures with consciousness (see Elliot, 1978; Williams, 1992, p. 64; and for a different view Attfield, 1992, pp. 86–88). So, it is doubtful that a successful liberal defence of environmentalism could develop along this path, appeals to human interests aside. And even if such a defence did succeed it would seem to miss the point of much concern about wild nature; that concern simply does not seem to have as its focus the rights of such items as trees, fungi, gnats, rocks and stalactites, or, more grandly, species, ecosystems and the biosphere.

If one does regard nature as possessing intrinsic value and if one is swayed by the norm of liberal neutrality, then an option worth pursuing is to attempt to articulate what it is about wild nature that underpins its intrinsic value. To get others to perceive nature as one does oneself, and obviously that will be no simple feat, is a step towards making a central element of one's own conception of the good a central element of their conception of the good. And the pursuit of environmentalist policies by the liberal state does not violate the requirement of neutrality where citizens agree that nature has intrinsic value and consequently desire that it be protected and preserved.

The Basis of Nature's Intrinsic Value

Some might suggest, as I have, that the property of being naturally evolved is a basis of nature's value (Elliot, 1982; 1992, pp. 151–155). If this is just to say that nature has intrinsic value because it is natural, then it says little, but it does provide the starting point for a fuller account. As Williams says, 'the idea of "raw" nature, as opposed to culture and to human production, comes into these matters, and fundamentally so' (Williams, 1992, p. 65). The suggestion is that it is the otherness of nature, its separateness and distinctness from creatures such as ourselves who are produced and produce within culture and technology, that underwrites its intrinsic value. Our sense of nature's otherness sparks the valuing response (see also Attfield, this volume, p. 46; Lee, this volume, p. 94).

Sense of otherness, however, is not sufficient by itself. For, as Williams implies, the sense of nature's otherness might engender pervasive and overwhelming fear (Williams, 1992, pp. 66-68). The sense of otherness needs to be combined with other elements in order to produce the valuing response. I think there are two candidates. The first is an appreciation of nature's aesthetic value. This aspect of nature is manifested through properties such as diversity, stability, complexity, beauty, grandeur, subtlety, harmony, creativity, organisation, intricacy, elegance and richness. And these are properties that ecology can assist us to perceive, inviting us to look beyond what initially strikes us in our observations of the natural and to notice relationships and qualities hitherto unnoticed. The addition of aesthetic value is not quite sufficient, though, to provide a distinctive value perspective on nature. After all, there is much outside nature that has aesthetic worth and it might be suggested that its creation can compensate for the destruction of natural aesthetic value, a suggestion which I reject. This is where the second candidate comes in. What distinguishes the aesthetic value of nature is that it is achieved without intentional design, without purposive intervention.[1] Again, ecology as well as other sciences

[1] One implication is that if the universe were the creation of a divine being and is the expression of some divine plan, then it could not have value in the same way, for the same reasons, as the universe I think we inhabit, although it could have equal value. Not all theisms will have this implication. Whether they do will depend on whether the creation of the universe is construed as the setting in motion of a plan. A theism involving only an indifferent divine being would not have the implication.

helps us to comprehend the evolutionary and other natural processes that have led to natural organisation, complexity, diversity and so on. Ecology as well as other sciences contributes to the elimination of that fear of the natural which derives from bewilderment and the absence of understanding.[2]

Some Claims of Restoration Ecology

Restoration ecology is the enterprise of 'returning a site to some previous state, with the species richness and diversity and physical, biological and aesthetic characteristics of that site before human settlement and the accompanying disturbances' (Morrison, 1987, p. 160). Or, more broadly, restoration ecology might be taken to include returning a site to an original state after any significant disturbance, whether its cause be human activity or some unambiguously natural phenomenon such as volcanic eruption or meteor strike.

There has been some theorizing associated with restoration ecology which threatens the claims I have made about the basis of nature's value, particularly the claim that its value derives from its being naturally evolved. It might be thought that my claim about naturalness as a basis of intrinsic value implies that successfully restored environments would have less value than the original environment. It might also be argued that if the restored environment has the same value as the original, then naturalness cannot be a basis for the intrinsic value of wild nature. Finally, it might be argued that the restored environment does have the same value as the original. This line of argument is present in some restoration ecology theorizing but the crucial alleged implication, on which its success depends, is illusory. Obviously all that follows from my claim about naturalness as a basis of intrinsic value is that the value of the restored and original environments respectively must have at least a partially different basis.[3]

---

[2] Some might suggest that the understanding afforded by the sciences is itself a kind of conquest, domestication and humanising of nature. The concern might be deepened by the suggestion that the nature to which we seem to have access through our senses and their technological extensions is not nature as it is in itself, there being no such thing. (For a response see Elliot, 1989, pp. 197–198.)

[3] We should also note that restoration ecology is, for reasons to do with limited manipulative capacities, imprecise knowledge of ecological processes, imprecise knowledge of original sites, cost, irretrievable loss of ecosystemic components, and the like, more theoretical than practical.

According to C. Mark Cowell, Peter Losin, a restoration ecologist, argues that 'human influence need not always be considered bad or unnatural, and . . . restoration salvages natural values that would otherwise be lost' (Cowell, 1993, p. 25). Cowell represents Losin's view as casting doubt on the claim that naturalness is a basis of intrinsic value. On Cowell's account, Losin appears to be making three distinct claims. First, he seems to be saying that human influences on the natural environment are not always bad; second, he seems to be saying that human action should not always be seen as unnatural; third, he seems to be saying that restoration ecology can preserve certain natural values. I shall discuss these claims in turn and ask whether any of them, to the extent that they are true, casts doubt on the claim that naturalness is a basis of intrinsic value.

The first claim is true for two sorts of reason. For one thing, human influence can preserve nature through the designation of wilderness areas in which human activity is, through the enactment and enforcement of legislation, kept at a minimum. This might provide the basis for an argument along the following lines. The value of nature within such a designated area is the same as the value of an exactly similar area of nature that was not preserved through human influence but which unambiguously naturally existed. Moreover, so the argument might run, the role of human action in preserving the first area subverts, if not destroys, its naturalness. The thought is that in such acts of preservation, just as in acts of restoration, 'we impose our anthropocentric purposes on areas that exist outside human society' (Katz, 1992a, p. 235). So, it might be inferred, naturalness cannot be the basis of nature's intrinsic value.

This argument is flawed, however, because it neglects to emphasise the fact that artificial processes do not generate or give rise to wild nature but rather artificially prevent the destruction of something which has naturally arisen. To a large degree it is true that, within the boundaries of the wilderness area, ecological and other natural processes remain at work. And certainly the explanation of the structure of nature within the designated area is explicable without reference to human purposes: it is nature's project, not ours. (See Rolston, 1988, pp. 192–201 on *projective nature* and Sylvan, 1990, pp. 7–28 on *purposive nature*.) All that can be said about the role of human activity is that it partially explains how nature's project in this particular area continues. In the case of restored nature, by contrast, human purposes and human activity play a central role in explaining how the restored environment came to have the structure it has. It does not seem that artificial protection compromises the naturalness of wilderness. We let it alone by ensuring that it is left alone, and that does not strike me as paradoxical—although Williams seems not to agree (Williams, 1992, p. 68).

There is, of course, a reply. The restoration ecologist might concede that the act of preservation itself does not compromise the area's value-adding naturalness but argue that human activity does influence the ecological development of the area. It does this because the effects of human activity are all-pervasive and compound over time to impact significantly on apparently pristine nature. For instance, pollution from human industrial activity or from concentrations of human population will enter into evolutionary and ecological pathways leading to, for example, species variation and even broader ecological restructuring. But this reply shifts the criticism of my claim that naturalness is a basis of intrinsic value in a direction that brings it close to a view I shall later discuss.

The second reason why Losin's first claim is correct has to do with value pluralism, that is, the view that there is a variety of bases of intrinsic value. Value pluralism makes space for both the claim that naturalness is a source of intrinsic value and the claim that the restored environment might possess as much intrinsic value as the unambiguously naturally evolved one. So, we must distinguish between the claim that equal value is restored and the claim that equal and similarly structured value is restored. Equal value is restored if and only if the total value of the restored area is the same as the total intrinsic value of the original area. And value is similarly structured if it supervenes in the same way, is based on the same value-adding properties, as the equal value of the original area. It is clear that even if restoration ecology could deliver equal value it might not be able to do so in a way that is similarly structured, in which case the claim that naturalness itself is a basis of intrinsic value is saved. Only where the equal value is similarly structured may we say that value has been fully restored.

An analogy might make the point clearer. Consider a chair that I might make from a tree that I fell. The chair may possess the same value as was possessed by the tree. However, the value-adding properties in virtue of which the chair has intrinsic value differ from the value-adding properties in virtue of which the tree had intrinsic value. The chair may exemplify certain aesthetic properties, it may be pleasingly delicate and finely proportioned, and in virtue of that have intrinsic value. The tree may exemplify quite different value-adding aesthetic properties, being neither pleasingly delicate nor finely proportioned. Or we might judge it to have

39

intrinsic value in virtue of exemplifying organised life. Indeed part of the chair's intrinsic value may derive from the relational fact that its production involved the transformation of the bases of value. In making the chair I may compensate for the value lost from the world when I felled the tree but that compensation does not involve, in the sense defined above, full restoration. So, there is no suggestion that restored nature cannot have the same value or even greater value than original nature, although as a matter of fact, given the comparative crudeness of restoration ecology, it does not. Indeed I would urge that there is another, perhaps more significant reason, namely, that the property of being naturally evolved is intensely value-adding. It is a source of value for which it is difficult to compensate. I would, moreover, seriously entertain the view that the property of being naturally evolved is absolutely value-adding. And a property is absolutely value-adding if any state of affairs exemplifying it has more value than any state of affairs not exemplifying it (Chisholm, 1986, pp. 93–94).

It is important to mention another source of value associated with ecological restoration which might mislead some to accept a strong version of Losin's first claim. Intrinsic value might be generated by the fact that restoration is restitutive. The property of being a restituting state of affairs or the property of being an act of endeavouring to bring about such a state of affairs could sustain intrinsic value. As Sylvan, Taylor and Gunn urge, we are morally responsible for our despoiling acts and, arguably, for the despoiling acts of others from which we have benefitted, and we have a duty to restore value that has thereby been obliterated or eroded (Sylvan, 1988, p. 14; Taylor, 1986, pp. 304–306; Gunn, 1991, p. 308). Discharging this restitutive duty is both deontologically required and has positive intrinsic value. So, intrinsic value attaching to acts of restitutive restoration and to the resultant state of affairs, in virtue of the restitutive motivation, would offset the value loss caused by degradation. But it is doubtful that the intrinsic value produced through restitution makes up for the value lost through the degradation of wild nature. It would have been better had restitution not been required.

Turn now to Losin's second claim, that human action should not always be seen as unnatural. Again I think that this is correct but not in any way that is particularly helpful to the view that restoration ecology can in principle restore full value. Certainly humans are part of nature; our species is an item in nature's evolutionary project. There is, however, a sense in which humans have transcended nature or are outside nature. In so far as humans are creatures who make extensive use of technology and are thorough-

ly enmeshed in culture, they are more properly thought of as outside the bounds of the natural: human actions which employ technology and have a basis in culture are not natural. Or so I hope to
suggest.

Losin's claim is echoed by other restoration ecologists. William
Jordan, for instance, complains that 'much environmental thinking
. . . takes for granted that the world, the rest of nature, is something "out there" and that human beings are somehow outsiders,
alienated from this other world' (quoted in Cowell, 1993, p. 26).
Furthermore, Jordan depicts humans as natural inhabitants of
ecosystems 'in intimate contact with nature, changing the landscape
unapologetically as all creatures do' (quoted in Cowell, 1993, p. 27).
And others complain that the distinction between the natural and
the non-natural, on which my claim concerning naturalness as a
basis for intrinsic value depends, reflects 'the modern estrangement
of humans from nature, derived from the Cartesian subject-object
dualism' (Cowell, 1993, p. 27). This objection is sometimes associated with the view that restoration ecology has point in part
because it involves a harmonious re-entry into nature. The thought
seems to be that human intervention in the environment need not
amount to laying waste to nature but may instead take the form of a
co-operative transformation in a way that preserves certain values
but involves a purposive role for humans in reshaping, even
improving, nature (see Callicott, 1991; 1992). An example might be
the purposeful introduction by humans of a species into an area in
which it has hitherto not been present, perhaps to save it from
extinction or biologically to enrich an area.

Despite these objections I think there is a recognisable point to
the distinction between the natural and the non-natural. And there
is a recognisable point to the claim that even the harmonious
transformation of nature drains it of significant intrinsic value,
contaminating it with human purposiveness. After all, human
agency is strikingly different from other kinds of agency, such as
the agency of most nonhuman animals, of plants, of acids, of geophysical forces and the like. It involves an array of higher order
intentional states; it is mediated by a heavy intrusion of culture,
social organisation and highly structured economic arrangements;
and it is exaggerated by extensive technological capacities. While
humans result from, are embedded in and exemplify natural
processes, including cosmological, evolutionary and biological
processes, they have at least partially transcended the natural.
Rolston (1991) helps us to see this. He notes, for instance, the different modes of transmission of information in nature as against
culture. In the former it is transmitted genetically and it does not

include acquired information. In the latter it is transmitted through language in particular but also through other elements of culture such as rituals. In culture, moreover, the transmission of acquired information is comparatively fast. Or again, culture and technology insulate humans from natural processes, particularly natural selection, as when we use medical technology to assist other humans. Certainly technology makes possible massive interventions in ecosystems. And cultural structures, such as economic and political systems, drive such intervention. We have, as well, a capacity for active decision-making or goal modification, involving culturally constructed attitudes, desires and preferences. The upshot is that our propensities are more malleable than those of other organisms.

The distinction between culturally and technologically mediated human agency and the agency of other living and non-living things is so profound that it is grotesque to think of ourselves as simply another species embedded, and striving to make a living, in nature. And while the distinction between the natural and the non-natural may be blurred at the boundary, we have no reason to give it up as a basis for making value distinctions. Moreover, the distinction does clearly pick out and sharply differentiate substantial non-contiguous parts of a continuum.

Losin's third claim is that restoration ecology can preserve certain natural values. Again I think that there is some truth in this which is nevertheless consistent with the claims that restoration erodes one significant basis of intrinsic value, namely naturalness. Consider the restoration of a species through a genetic recovery programme and its reintroduction into areas from which humans earlier caused it to disappear. Its reintroduction may stabilise the ecosystems in question, preventing their unnatural simplification or collapse. The example compels the concession that ecosystems may be to varying degrees natural (see Elliot, 1994). The reintroduced species is in the ecosystem non-naturally but being there stabilises natural structures. Moreover, the recovery and reintroduction of the species amounts to a reinstantiation of a natural design. While the process is not natural, much of what it results in, and much of what it utilises, is. While value is not fully restored, what natural value remains is preserved. And that is a good thing.

Conclusion

I have distinguished between non-anthropocentric meta-ethics and non-anthropocentric normative ethics. My suggestion was that the former is not possible; all values that I take seriously are values that I find myself with, perhaps after critical reflection, in a particular place at a particular time. But others are to a large extent like me and our value perspectives overlap to varying degrees even if they do not coincide. Still, there is space for non-anthropocentric normative ethics. This brought us to Williams's question of how the normative shift away from the narrowly anthropocentric might be achieved in those who are initially disinclined to perceive intrinsic value in nature. I suggested that the otherness of projective nature in concert with its positive aesthetic worth is the significant basis of its intrinsic value. And I have endeavoured to articulate and defend this suggestion in the context of some apparently contrary claims of some restoration ecologists.

Rehabilitating Nature and Making Nature Habitable

ROBIN ATTFIELD

Can nature be reconstituted, recreated or rehabilitated? And would the goal of doing so be a desirable one? There again, is wild nature intrinsically valuable, or are parks, gardens and farms sometimes preferable or of greater value? This cluster of questions arises from recent debates about preservation, restoration, wilderness and sustainable development. In discussing them I hope to throw some light on both the concept and the value of nature, and in due course on the attitudes which people should have towards it, the policies which should guide their practice, and thus on the proper role of humanity with regard to the natural world.

To begin with, we need a clear sense of 'nature', and thus to turn to John Stuart Mill's celebrated essay on that subject (Mill, 1874). Now when the possibility of nature being restored is at issue, 'nature' cannot be used in Mill's first sense, 'all which is— the powers and properties of all things'. For in this sense there is no possibility of nature being destroyed or damaged, let alone reconstructed. Mill's second sense of 'nature', rather, is the relevant one: 'what takes place without . . . the voluntary and intentional agency of man [sic]'. Nature (in this sense) can obviously be modified by human activity. Moreover a difficulty already emerges about the possibility of restoring it: how can anything be restored by human agency the essence of which is to be independent of human agency? This is a question to which we shall return.

Meanwhile it is apposite here to remark that Mill argues against the desirability of imitating nature (in this sense), holding that civilization has made progress precisely through turning its back on this policy, and that nature is not an exemplar fit to be followed. His case is, indeed, well made. It may further be noted that his own understanding of the tendency of humanity to value nature is that this tendency arises from the vastness of natural forces; but the astonishment and awe which are thus inspired are said to be prone to 'intrude into matters with which they ought to have no concern' (Mill, 1874, pp. 26f). They are, in particular, no guide for ethics or conduct.

This essay was composed during the 1850s, before Darwin's theory of evolution was published. Thus, conservationist as he was, Mill was in no position to appreciate the evolutionary systems and networks which are among the modern bases for the appreciation of nature. Yet more than this is missing from his account of responses to nature. He grasped the terror-inspiring vastness of natural forces, and to this he ascribed their sublimity; but he seems to have omitted the sense of nature's otherness or strangeness, and the importance that this has in renewing both wonder and perspective. Nor does he mention another aspect of nature's strangeness, its inexhaustible diversity; while little is said, beyond the passage about sublimity, about natural beauty. Since so much that he says about nature is convincing, it is worth drawing attention from the start both to his omissions and to these further grounds for valuing nature.

But this does not show that whatever is natural is invariably valuable. Robert Elliot, whose views on attempts at the restoration of nature will shortly be discussed, recognizes this at the outset of his essay 'Faking Nature'; treating 'natural' as meaning (approximately) 'unmodified by human activity' (Elliot, 1982, p. 84), he gives sickness and disease as examples of natural phenomena which are not good, and mentions how fires, hurricanes and volcanic eruptions can alter landscapes for the worse. He does claim, however, that 'within certain constraints, the naturalness of a landscape is a reason for preserving it, a determinant of its value'. One constraint which he supplies is this: 'Artificially transforming an utterly barren, ecologically bankrupt landscape into something richer and more subtle may be a good thing'. Here the naturalness of the landscape is not regarded as a sufficient reason for preserving it. Nevertheless, he argues, the natural origin or genesis of a feature or landscape is always a factor which contributes to its value (Elliot, 1982, p. 87); and to this conclusion I shall be returning.

A rather stronger position about the value of nature is taken by Eric Katz (Katz, 1992a). Katz basically defines 'natural' as 'being independent of the actions of humanity', and less basically as 'objects and processes that exist as far as possible from human manipulation and control' (pp. 238f). The key characteristic of natural individuals is that they 'were not designed for a purpose', but 'evolve to fill ecological niches in the biosphere', unlike artefacts, which Katz represents as created for human purposes, and thus 'essentially anthropocentric' (p. 235). Further, 'natural entities are autonomous in ways that human-created artefacts are not'; thus 'When we . . . judge natural objects, and evaluate them more highly than artefacts, we are focussing on the extent of their independence from human domination' (p. 239). For the pre-eminent value is self-realization, and that is what natural entities, being autonomous, are free to pursue (pp. 239f). Katz, like Elliot, uses his metaphysical and axiological claims about nature to argue against attempts to restore damage caused by human interventions.

For his part Elliot maintains that if a reconstituted natural setting is qualitatively indistinguishable from other natural settings or from its own earlier condition, its value is less because it is a 'fake', lacking the right kind of origin. Just as the value of works of art depends on their having the right sort of provenance, so too the value of apparently wild and natural settings depends in part on their being genuinely so, and having originated through natural processes and not through artifice (Elliot, 1982, pp. 87–89). Elliot adds that it is wise for conservationists to argue in addition the inadequacy of the restorations which developers promise (p. 92); but he believes that in protesting that even the best of restorations lacks the value had by what is to be restored simply because it is a fake they already have a rational case (pp. 83, 92).

To this case, Katz and Richard Sylvan, conservationists both, reply that actual deception is rarely in question, and thus that little is achieved by representing restoring as faking or restorations as fakes (Katz, 1992a, pp. 237f; Sylvan, 1992, pp. 11–13). While this reply is apposite, Sylvan finds merit all the same in Elliot's arguments in favour of the significance of an item's origins and history for its value, taking the view that this is where the strength of his case really lies, and not in the faking analogy (Sylvan, 1992, p. 13).

Now certainly the symbolic and aesthetic value of an item can depend in part on its origins and history; but this approach puts the value of natural items with the right kind of origins in much the same position as that of cultural artefacts such as vases or paintings, despite the manifest differences between art appreciation and nature appreciation, differences which Elliot well recognizes and expresses (Elliot, 1982, p. 90). And plausibly the value of such items is what Frankena calls 'inherent value' (Frankena, 1979); it depends ultimately on the actual or potential appreciation of valuers, rather than supplying grounds for preservation independent of psychological states of valuers in the way that intrinsic or independent value is held to do. Certainly this appreciation is itself sometimes dependent on the valued item having the right kind of origin or history, and that is an independent characteristic of the item in question, as Elliot points out (pp. 87f). But this does not serve to make the case for its preservation (and thus for its non-replacement) any stronger than the like case for the preservation of cultural artefacts. Indeed unless it has further grounds, its

strength is surely proportionate to the number of humans susceptible to the right kind of appreciation.

While for Elliot restorations of nature are possible but of inferi-
or value, for Katz they are impossible. Restorations are artefacts,
which are invariably anthropocentric; whereas nature is without
design, is capable of self-realization and is precisely not an artefact. Most of this, however, is open to challenge. For the moment
I set on one side the reply that most areas of the earth, however
apparently natural, have in fact been influenced by human activity,
and thus would have to be seen by purists as artefacts. Further
replies concern restorations of nature specifically, and are raised
by Sylvan. Thus restorations of nature are largely achieved 'by
nature doing its own thing' (what used to be called *natura
naturans*), and are not the products of human making or human
creation. Humans weed them or remove rubbish, but their contribution amounts to helping along a natural process of healing.
Thus Katz has illicitly extended the meaning of 'artefact' to
restorations, which, unsatisfactory as they standardly are, should
still not be regarded as artefacts (Sylvan, 1992, pp. 22f).

Sylvan here adds that the point of restorations is not invariably
human pleasure or human use, and is often 'the welfare and persistence of other creatures and natural features', or alternatively the
enrichment or enhancement of an area's value. Thus restorations,
albeit designed by humans, need not have a shallow or 'anthropocentric' motivation, and need not conflict with the natural
development of natural creatures. Even if artefacts were essentially
anthropocentric, which they are not, this would still not apply to
restorations. Sylvan does not discuss Katz's contentious claim that
the pre-eminent value is self-realization, but does not need to do
so to make the point that the case for restorations is liable to concern whether there is an increase in value, as there sometimes is,
and not a false metaphysical account of their essence. He gives the
example of an ecosystem which has been impoverished by 'cream-
ing', and which is restored by reintroducing the creamed species
from elsewhere; here value is clearly enhanced (Sylvan, 1992, p.
23).

Sylvan goes on to recognize the many problems facing attempts
at rehabilitation of a natural setting. Besides obvious practical
obstacles there are problems deriving from lack of information and
also from lack of suitable technology. Yet 'technology-assisted
restoration nonetheless has a point and place'. The modest role
envisaged here for technology is in complete contrast to belief in
'universal technological repair and . . . total rehabilitation', or in
there being a technological fix for each and every ecological prob-

lem, something against which Katz is right to protest (Sylvan, 1992, p. 26). Even former wildernesses can sometimes be restored, by closing off the roads which enter them (p. 27). Rehabilitation is thus possible, and sometimes admissible and worthwhile. For societies (as opposed to individuals) able to put this into effect it can actually be obligatory, just as it is obligatory to reduce the erosion of substantially natural environments. But there is nothing glamorous about it; it is the cleaning up of some of the appalling mess around us, and resembles, as much as anything, 'housework in a slum' (p. 28). This does, however, show that 'Letting Be' (what Hargrove calls 'therapeutic nihilism' (Hargrove, 1989, pp. 160f)) is frequently inappropriate, at least for disturbed areas (Sylvan, 1992, pp. 29f).

While I consider that Sylvan's critique, as just presented, can largely be accepted, it raises certain problems of both metaphysics and ethics which call for further investigation. In particular it recalls the metaphysical problem mentioned above when Mill's second sense of 'nature' was introduced: how can anything be restored by human agency the essence of which is to be independent of human agency? Indeed it further raises the whole question of the role of humanity *vis-à-vis* nature, and the related ethical questions of the principles by which conduct and policy should be guided with respect to an environment mostly already heavily affected by previous use, in circumstances when pressing human needs require its further use for as long as the future can be foreseen.

To tackle the metaphysical problem first, there certainly is a paradox concerning human agency restoring what is essentially independent of human agency. But it should also be noted that there is no question of this where nature is undamaged and wilderness untrammelled. Intervention could certainly be required to prevent disturbance (and on occasion could be justifiable), but this would not be restoration. Only where disruption has already taken place, as, however, is the case in most of the areas of Britain recognized as 'ancient forest', is restoration or rehabilitation possible; and what is sometimes possible is reversing the damage and returning an area to a condition closely resembling its erstwhile condition in which evolutionary processes proceed independent of further human agency. Sylvan's example of returning creamed species could be a case in point. Although Elliot's historical requirement for nature to have its full aesthetic value is not satisfied, and the area cannot be regarded as in all respects wild, there could in theory be the same blend of creatures each living in accordance with its own nature, and jointly forming a system just like the pristine one which preceded human intervention. Although the outcome is, broadly, what human agency intended, it is still equivalent to what unimpeded nature would have produced. Besides, if there is intrinsic value in the fulfilment of the capacities of the various natural creatures, each in accordance with its own nature, as I have argued elsewhere, then there is present the same intrinsic value as there would have been if humanity had never intervened. Further, if the area was ever to regain this condition, nothing but the intervention of an intentional agency could bring this about. Indeed the paradox is perhaps no stronger than that involved when the agency and interventions of parents bring about the possibility of autonomy for their children as they grow to adulthood; though here autonomy is of course initiated rather than restored.

The deliberate restoration of nature (to something like the condition of wilderness) is thus a possibility. So is the preservation of nature, where intervention prevents the natural course of events being disturbed. Yet the difficulties, including those mentioned by Katz and Sylvan, will often make this more a theoretical than a practical possibility. Katz objects that even if there were a plan in a natural system, we could not know it (Katz, 1992a, p. 236); while we might in theory know how to rectify the *status quo ante*, without knowing the full story of how this particular ecosystem works we are most unlikely to, or to act in a manner precisely proportioned to what we should need to know. And so on. Yet it would still be possible (as Sylvan says) to enrich the area and increase its value; and where the enrichment was considerable, this might be regarded as rehabilitation, even if it would not technically be restoration. For the outcome could still (at least in theory) be an area in which, without further human intervention, evolutionary processes produced ever new communities of thriving wild creatures, much more than was possible up to the time of intervention, and this would surely count as rehabilitation if anything ever would. Whether a particular act of rehabilitation is justified would, however, often turn on further factors, such as whether value could be enhanced in an alternative way, or whether the proposed rehabilitation was a ploy proposed to offset environmentalist criticism of a destructive development like strip-mining which the proposers intend to carry out first.

Indeed not too much can be derived from these possibilities about the role of humanity *vis-à-vis* nature; for humanity has many obligations besides wilderness preservation, restoration and rehabilitation, if indeed these are obligations. The suggestion that they are not, together with several related issues of ethics and policy, has recently been debated by J. Baird Callicott and Holmes Rolston (Callicott, 1991; Rolston, 1991); a brief account of this debate is now in place, before the outstanding metaphysical, ethical and policy issues are further tackled.

Callicott ascribes to Aldo Leopold support not only for preserving wild sanctuaries but also for the view that human activity sometimes enhances ecosystems (Callicott, 1991, pp. 235–238). He proceeds to question the viability of wilderness preservation, and then to criticize the very concept of wilderness as unnecessarily dualistic, and objectionably ethnocentric and static (pp. 238–242). Conservation, he suggests, should rather be blended with sustainable development, economic development being at the same time reconceived in the light of ecology, with (for example) reintroduced native ungulates both sustaining New World ecosystems and being ranched to feed humans there (pp. 239, 242–245).

Rolston for his part ably defends the concept of wilderness. The concepts of nature and culture are fundamentally distinct (as indeed has effectively been shown also in the passages concerning Mill, Elliot and Katz, above), and the concept of wilderness preservation need not be ethnocentric, and does not ignore temporal change (Rolston, 1991, pp. 370f, 373–375). There are values intrinsic to wild nature, which thus ought to be preserved both for its own sake and for the good of humanity; wilderness advocates recognize values which do not depend on human valuations, but which humans nevertheless ought and need to affirm (pp. 371, 375). Rolston accepts the importance of sustainable development within the realms of culture and cultivation, but rejects the possibility of wilderness management and that of humans improving wild nature as contradictions in terms (pp. 371f). He also regards as inadequate Callicott's anthropogenic value-theory, which makes values ultimately dependent on human valuations (pp. 370, 376).

As will already be apparent, there is no alternative but to recognize the conceptual case for the impossibility of managing or enhancing areas of pure wilderness. Yet rather little of the earth's surface amounts to pure wilderness, and in Europe virtually none. There is a strong case for preserving such areas as there are, for the sake of the creatures within them, because of the needs of human science, and because of the value to humans of the availability of what is wild and wholly other; and this applies both to untouched wilderness and to wilderness (or semi-wilderness) only lightly affected by humanity, as by the primitive technology of forest peoples—as long as these people are not excluded from their own forests. But it is at least equally important to reflect on how best to treat the remaining areas of the earth which have ceased to be wilderness, but remain significantly wild, and a vital contrast to the frenetic life of cities and motorways. As has been seen, the possibilities of enhancing, rehabilitating and even restoring such areas certainly can arise. Indeed, conservationists cannot afford to reject the enhanced value of restored wilderness, despite what Rolston calls its 'different historical genesis' (Rolston, 1991, p. 372). While there is, as Rolston (in line here with Elliot) says, 'a radical change of value type' (p. 372), the deficiency (I have suggested) concerns one particular kind of aesthetic value, while much which is of intrinsic value remains, together with the restored intactness of ancient ecosystems.

Next, to be fair to Callicott, his idea of wilderness management should not be ruled out entirely, despite the contradiction which it generates where the express aim is wilderness preservation, and despite the strong ethical case for preserving wilderness untrammelled. Callicott writes of management with a view to the vital part which wilderness can play in biological conservation, by which he could easily mean 'species conservation'; and if a species whose original habitat has ceased to be viable can only be preserved (or can best be preserved) by its introduction into a wilderness (which its introduction would admittedly modify), the implicit clash of values confronting decision-makers would not seem to produce a clearcut case every time against introduction. But this minor rehabilitation of the case for wilderness management does not make and should not be taken as a case for the management of wildernesses in general, which, as Callicott acknowledges, might 'artificialize' any wilderness to which it is applied (Callicott, 1991, p. 239).

This discussion of restoring wilderness and of managing wilderness does, however, serve to bring to light the way Rolston sometimes overstates his case. Rolston writes that it is a 'fallacy to think that a nature allegedly improved by humans is any more real nature at all', and goes on to claim that 'the values intrinsic to wilderness cannot, on pain of both logical and empirical contradiction, be "improved" by deliberate human management, because deliberation is the antithesis of wildness' (Rolston, 1991, p. 371). This is the passage which leads up to the claim that wilderness management is a contradiction in terms. Though the context concerns wilderness, the claim here about nature happens to imply both that areas like parks and gardens, designed and intendedly improved by humans for the sake of beauty and its aesthetic enjoyment, contain neither natural creatures nor natural processes, and also that the species modified for agriculture have ceased to have natural capacities and propensities, and thus a good natural to their kind. Yet natural goods can in fact persist far away from wilderness; and this is just as well for the citizens of modern urban and rural areas alike, for the creatures they cultivate and for the ethics of the treatment of those creatures.

Relatedly, the values intrinsic to wilderness include the intrinsic value of the flourishing of the creatures which originate there, the value of intact ecosystems, and the value of the human appreciation of wildness, of otherness, and of living systems which originate from evolution alone and lack any human modification. But only some of these values are distinctive of pure wilderness. While restored wilderness lacks only the last-mentioned value (living systems originating from evolution alone), the intrinsic value of the flourishing of natural creatures occurs wherever they are to be found throughout the earth, and not only in wilderness. While this does not of itself affect Rolston's point about wilderness management, it does show that the value of wilderness does not only consist in its wildness; indeed it suggests that it does not principally consist in this. And if so, the wildness of wilderness might not be a conclusive ethical reason against proposals to manage it; indeed much that is wild ought to be managed more than it is, including certain philosophical theories (but I am not referring here to Rolston's). In any case some of the values originating in wilderness are transferable out of the wild without ceasing to be natural, when, as Rolston goes on to remark, humans rebuild the natural world they inherit. And this too is important, as the appreciation of nature, and to a limited extent of its otherness and even of its wildness, can be significantly available even in places like Europe, where wilderness has virtually ceased to exist, and in Third World settings, where, as Callicott points out, most landscapes have long been inhabited by *Homo sapiens* as well as by other species (Callicott, 1991, p. 242).

These considerations are not without their importance when, as I shortly shall, we turn to the role of humanity *vis-à-vis* nature. The importance of sustainable development is recognized both by Callicott, who regards it as the main route to conservation, and by Rolston, who reasonably enough requires that there be some wilderness preservation independently of it, but who implies too great an absence of the natural within the sphere of human culture and cultivation. Sylvan too recognizes that sustainable development may have much merit, but rapidly adds that it is 'not nature *enhancing* but rather purports to limit further rot and decline', that it is less benign than nature rehabilitation, and that it and its sub-types, sustainable forestry and sustainable agriculture, are typical of a shallow (i.e., anthropocentric) rather than a deep value-theory

(Sylvan, 1992, p. 28). While his context concerns nature restoration, these remarks still gravely underestimate the values which sustainable development can uphold and which often motivate its advocates.

To take the last point first, sustainable development is aimed at satisfying future as well as present needs, and not only human needs at that. For sustainability involves the preservation of ecological systems. As Callicott puts it: 'We conservationists . . . may hope realistically that in the future, ecological, as well as technological feasibility may be taken into account in designing new and redesigning old ways of humans living with the land' (Callicott, 1991, p. 236). This well conveys the approach of enlightened human self-interest; but the Brundtland Report, the deservedly influential text which continues to inspire the advocacy of sustainable development, is clear that ecological systems are also to be preserved for the sake of non-human species and of their own intrinsic value, and proceeds to urge a considerable amount of wilderness preservation alongside its advocacy of sustainable production. To cite a relevant passage: 'The case for the conservation of nature should rest not only with development goals. It is part of our moral obligation to other living beings and future generations' (World Commission on Environment and Development, 1987, p. 57; on wilderness preservation, and on there being ethical as well as economic grounds for it, see ch. 6).

Thus, while sustainable development is not specifically focused on nature *restoration*, it is not, essentially or centrally, an anthropocentric or shallow policy; indeed the pursuit of sustainability is, to say the least, compatible with the restoration of forests, and may sometimes require it. Thus Rolston too is adrift when he declares that 'Sustainable development is, let's face it, irremediably anthropocentric' (Rolston, 1991, p. 376); it should, however, be acknowledged that he endorses much that Callicott says in its favour, including the apparently non-anthropocentric remark 'Human economic activities should at least be compatible with the ecological health of the environments in which they occur' (Rolston, 1991, pp. 370, 375; there he quotes Callicott, 1991, p. 239). Callicott in fact goes further, advocating (under the banner of sustainable development) 'economic activity that positively enhances ecosystemic health' (Callicott, 1991, p. 243); there is, as has already been seen, no contradiction in this, and conservationists can and should welcome this suggestion for a wide range of ecologically impoverished environments.

Sustainable development has the further merit that it takes seriously people's obligations to satisfy human needs both in the present and into the indefinite future. Since the development thus facilitated of essential human capacities has intrinsic value, as also has the flourishing of non-human creatures (or so I have argued elsewhere (Attfield, 1987, chs. 2–5)), a policy which promotes or sustains both these tendencies yields greater value and enriches the world much more than a policy (such as the restoration of wilderness) with only one of these outcomes. This does not show that the entire surface of the planet should be devoted to processes of sustainable development, not least because this would undermine numerous non-human species (see also Katz, 1992b); but it does suggest that there is in general a stronger obligation to support and implement sustainable development than there is to enhance the value of natural areas.

Not too much more can be said here about priorities, but what has just been said has important implications. Thus whether an area should be restored, or even first mined or felled and then restored, depends not only on the value implications for non-human nature, as the general tone of Sylvan's remarks suggests, but, as Elliot says, on the whole range of relevant ethical considerations, and thus on the overall balance of values at issue (Elliot, 1982, pp. 82f), for all that Sylvan takes him to task for saying so (Sylvan, 1992, pp. 9f). The ethical verdict may thus not always come out as conservationists would wish; but that is no reason for regarding the value-theory which makes this possible as shallow. (It might be shallow in another sense if it did not underwrite protests against exploitation and injustice; but it does.)

Thus the role of human beings is not only that of preservers of nature, not even when the role of restorers is added to that of preservers. Besides the role of rehabilitating nature, people have the role of making nature habitable, and sustainably so—habitable for human beings of the present and the future and also for those non-human creatures which they rear or cultivate as part of their civilization or their culture—without at the same time undermining those whose wildness and otherness they need or whose flourishing is of value in itself. Unsustainable processes of agriculture, forestry and industry can seldom contribute to this, except where they are needed as initial investment to inaugurate genuinely sustainable processes. Among sustainable processes, those which are globally sustainable are preferable to those which are only sustainable in some regions at the expense of others; likewise those which take into account the full range of values are preferable to those with any kind of discriminatory tendency. The suggestion that humanity should cultivate the earth and through skills and crafts make it habitable (though not for humanity alone) is an ancient one, put forward originally by such Church Fathers as Basil, Gregory, Augustine and others as work which fulfils the purpose of the creator (see Glacken, 1967, pp. 298–301; for some counterpart modern views, see Cowell, 1993, pp. 19–32) and it is none the worse for that. That humanity has this role (whether with or without these theological overtones) is also a key part of my present conclusion, without negating the conclusion that the proper role of humanity also includes preservation and rehabilitation.

This is not the place to discuss in depth whether the particular strategies urged by Callicott are the best way to fulfil these roles. His proposals for the ranching of ungulates in their original habitats has much to commend it, but may perhaps pay too little regard to the interests of the ungulates themselves. His proposals that designated wilderness areas serve as '*refugia*' for the less tolerant or the less easily tolerated species (Callicott, 1991, pp. 236, 237f, 240) are trenchantly criticized by Rolston (Rolston, 1991, pp. 373f, 376f), as are his attempts to represent human activities in general as natural; yet the idea of *refugia* may have a point in some cases in connection with species preservation, especially 'for species not tolerant of or tolerated by people' (Callicott, 1991, p. 236). And his remarks about the symbiotic relations of the Kayapo Indians of the Amazon and their rainforest reveal an apparent paradigm of sustainability there, and strengthen the belief that designs for nature reserves can and should (where it is viable) 'require planners to take account of and integrate local peoples culturally and economically', as United Nations policy apparently already enjoins (Callicott, 1991, p. 239).

But all this would come to very little if Callicott's or similar accounts of the nature of value and the status of value-language were granted; accordingly a brief mention of meta-ethics is finally in place. As Rolston reminds us, Callicott maintains that 'Intrinsic value ultimately depends upon human valuers' (Callicott, 1984, p. 305, cited by Rolston, 1991, p. 376) and that 'Value is, as it were, projected onto natural objects or events by the subjective feelings of observers' (Callicott, 1986, p. 156). Thus nothing would be of value unless valued by humans (or other valuers) in at least some possible world. Partially similar conclusions are maintained by Sylvan, whose 'nonjectivism' is as much intended to deny the independence of value from valuers as to deny that it is a quality of valuers, i.e., to reject both objectivism (both naive and sophisticated) and subjectivism too (thus Routley and Routley, 1980, pp. 154–157). Thus Sylvan too implies that there would be no value if there never were any valuers. Meanwhile Elliot, without relativising value to valuers, still represents it as always relative to a valuational framework; and while any given framework offers interpersonal reasons, ultimately there are apparently no reasons for preferring one valuational framework to another (Elliot, 1985).

Thus in some ways it is here that Rolston makes his most trenchant and possibly most important contribution to the debate, maintaining that Callicott's is a truncated theory of value, making wild nature valueless without humans, and that on the contrary wild nature is of value and would still be valuable even in the complete absence of valuers and their valuations (Rolston, 1991, p. 376). There can be little doubt that he is committed to saying much the same about the theories of Sylvan, and perhaps to a corresponding response to the valuational subjectivism of Elliot too. While Rolston does not here expound the meaning of 'value' in this objectivist sense, there would seem to be no problem about it meaning 'supplying interpersonal reasons for being fostered, promoted or preserved', as I have suggested elsewhere (Attfield, 1991, p. xiii). Indeed, with Rolston, I maintain that intrinsic value of this kind attaches to the flourishing of living creatures, and would still so attach even in the absence of all valuers both actual and possible; and also that such valuational frameworks as would preclude this value are objectively inferior to those which do not. But this is not a point which can be further elaborated or defended here, especially as it has received detailed treatment elsewhere, both from Rolston and myself. (For further discussion of these matters, see Attfield, 1987, chs. 10–12. Rolston's own case against Callicott's meta-ethics is more fully expressed at Rolston, 1988, pp. 112–117.)

Rolston suggests that Callicott's truncated value-theory accounts for his truncated account of biodiversity preservation (Rolston, 1991, p. 376). There must indeed be at least a risk that a meta-ethics which effectively undermines any ethics, whatever its content, reduces the likelihood of a defensible ethics being adhered to, not least in matters of preservation, though, as I have argued, some of Callicott's latest views, such as his advocacy of sustainable development, are eminently defensible. Yet it remains importantly true that sound and stable environmental policies are liable to require not only stable foundations by way of a sound value-theory and ethics, but the underpinning of an appropriately robust metaphysics and meta-ethics too.

Personalistic Organicism: Paradox or Paradigm?

FREDERICK FERRÉ

Many environmental thinkers are torn in two opposing directions at once. For good reasons we are appalled by the damage that has been done to the earth by the ethos of heedless anthropocentric individualism, which has achieved its colossal feats of exploitation, encouraged to selfishness by its world view—of relation-free atoms—while chanting 'reduction' as its mantra. But also for good reasons we are repelled, at the other extreme, by environmentally correct images of mindless biocentric collectivisms in which precious personal values are overridden for the good of some healthy beehive 'whole'.

My aim here will be to examine this tension between the imperatives of personalism and organicism. I shall argue that although contrasts are sharp, the quest to harmonize vital intuitions reflected by these imperatives is not futile. Their combination may be paradoxical, at first blush, but this paradox admits of coherent resolution. Still more, such a resolution, legitimating the logical possibility of a Personalistic Organicism,[1] may provide a paradigm for resolving other intellectually (and environmentally) dangerous dualisms that sunder civilization from nature, mind from body, and intrinsic from instrumental values.

The Paradox

One side of us strongly affirms Aldo Leopold's classic dictum that the human species should live in its proper place, not as conqueror of the land-community, but as 'plain member and citizen' within it (Leopold, 1966, pp. 219–220). From this modest forester's moral intuition much has followed.

Arrogant anthropocentrism has been a favourite target of environmental thinking rooted in Leopold's land ethic: 'A thing is right when it tends to preserve the integrity, stability, and beauty of the biotic community. It is wrong when it tends otherwise' (Leopold, 1966, p. 240). Human pride, human greed, even human

---

[1] This paradox-prone term was first proposed in Ferré, 1989. See especially pp. 238 ff.

Frederick Ferré

convictions that God created the earth for our species' dominion (see White, 1967), have laid waste to nature and deeply upset the stability of the biotic community from Alaska to the Amazon. The philosophical fight against such arrogance has seemed a clearly virtuous cause.

On one front, the epistemological, the battle was joined against the sort of analytic, reductionist thinking that allows human exploiters to tear at the delicate web of life without noticing how, in Barry Commoner's words, 'everything is connected to everything else' (Commoner, 1972, pp. 29–35). In place of trying to understand nature primarily in terms of ever-smaller parts, this argument contends, we should attempt first to appreciate the natural wholes that give context and significance to their parts. This different way of thinking would put priority on understanding whole organisms, populations, habitats, and ecosystems, rather than on the cells and molecules so beloved by modern analysers. The postmodern science of ecology, instead of hypermodern molecular biology, should lead the way in developing responsibly rigorous, holistic thought-patterns for an environmentally sensitive world (Ferré, 1993a, chs. 2, 3, 6, 7, 16).

On another front, the ethical, organismic holism has been widely identified with egalitarianism across the biotic community. If we human beings are to play our proper democratic parts as 'plain citizens' in nature, we must weed out from our policies those prejudices which automatically favour our own kind. As the pioneer of deep ecology, Arne Naess, put it: 'To the ecological field-worker, *the equal right to live and blossom* is an intuitively clear and obvious value axiom' (Naess, 1973, p. 96).

Naess, even as he wrote this, acknowledged that 'biospherical egalitarianism' could be affirmed only 'in principle'. 'The "in principle" clause is inserted', he noted, 'because any realistic praxis necessitates some killing, exploitation, and suppression' (Naess, 1973, p. 95). Naess and his followers have taken this principle, nevertheless, as a necessary condition for deep ecological thinking. George Sessions, for example, excludes A.N. Whitehead's organismic ecological ethics from deep ecology solely on the ground that it allows for gradations of value, depending on the quality of experience enjoyed by different forms of life. 'The point', he writes, 'is not whether humans in fact do have the greatest degree of sentience on this planet . . . . deep ecologists argue that the degree of sentience is *irrelevant* in terms of how humans relate to the rest of Nature. And so, contemporary Whiteheadian ecological ethics does not meet the deep ecology insistence on "ecological egalitarianism in principle"' (Sessions, 1979, p. 18).

This insistence, affirmed not only as standard for 'depth' but also as criterion for virtue, motivates the charge of speciesism against those who do not adopt it. Arguing from the analogy of racism, sexism, and other such groundless prejudices against victims of exploitation, some vigorously condemn any who cling to the view that the human species is special in any morally relevant way.[2] And from such condemnation of systematically pro-human outlooks it is a short step to systematic condemnation of the human as such. Our species has in truth done vast, irreparable damage. Humans have much to answer for. A misanthropic cast is frequently found in much organismic rhetoric. As Baird Callicott observes: 'The extent of misanthropy in modern environmentalism . . . may be taken as a measure of the degree to which it is biocentric' (Callicott, 1980, p. 326).

Starting from the need for newly holistic, ecological thinking and a modest alternative to overweening human attitudes toward nature, we have been moved, by degrees, to a doctrine of organicism which rejects all claims for a morally relevant special status for humanity. Indeed, such organicism may find itself ashamed for the human race, regretting as demonic our presence on the earth. If this is what organicism means, what place can remain for personalism? Must it not be cast out as an embarrassment by deep environmental thinkers?

One striking answer in defence of personalism is to cast the question on its head. Who or what, except for persons, can aspire to be *thinkers* at all, shallow or deep? Who or what, besides persons, can suffer *embarrassment* at the disparity between *ideals* and sordid reality? Who or what, besides persons, can experience *moral shame* from *remembering* past acts of unrestrained exploitation? And who or what, besides persons, can *resolve purposefully* to put deliberate limitations on selfish urges in order to *plan* a better long-range future?

Richard Watson develops these lines with fine irony. Unless we appeal to the uniquely personal capacities of the human species, we have no leverage for self-restraint, no basis for an ecological ethics. Taking a purely organismic view of nature, including the human as literally no more than one more 'plain citizen', our species should be allowed to live out its 'destiny' without any more moral censure than is applied to other species that trample and consume.

[2] See, for example, Regan, 1990, p.78; but see also Midgley, 1983, ch. 9 for a characteristically sensible antidote.

> Human beings do alter things. They cause the extinction of many species, and they change the Earth's ecology. This is what humans do. This is their destiny. If they destroy many other species and themselves in the process, they do no more than has been done by many another species. The human species should be allowed—if any species can be said to have a right—to live out its evolutionary potential, to its own destruction if that is the end result. It is nature's way. (Watson, 1983, p. 253)

The opposite conviction, that more should be expected of the human race, is a form of anthropocentrism, Watson points out. Thus if 'the posing of man against nature in any way is anthropocentric' (Watson, 1983, p. 252), then deep ecological thinking, which seeks deliberate moral controls on organic human urges to multiply and consume, has not escaped.

> If man is a part of nature, if he is a 'plain citizen', if he is just one nonprivileged member of a 'biospherical egalitarianism', then the human species should be treated in no way different from any other species. However, the entire tone of [deep ecological thinking] is to set man apart from nature and above all other living species. Naess says that nonhuman animals should be 'cared for in part for their own good'. Sessions says that humans should curb their technological enthusiasms to preserve ecological equilibrium. Rodman says flatly that man should let nature be. (Watson, 1983, pp. 251–252)

Thus, the deep ecologist is a personalist *malgré lui*. Personalism may be scorned in the rhetoric of organicism and biocentric egalitarianism, but it cannot be avoided. Deep ecologists, like it or not, think, write, deliberate, plan, and preach as personal women and men. Thus, as Watson concludes: 'Man is privileged—or cursed—at least by having a moral sensibility that as far as we can tell no other entities have' (Watson, 1983, p. 256).

To heighten our paradox one final notch, we should note that some personalists argue forcefully that this privilege (or curse) of personal existence makes the application of organic categories to human beings wholly inappropriate. Of course it is granted that our bodies are living and organic; but we fail to understand human individuals or human societies by subsuming them under the principles of biology. As John Macmurray proclaimed in his distinguished Gifford Lectures:

> We are not organisms, but persons. The nexus of relations which unites us in a human society is not organic but personal.

Human behaviour cannot be understood, but only caricatured, if it is represented as an adaptation to environment; and there is no such process as social evolution but, instead, a history which reveals a precarious development and possibilities both of progress and of retrogression. (Macmurray, 1961, p. 46)

Macmurray points out that organic categories are applied to human affairs only by analogy and that they do not function empirically (as often assumed) but *a priori*, being imposed as an explanatory model drawn from another field of data. And since the uniquely personal traits, like freedom and deliberate action, are absent from that other field, these traits are overlooked or explained away when the theory is applied in the human domain.

The practical consequences are in the end disastrous; but they do reveal the erroneous character of the assumption. To affirm the organic conception in the personal field is implicitly to deny the possibility of action; yet the meaning of the conception [of the personal] lies in its reference to action . . . . We say, in effect, 'Society is organic; therefore let us make it organic, as it *ought* to be'. The contradiction here is glaring. If society is organic, then it is meaningless to say that it ought to be. For if it ought to be, then it is not. The organic conception of the human, as a practical ideal, is what we now call the totalitarian state. It rests on the practical contradiction which corresponds to this theoretical one. 'Man is not free', it runs, 'therefore he *ought* not to be free'. If organic theory overlooks human freedom, organic practice must suppress it. (Macmurray, 1961, p. 46)

Here is the paradox. Just as one side of us resonates favourably to Aldo Leopold's call for human modesty among other organisms, so another side responds to Macmurray's warning not to lose sight of the uniquely personal among organic metaphors. It is true, he admits,

that the personal necessarily includes an organic aspect. But it cannot be defined in terms of its own negative; and this organic aspect is continuously qualified by its inclusion, so that it cannot even be properly abstracted except through a prior understanding of the personal structure in which it is an essential, though subordinate component. A descent from the personal is possible, in theory and indeed in practice; but there is no way for thought to ascend from the organic to the personal. The organic conception of man excludes, by its very nature, all the characteristics in virtue of which we are human beings. To include them

63

we must change our categories and start afresh from the beginning. (Macmurray, 1961, pp. 46–47)

The Resolution

Start afresh we must. But not quite from the beginning. Rather, we need to look again at this familiar terrain with an eye more guarded against 'either/or' thinking, or against seduction by what we might call the 'Fallacy of All-or-Nothing'. A great part of the apparent opposition between organicism and personalism (and therefore most of the force behind the seeming paradox of Personalistic Organicism) is generated by taking for granted two major types of dichotomies. First, we have been dealing with a binary ethics on which *either* all organisms have equal intrinsic value *or* only human persons have value and everything else has none. Second, we have been assuming a binary ontology recognizing *either* persons *or* non-persons, *either* organic *or* inorganic entities. I recommend, instead, a value-theory capable of recognizing degrees of intrinsic (as well as instrumental) value, and an ontology in which fundamental organic unities are recognized both 'downward' indefinitely toward predictable, stable simplicities and 'upward' indefinitely toward increasingly free, originative complexities.

An encouraging model for such both/and thinking can be found in the epistemology of holism as disciplined in rigorous ecological science. Here, in what I think of as the bell-wether postmodern science (Ferré, 1982, pp. 261–271), major advances have been made in the fight for understanding in accordance with Commoner's earlier cited dictum that 'everything is related to everything else' (Commoner, 1972, pp. 29–35), but without refusing aid from analytical weapons forged by modern biochemistry, microbiology, or from the panoply of all the other modern sciences. It is not necessary to think *either* wholes *or* parts; both are important levels for understanding. The whole, seen as a system, gives context and significance to its parts. The parts, in turn, show the fine structure of the whole. Moreover, the parts, looked at closely, are themselves each systems with fine structures of their own and therefore become wholes relative to their sub-parts. Equally, the larger, context-conferring system, seen in its own context, is itself part of a still more inclusive system. What we should find objectionable about analytical thinking is not that it engages in close examination of parts, or that it conceptually divides its subject matter for rigorous study, but rather that analytical thinkers have too often lost sight of (or interest in) the very contexts that give point to the analytical process itself. They have lost themselves in fascination with the parts. But it is not necessary to choose sides. Epistemological holism can (and in ecological science effectively does) embrace analytical thinking, enriching detailed knowledge with wider understanding even as analysis provides rigour in the appreciation of detailed relations.

On this both/and model, if we can reasonably extend it to ethics and ontology, we should be able to get beyond the seeming impasse of personalism *versus* organicism. With this in mind, let us first consider the principal features of personhood and ask whether we do not find continuities with most of them in organic life; then let us reflect on the main traits of healthy organic existence and ask whether these do not lend themselves to characteristic personal expressions.

I propose that we take full personal existence, at the height of its expression in mature, healthy human beings, as characterized by six major capacities. These are the powers of (1) enjoying consciously (including the ability to receive and appreciate experiences of senses or imagination), (2) thinking logically, (3) remembering, (4) planning, (5) preferring or judging, and (6) acting with moral responsibility. These powers constitute the basis for the best and the worst—for the heights of aesthetic achievement and religious ecstasy, the depths of philosophic reflection and scientific penetration, the tenderness of regret, the eagerness of hope, the seriousness of choice, and the nobility (or baseness) of responsibility. These capacities have been refined in human civilization over the millennia, while beauty has been created and profaned, opportunities grasped and missed, good achieved and destroyed. They constitute the humanist's pride and (all too frequently) the environmentalist's despair.

Personal capacities are not, however, without their analogues and continuities in the nonhuman world. We hardly need to attribute full self-consciousness to experience to acknowledge that it is experience. Our own lives abound with examples in which we find fluctuating degrees of less and more self-consciousness. At times of greater awareness we may realize that we were certainly experiencing—perhaps a discomfort or a pleasure—but were not sharply aware at the time of our personal selves as enjoying these experiences. It is possible for me to be a subject, that is, without full awareness that it is 'I' who am aware. If these grades of subjectivity are present in human life, there should be no paradox in holding that significant subjectivity is present in the nonhuman world, though very probably not at the level of full personal self-consciousness. Mammals are certainly aware. They are undoubted-

65

ly capable of enjoyments, appreciations, and pains. They need not be capable of the full personal heights and depths of such subjectivity in order to be, as Tom Regan puts it, genuine 'subjects of a life' (Regan, 1983, p. 245). But if mammals can, and do, manifest significant subjectivity, is it not arbitrary to draw lines against the possibility of some degree of subjectivity in other living organisms? Such acknowledgment of course does not imply that the subjectivity of a butterfly is equivalent to that of a bird, or the bird to that of a human gardener; but there seems no reason in principle to deny any one of them a degree of appreciation of the flowers they all attend.

The Cartesian prejudice against granting even the possibility of an inner life for nonhumans was based on the *a priori* application of mechanistic models of understanding to all *res extensa*, not on empirical appreciation of nature. More empirical, and more adequate, would be inductive generalization from the evidence of our own subjective interiority to the acknowledgment of interiority, of some grade or other, everywhere around us.

Not only interiority, the capacity to be a subjective centre for aversion or appreciation, but also mentality or thinking is one of the primary capacities of which personalists tend understandably to be proud. It would be hazardous (and probably quite wrong) to suggest that thinking is as widespread in nature as subjectivity, but it would seem sheer dogma to insist that human beings are the only subjects who also manifest logical thought at some level. H.H. Price was right to declare that logical thought functions long before language. Thought itself is the capacity to take relevant account of the absent. Thought thereby extends the environment beyond the immediately given in space and time. Thought under methodological discipline, whether expressed in symbols or in bodily alertness, qualifies as logical. Price reminds us:

> It is usually supposed that the logical notions of *not*, *or*, *if*, etc., play no part whatever in pre-verbal thinking, and this is one of the grounds for the opinion that such thinking cannot 'really' be thinking at all. Logic, it is supposed, is the study of talk, or even of print; or rather, it is one way of studying them, concerned with the formal factors which are detectable in spoken or written sentences, or perhaps only in written ones. I believe that these opinions are mistaken. These formal factors, though they are more obvious and explicit in verbalized thought, are already present in pre-verbal thought, and even in that 'enacted thought' or 'thinking in actions' which is mistakenly supposed to be nothing but bodily movement. (Price, 1962, p. 123)

The cat, crouched before the mouse, is in its organic alertness manifesting the logical disjunctive: '*Either* the mouse runs this way *or* it runs that way'; and tabby is taking account of the conditional: '*If* the mouse runs in that direction, *then* leap just so far', etc. (Price, 1962, p. 129). For Price, as for any philosophically unprejudiced observer of animal intelligence in action, there is no good warrant for denying some degree of logical thought in non-human species.

Likewise, memory and anticipation are present to some degree in all organic entities. Every organic process, however primitive, involves a flow from some influential past condition toward some guiding future condition. What the process is depends on what was the case in its immediate—and sometimes in its significantly removed—past; but also what a process is can only be understood in terms of where it is heading. Organisms, in other words, have an irreducible capacity for what even Jacques Monod, fierce opponent of mind or purpose in nature, calls 'teleonomic' behaviour:

> science as we understand it today . . . required the unbending stricture implicit in the postulate of objectivity—iron-clad, pure, forever undemonstrable . . . . Objectivity nevertheless obliges us to recognize the teleonomic character of living organisms, to admit that in their structure and performance they act projectively—realize and pursue a purpose. (Monod, 1972, pp. 21–22)

Judging, or preference, is also found everywhere within organic nature. Preference (e.g., for one sort of food or another, for avoidance of one sort of aversive stimulus or another) is exactly what steers organic teleonomic processes. For personalists to deny that human judgment is on a continuum with analogous activities in organic nature is an odd exercise in selective seeing.

My argument against the extremes of personalism, then, is that if human persons rightly can claim intrinsic value by manifesting subjective interiority, logical thought, memory, anticipation, and judgment, then humans should not fail to honour the same capacities when found elsewhere in the organic world. These capacities are not expressed in the same way or to the same degree as is granted creatures equipped with symbolic speech. Claims for 'equivalency' or 'equality' are not supported by my observations. But the organic must not be taken as the simple 'negative' of personhood. There are still important matters of degree to consider. Still, the 'All or None' attitudes that give rise to the apparent paradox of Personalistic Organicism should now be firmly set aside.

Frederick Ferré

They are as unhelpful in attaining cognitive clarity as they are in finding ethical balance.[3]

Ethics itself, however, may be the one place where there may be some justification for drawing an empirically legitimate line between paradigmatic human persons and all other known organisms. I have argued that most of the key marks of personhood can be found, in germ, within the nonhuman order; but moral responsibility, vulnerability to the claims of ethical obligation, seems not to apply outside fully developed human persons. Even many human beings—babies, growing children (to an indeterminate point), and a disturbingly large number of human adults—seem to have nonexistent or weakly developed intuitions of moral responsibility. Perhaps one could argue that some domesticated species (especially dogs) manifest what looks like guilt after an infraction of learned behavioural norms. Admittedly this behaviour could simply be fear of anticipated punishment—but so it may be with many human transgressors as well. This is a difficult issue to resolve. Still, it is not a matter on which all humans fall on one side of a great divide and only nonhumans fall on the other. It may be that in the matter of moral responsibility we encounter the flickering of an emerging property, uniquely human even if far from perfectly distributed among humans, through which we may justifiably distinguish our species as a necessary condition for its appearance. But if so, it is a distinction which, the more deeply we attend to it, the less prideful (on its own showing) we are permitted to be.

It is, after all, this fault of human pride—arrogant disregard for the other—that grounds what is legitimate in the complaints of the organicists. Denunciations of 'hierarchy' from deep ecologists gain their proper force not from our recognizing the obvious facts of superior human capacities—that human beings are capable of remembering more effectively and planning more remote outcomes, or are more capable than other animals of redirecting natural processes by taking thought and making tools—but from the morally blameworthy arrogance with which many humans have used these capacities to ride roughshod over the feelings, endeavours and values of differently endowed other creatures. To our shame, we see around us all too clearly the same unfeeling arrogance, the same failures of empathy, and the same heartlessness in the treatment by some humans of other less powerful fellow-humans. Arrogance and exploitation are, indeed, indivisible evils in our suffering world, both natural and social.

[3] For further support of the present both/and argument, see Midgley, 1978, ch. 10, 'Speech and Other Excellences', and ch. 11, 'On Being Animal as Well as Rational'.

Personalistic Organicism: Paradox or Paradigm?

The problem then is not so much 'speciesism', at bottom, as egoism.[4] For this, the remedy is not some theoretically inconsistent and practically unsustainable doctrine of biocentric egalitarianism (Watson, 1983, pp. 251–252, 256), but clearer understanding, widened sympathies, and trained habits of self-limitation based on due respect for all types and degrees of value, wherever found.

Values should be respected, whether they are *intrinsic*, based on the capacity of organisms to be the 'subject of a life', thus having interests and preferences of importance to themselves, or whether they are *instrumental* for the satisfaction of those interests and preferences—and thus helpful for the enhancement of the quality of subjectivity in organisms. It is quite possible for an entity to have both sorts of value at once. In my view, even the inexpressive oyster has some intrinsic value for itself, at least in the slow satisfactions of metabolism and perhaps in other forms of appreciation of which we are ignorant. But the oyster also contributes instrumental value to the food-chain of which it is a part. Whether devoured by starfish, sea birds or sailors, oysters count as instrumental values to those who find nourishment and delight through them.

We must not confuse intrinsic with instrumental values; the latter are always and only for the sake of the former. Were there no intrinsic values, there could be no instrumental ones. But we must equally avoid the common error of supposing that only intrinsic values are real or important. Grass may have some modicum of intrinsic value, on my view, but not very much. Still, the instrumental value of grass may far outweigh the higher, more intense intrinsic values of particular mammals which graze upon it. If there are any wholly inorganic aspects of habitat, by the same token, these may deserve great respect (and morally motivated protection) for what they contribute in instrumental value, though *ex hypothesi* they may be entirely devoid of significant subjectivity and therefore empty of intrinsic value.

Still, it is reconciling the organic and the personal, both domains of intrinsic value, that principally concerns us here. We have seen how key traits that personalists admire can be recognized in nonhuman organisms; is there a reciprocal move from what organicists see as the 'wisdom of healthy life' to the personal? I believe so. All healthy organic life shares three great characteristics, worthy of admiration in their interactive tension: creativity, homeostasis, and holism. (1) *Creativity*: healthy life grows, innovates, spreads, devours, evolves. (2) *Homeostasis*: healthy life

---

[4] On this, and other related issues, see Merchant, 1990, for a thoughtful exploration of 'egoistic', 'homocentric', and 'ecocentric' ethics.

defends itself from overgrowth and collapse by many mechanisms, both at the individual and population levels. (3) *Holism*: healthy life makes both creativity and homeostasis possible by intricate networks of information feedback in which diversified elements are relevantly linked for the benefit of the whole system (Ferré, 1976, ch. 6).

Personal existence transforms the ways in which these great organic achievements are expressed, but in principle they can still be found underlying normative personalism. The thrust to create, to innovate in the arts as well as in the homely circumstances of daily life, is part of the quest for increased quality of intrinsic subjective satisfaction. Controls, however, are also needed against what Whitehead called 'mere anarchic appetition' (Whitehead, 1929, p. 34). These controls (homologous to the salutary mechanisms that guard organisms against self-destructive growth) are those of logic and ethics; that is, these serve, if utilized, as internal homeostatic limitations on the sheer freedoms of thought and action that come with the emergence of personhood. And, finally, the prime condition of successful working for logic and ethics within the realm of the personal is holistic intelligence, the developed capacity for giving and receiving complex symbolic information, the readiness to enter sympathetically into and to empathize with initially alien diversity, the melding of respect for otherness—including proper respect for the intrinsic value of one's own uniqueness—with mutuality in co-operative social functioning. All this we can learn as persons, without minimizing the immense respect due to the uniquely valuable achievements of personhood, if we will observe and take voluntarily to heart the basic wisdom of healthy organic life.

The Paradigm

If the apparent paradoxicality of Personalistic Organicism gives way to resolution, in principle, along the lines I have now briefly sketched, we should grant ourselves a few final reflections on what this approach could mean for epistemology, ontology, and ethics. Far from posing a paradox, Personalistic Organicism may well offer a paradigm for the avoidance of dualisms and dichotomies that have too long plagued environmental philosophy and philosophy in general.

First, on methods of thought, the approach through Personalistic Organicism recommends *distinguishing* what is different, but not *separating* it without necessity. The dominant tendency in modern philosophy, encouraged by both René Descartes among the rationalists and David Hume among the empiricists, has been to tear apart what seems distinctly conceivable alone. Such abstraction from the real connectedness of things encourages cognitive simplicity and has its place, as we have seen, as a subordinate tool in the quest for understanding. But in excess it is a serious mistake. Holistic thinking warns that a subject-matter shorn of its relations is not the same subject-matter with which we began. Things are not so conceivable alone as may appear. Organism without its proto-personal traits is not fully organism, just as personality without its organic context is not fully personality.

'Writ large', the moral is to avoid as far as possible our temptations towards either/or thinking. Categorizing in 'on-or-off' or 'in-or-out' terms comes easily to our modern minds after centuries of custom now reinforced by our environment of electric switches and binary computer circuitry. But the lessons of Personalistic Organicism teach us—for the sake of fuller understanding—to resist this comfortable habit. Allied to sciences such as ecology and systems theory, our paradigm leads us to prefer 'both/and' approaches. Culture *and* creation, human *and* animal, even artificial *and* natural need to be seen together, questions of degrees, not conceptual contraries (Ferré, 1988, pp. 27–29). The Fallacy of All-or-Nothing has too long imposed its abstract frameworks on our attempts to see the world. Our paradigm teaches us to see differences clearly, but to look wherever possible at these differences not as mere contrasts but as polarities in tension within complex fields of relations.

Just as in every epistemological paradigm, such a heuristic is linked, of course, to a corresponding ontology. Personalistic Organicism suggests a world of real relatedness. Just as we see organisms and persons as essentially what they are because of their reciprocal connections, so, more broadly, we are offered a metaphysical paradigm that is neither materialist nor idealist, nor (certainly) dualist. Since on this paradigm body and mind *begin* by being joined, as functional polarities within a common field of energy-with-interiority, as intimately related networks of events that are past-inheriting and future-regarding, we never fall into the insoluble puzzles of modern philosophy. No need to speculate how mind-stuff can influence or be influenced by body-stuff. Those theoretically incompatible 'stuffs' are abstract fictions, products of either/or thinking. No need to question how ideas can be efficacious in a theoretical physical world made up only of matter in motion (Ferré, 1993b). The actual physical world is far richer. It contains subjectivity, life, preference, projects, freedom, and value.

Frederick Ferré

Mention of value leads to a third major area, ethics, in which Personalistic Organicism may provide a paradigm for breaking out of old dilemmas. Ethical theory is hindered when one assumes, on either/or thinking, that an entity can have only one type of value, *either* intrinsic *or* instrumental. Likewise ethical penetration is crippled by the All-or-Nothing Fallacy when one insists that intrinsic value does not come in degrees of greater or less, but that something either has, as it were, all value or none. Such gratuitous disjunctions lie behind most of those rhetorically glib but ill-considered proposals of 'biocentric egalitarianism' that have gained the status of dogma in some environmental circles.

Personalistic Organicism, as we have seen, acknowledges types as well as grades of value. The universe is full of intrinsic values, importantly including human persons but extending far beyond, perhaps even beyond what we normally recognize as the living world. These all deserve ethical respect to the degrees appropriate to the intensity of the values concerned. The world is likewise full of instrumental values with all ranges of importance. Both sorts are difficult to measure and even more difficult to weigh against one another, but on this paradigm they are openly recognized and held together in dynamic tensions that—given hard work, patience, and good will (or what William Frankena calls 'the moral point of view' (Frankena, 1973, pp. 68–70))—can energize personal ethics and transform social policy. No one ever promised that clarifying and applying ethical theory should be easy. But it is morally obligatory on moral agents to try.

So far as we know, the only moral agents on earth are human beings. Does this make Personalistic Organicism 'anthropocentric' in any objectionable way? I think not. We have no choice but to think as humans, to take a human point of view even while we try to transcend egoism by cultivating sympathy and concern for other centres of intrinsic value. Fate forces at birth what, in a harmless sense, we might call 'perspectival anthropocentrism'. But this carries no moral penalty, since ought implies can, and we literally *can* do no other than see from our own point of view. In another harmless sense, we are obliged to measure values (and all else) as humans. This might be called our unavoidable 'anthropometric' condition, as Alan Wittbecker suggests (Wittbecker, 1986, p. 261). Some have mocked anthropometric efforts to define and measure values as inevitably self-serving, since quality of experience is the only thing that human beings can know as intrinsically valuable, and our species starts with a large advantage (so we usually conclude, on neurological and behavioural grounds) in the explicitness, complexity, refinement, and power of our experience, as compared to oysters, tadpoles, birds and even other mammals. To this Personalistic Organicism offers a two-part reply. (1) The mocker is challenged to come up with a coherent alternative account of intrinsic value, one not resting, finally, on quality of some subjectivity; this will not be easy, since intrinsic value that is not valuable for any experiencing valuer is a vacuous concept. (2) On any measure of intrinsic value, including quality of experience, if the moral point of view is assumed, self-serving egoism is *ex hypothesi* ruled out. 'Due respect for value wherever found' is not an automatic pass for human interests when they are dispassionately found to conflict with significant nonhuman intrinsic values or crucial instrumental values leading to a wider good. It seems then that such mockery is only a thin disguise for cynicism about the very possibility of genuinely moral thought and action by human beings. The distribution of moral responsibility among persons may be thin and uneven, as we noted above; but to doubt its very possibility, since humans (inevitably) must do the defining and be the agents, slides too far toward nihilism and misanthropy.

If we humans are both persons and organisms, as on this paradigm we are found to be, then we are not forced to choose between 'biocentrism' and 'anthropocentrism', as though these were in opposition. We are organisms; we are persons. We are in nature; we are in culture. The point is not to choose some other ethical perspective, as though embarrassed to be human. The point, rather, is to enlarge, deepen, and refine the one we have from birth. To this end it would be no mistake to continue exploring a relational view that is in itself healthily 'polycentric', Personalistic Organicism.

Values, Reasons and the Environment

ROGER CRISP

I

By 2030, according to one reliable source, the world's population will have increased by 3·7 billion, demand for food will have nearly doubled, and industrial output tripled (World Bank, 1992, p. 2 and *passim*).[1] Consider two possible histories of the world in this period:

The Admirable (A) History. Wastage of energy and natural resources is reduced, as is poverty in developing countries. Pollution decreases. Greenhouse warming slows. Biodiversity is preserved. The natural environment is protected. Food is not short.

The Bleak (B) History. Widespread wasteful consumption practices continue. Air pollution increases. Greenhouse warming continues. Biodiversity decreases. Water contamination, deforestation and desertification are widespread. Sea levels rise. Food shortages cause local wars.

It is obvious that, other things being equal, the history of the world will be better the closer it comes to the A-History. But it is less obvious why it is better, or quite what its good aspects might be. One might ask, for example, whether the 'deep ecological' view is correct that the condition of the environment in itself contributes to the superiority of the A-History (see Naess, 1973; Rolston, 1986a, esp. part II; Taylor, 1986; Rolston, 1988, esp. ch. 6; Callicott, 1993).

These are the first questions I shall consider (in §§ II–VIII). I shall then move on to the implications of my answer to these questions for the content and strength of our reasons to live or to act in one way rather than another in the light of the above projections.

II

If I were to say that a certain history of the world is good overall, I would mean that it is better overall that this history should have

---

[1] See Schelling, 1983, for caution about predictions such as these. My argument does not depend on their truth.

occurred than no history. It is not implausible to suggest that there are certain aspects of the A-History which make it just good, or 'good, period' as one might put it. These aspects are roughly what Robert Elliot describes as 'value-adding properties' (Elliot, 1992, pp. 138–139).

Some philosophers (e.g., Williams, 1985, ch. 6; Foot, 1988) find this use of 'good' unintelligible. If a history of the world is to be said to be good, they argue, it must be said to be good *for* some being or beings or good *from* some point of view. But common usage suggests that most people find no difficulty with the notions that the A-History is just better than the B-History, that certain aspects of the A-History are just good, or that it is just good that the world turn out in some way rather than another.

Thomas Hurka even suggests that because it is multiply ambiguous we banish the expression 'good for' from our ethical language (Hurka, 1987a). I intend that expression to be taken to refer to 'that portion of the good . . . that falls within a person's [or being's] own life', and Hurka's recommendation here is that I speak instead of 'a good in [a] life' (Hurka, 1987a, p. 73). But since this is what is often meant by 'good for', and since anyway I have stipulated what I mean by it, I shall not abandon the phrase (though I shall qualify it slightly in §VII, below).

The notion of 'good', then, is so far from being unintelligible as to give content to the notion of 'good for'. Nothing can be good for any X unless it is good; and anything is good for any X only to the extent that it is good.

III

I am suggesting that the value of the A-History is to be understood in terms of those aspects of it that make it good, period. Another philosophical objection, related to but less sweeping than that alleging the unintelligibility of 'good', might be raised at this point. Some writers speak of agent-relative or personal values (see e.g. Nagel, 1986, p. 154 and *passim*). They will claim that giving an evaluative account of the world *purely* in terms of what is good (that is, good, period) will miss the value certain things, such as my learning modern Greek, have *for particular people*—in this case, for me. The answer you give to the question, 'What makes the world valuable?', will depend on your 'standpoint'.

The notion of agent-relative value, however, is unnecessary and implausible. Best sense can be made here by saying that my learning Greek has a certain value—other things being equal, it makes the history of the world better—and that this is the value it has for me. To be sure, it seems that I have a special *reason* to promote my learning which you lack. But it adds nothing to say that my learning has some personal value which cannot be captured from what we might call, if we must, the 'point of view of the universe' or the 'view from nowhere' (Sidgwick, 1907, pp. 382, 420; Nagel, 1986).

Let me give another example. My relationship with my child might be said to have agent-relative value. But in fact my relationship with my child is of no more value, other things being equal, than anybody else's relationship with their child. What makes it good for me or valuable for me is that its value is instantiated in *my* life. That does not add anything to its value, though it might be said to give me a special reason to promote that particular relationship.

IV

It is time that I offered an example of an aspect in which the A-History might be thought good. In the B-History, the natural environment is devastated, while in the A-History the beauty of, say, the Okavango swamp is preserved. Is beauty good? G.E. Moore's famous thought experiment in his discussion of Henry Sidgwick suggests that it is:

> Let us imagine one world exceedingly beautiful. Imagine it as beautiful as you can; put into it whatever on this earth you most admire—mountains, rivers, the sea; trees, and sunsets, stars and moon. Imagine these all combined in the most exquisite proportions, so that no one thing jars against another, but each contributes to the beauty of the whole. And then imagine the ugliest world you can possibly conceive. Imagine it simply one heap of filth, containing everything that is most disgusting to us, for whatever reason, and the whole, as far as may be, without one redeeming feature. Such a pair of worlds we are entitled to compare . . . . The only thing we are not entitled to imagine is that any human being ever has or ever, by any possibility, *can*, live in either, can ever see and enjoy the beauty of the one or hate the foulness of the other. Well, even so, supposing them quite apart from any possible contemplation by human beings; still, is it irrational to hold that it is better that the beautiful world should exist than the one which is ugly? (Moore, 1903, pp. 83–84)

Beauty, then, can be described as a value or a good. What makes anything, including a history of the world, good or valuable is the instantiation in it of certain goods or values. To the extent that beauty is instantiated in a world, that world is good. Some have argued that all environmental value is essentially aesthetic (for discussion, see Sober, 1986, pp. 189-191). I intend 'aesthetic' to be taken broadly so that, for example, integrity and diversity would fall under the aesthetic heading. But below I shall argue that there are other species of value.

V

In §§ II and III, I dealt with two objections to the claim that the world is good to the extent that it instantiates values. The first objection was that the notion of 'good, period' is unintelligible, while the second raised the possibility that I was ignoring agent-relative value. Let me now say something positive about my conception of the values I have in mind. To begin with, am I speaking here of 'intrinsic' value?

Christine Korsgaard (1983) has elegantly demonstrated the importance of keeping the notion of intrinsic goodness or value separate from that of goodness as an end or aim. Certain goods could be extrinsically valuable—on one understanding of the intrinsic/extrinsic distinction they might be good, for example, only on the condition that human beings existed—and yet be worth seeking as ends in themselves. Moore made it clear in what followed the passage quoted above that he saw beauty as at least a candidate end. Other things being equal, one should act so as to bring it about. Let me endorse that, noting that this is not endorsing intrinsic value understood as unconditional value or in any further sense.

John O'Neill has pointed out how the confusion between intrinsic value and non-instrumental value is common in environmental ethics, along with a confusion between intrinsic and objective value (O'Neill, 1992, pp. 119–125). If one says that the beauty of the environment is an objective value, one is claiming on O'Neill's view that the environment has value independently of the valuations of valuers. Again, in various senses of independence, that is something I am ready to underwrite. But objective value is not the same as intrinsic value.

Both Korsgaard (1983, p. 174) and O'Neill (1992, p. 120) quote Moore's account of intrinsic value:

> To say that a kind of value is 'intrinsic' means merely that the question of whether a thing possesses it, and in what degree it possesses it, depends solely on the intrinsic nature of the thing in question. (Moore, 1922, p. 260)

It does not depend, that is, on the contingencies of circumstance or causal laws (see Moore, 1922, pp. 256, 260, 268–270). If A has intrinsic value V, then A must have V in all possible worlds in which its intrinsic properties remain constant. As Korsgaard notes (1983, pp. 175–176), this view of intrinsic value as dependent on non-relational properties explains Moore's adoption of his 'method of isolation' to determine whether a thing has intrinsic value (see Moore, 1903, p. 91 and *passim*).

There is a value often alleged in the environmental ethics literature which clearly depends on relational properties: rarity. And if rarity is a value, I doubt that any important distinction between it and values such as beauty hangs on its dependence on relational properties. We could after all capture the necessity Moore is after here as well. In all possible worlds in which this relation exists, the rare objects will possess that value.

The method of isolation essentially involves considering a universe which contains only the candidate good. It is in fact useful independently of the relational/non-relational distinction in individuating candidate goods and evaluating them. But the lesson of the previous paragraph is that it should be employed primarily to work out which *qualities* are valuable, as opposed to which *objects* are valuable. The method *can* therefore be used to assess the claims of alleged values such as rarity. In this case, we should have to consider a universe containing many rare items. Again, we might conclude that beauty is a value after reflection upon a universe such as that described by Moore in the quoted thought experiment.

Moore, as the quotation shows, did not restrict the scope of the method to properties. Robert Frazier pointed out to me that axiology can be pluralist along two dimensions: that of which objects bear value, and that of what it is that makes these objects valuable. My view is pluralist in both senses: many kinds of 'object' can be valuable (physical objects, experiences, worlds, and so on), and there are several value-making properties (beauty, pleasurableness, and so on). In a further sense, however, the view is monistic along both dimensions: there is no more value than is located in worlds, and the only things that make objects valuable are straightforward properties (and not, say, mere existence). A great deal of relevant and important metaphysics is being left undeveloped here. Particularly important is the question of which values are functions of other values: is, for example, the value of a world reducible to the value of certain objects within it considered independently of one another, and, if so, which objects? Such questions are related to the issue of commensurability discussed in the text below.

Another important principle in using the method is to beware that value is not double counted. Having decided that, say, serenity is intrinsically valuable, we should refrain from counting in both the serenity of the Okavango and that part of its beauty which consists in its serenity.

In addition to the method of isolation, what we might call 'more-is-better' arguments are also important (see Aristotle, 1985, 15, 268–269 (1097b14–20, 1172b23–35); Crisp, 1994a). If I claim that the A-History is good *solely* because it instantiates values $V^1 \ldots V^n$, my claim will be shown to be incomplete if some further value V^{n+1} can be found instantiated in that history. For example, I might suggest that the A-History is good overall just because it includes both beauty and pleasure. But a more-is-better argument can be used against this suggestion: the A-History also contains, say, friendship, and friendship along with beauty and pleasure is better than the latter two alone.

Another ambiguous notion found in environmental ethics is that of 'anthropocentricity'. Many of the unclarities are teased out in Hargrove (1992). I hope I have said enough in this section to show that my view of value is in various senses non-anthropocentric. I would advocate an anthropocentric epistemology concerning many values. But it seems a purely contingent matter that non-humans can appreciate pleasurableness and not beauty. A more interesting epistemology might be zoocentric and hence non-naturalistic and anti-scientistic: values are discernible only from the point of view of animals engaged in the sort of lives animals live in our world and not from some scientific standpoint which aims to transcend these points of view (see Crisp, 1994b).

To sum up this section. Goods, valuable properties such as those which make the A-History better than the B-History, are: (i) good as ends, (ii) good in themselves, (iii) unconditionally good (since there are no conditions on which these goods depend), (iv) objectively good, (v) good in all possible worlds and (vi) possibly discernible only from a certain perspective. Further, a full account of the goodness of anything must enumerate all the values instantiated in it.

VI

To return to the values instantiated in the A-History. My example in § IV was beauty. When asked what it is that makes the A-History good, however, many will reply that its value lies solely in its being a history in which many individual human and non-human animals do well. This view is *welfarism*, of which utilitarianism is the most common example (see Sen, 1979). According to its adherents, what makes a world valuable is the welfare accruing to the beings that inhabit it and nothing else.

I intend to include under this heading those perfectionist theories according to which intrinsic value consists only in the development of the essential capacities of creatures, including plants.[2] Perfectionist theories, however, tend to employ the wrong notion of 'good for'. One can accept that water is in one sense good for plants without accepting that being given water or their being given water is valuable.

Part of the attraction of welfarism lies in the view rejected in § II that 'good, period' is unintelligible. But there is also an internal difficulty with it, viz. that any plausible theory of what welfare consists in implies that there are other values. Consider aesthetic pleasure, which is likely to feature at some level in most accounts of welfare. Properly characterized, aesthetic pleasure involves appreciating and enjoying certain characteristics of natural or artificial objects, broadly construed. These characteristics are evaluative: one enjoys the serenity of the Okavango in the evening, the drama and economy of the first movement of Beethoven's Ninth Symphony, the ingenuity of the Parthenon frieze.

Welfare values might be described as *essentially referential*. The pleasure I experience makes my life more valuable *for me*; whereas the serenity of the Okavango, though an evaluative property of the world, is not valuable *for* the swamp itself, the world or the universe. Welfarism, then, is not the whole story about value, since a plausible account of welfare must imply the existence of non-welfarist, non-referential values. I have assumed that the Okavango would be devastated in the B-History. Then one reason for the A-History's being more valuable will be the essentially referential pleasure taken in visiting it; but another will be the sheer existence of the swamp, or rather its serenity, beauty, and so on.

VII

In § II I suggested that A is good for P if and only if A is good, period, and is instantiated in P's life. But a further condition must now be added, which will explain why I used the notion of *essential* reference in the previous section.

[2] On perfectionism in general see Attfield, 1987, esp. chs. 3-4; 1991, esp. ch. 8. Perfectionist theories can be individualist, like Attfield's, or non-individualist, like that of Johnson, 1991, esp. chs. 3-4, who attributes independent moral standing to species.

It is hard to deny that aesthetic predications of people's lives make sense. My life might be described as well-balanced, fascinating, ugly or serene to contemplate. And the sense of these predicates is roughly the same when they are applied to more everyday aesthetic objects such as paintings or the natural landscape. The problem is that these values and disvalues appear to be instantiated in my life, to be properties of my life, and yet not clearly to be good or bad *for* me.

There are at least two options here. One would be to argue that in these cases the aesthetic qualities are also welfarist. It does not, however, seem likely that values such as these will play a role in the best account of welfare. The other option would be to suggest that welfare values are *essentially* referential, and other values essentially *non-referential*. Welfare values—pleasure, accomplishment, autonomy, understanding, friendship—make no sense outside the context of assessment of the value of human lives for those who live them. Aesthetic predicates make sense in a different context. Here the notion of different points of view might be more at home.

VIII

So far aesthetic and welfare values have featured in the evaluative account of the A-History. There is one other species of value. This species, like aesthetic value, is non-referential. I shall refer to it under the broad heading of 'moral value', to cover values such as justice, kindness and generosity. These properties are of course predicated of various items: persons, actions, states of affairs, institutions. And usually when instantiated they affect people's welfare. An unjust distribution of property, for example, is nearly always bad for particular people, viz. those deprived of their just entitlements (it is of course often good for those who benefit undeservedly).

Welfarists will claim that all apparently moral values are to be understood in referential and hence welfarist terms: there is nothing bad about injustice apart from its direct effect on the welfare of individuals. This is implausible. Just as the serenity of the Okavango is valuable in itself, so is the justice of an institution.

Consider another thought experiment. Take two versions of the A-History. In the first, certain people live lives of a certain value V, and are treated justly. In the second, this same group is treated unjustly, and yet the lives of its members are of the same value V (the welfare loss that accrues to them through the injustice is counterbalanced—though not compensated—by welfare gains *to them*). The second version is worse than the first, since it contains more injustice.

IX

What makes any history of the world valuable is its instantiating welfare, aesthetic and moral values, and it is valuable to the extent, and only to the extent, that it instantiates these values. The A-History is better (in part) because the human and non-human animals inhabiting the world are better off, the environment is better preserved, and there is greater fairness.

Any form of utilitarianism has two components: a conception of value as consisting only in utility or welfare, and a maximising principle. The first I have rejected, though welfare has been accepted as one among other values. Now consider the maximising principle. Should I agree that each of us is required to bring about the best possible outcome overall, i.e., to maximize the values identified above?

One reason for rejecting this proposal might be thought to be the incommensurability of values. I have allowed in not only three broad species of values, but countless individual types and tokens. Not only are aesthetic values not reducible to welfare values, but serenity cannot be understood to involve more of some substantive value also found in, say, sublimity. Surely pluralism of this kind rules out any conception of the best overall history of the world?

In fact it does not. In easy cases, such as that of the comparison between the A- and B-Histories, the right answer is clear. We can assume that there is a right answer in every case, allowing for the possibility of a certain amount of vagueness. This suggestion looks particularly plausible when we make the type/token distinction. Principles about trade-offs at the type level may be largely unavailable; but at the token level comparisons may be possible. It may be worth saving the Okavango, for example, at the welfare cost of slightly increasing the tax on tourists.

X

So maximisation is not ruled out by incommensurability. And there does indeed seem to be a clear link between justificatory reasons for living or acting in some way and values. If ever I am rationally justified in doing something, there must be some value grounding that justification. My jogging is justified if it promotes my health, which promotes welfare values good in themselves, such as pleasure. My campaigning to save the whale will be, in a sense, unreasonable if it is not grounded on some hope of making the world a better place and perhaps also a better place for whales and other animals. Further, the claim that it must be rational to bring about the best possible state of affairs has a great deal of intuitive force (Foot, 1988, p. 227).

Though one always has *a* reason to maximize, it is not one's only reason. It can be rational to bring about less than the best overall state of affairs. Values do not ground reasons in as straightforward a way as the maximizer claims.

The explanation for this is that, though there are no agent-relative values, there are agent-relative reasons. Nagel defines a reason as agent-neutral 'if it can be given a general form which does not include an essential reference to the person who has it', and an agent-relative reason as one which does include such a reference in its general form (Nagel, 1986, pp. 152–153). Thus the fact that doing X would produce the best outcome is an agent-neutral reason for doing it, while the fact that Y will benefit *me* provides an agent-relative reason for me to do Y.

Now consider another thought experiment. There are two options open to you concerning how to live your life. If you live your life in the first way, the A-History will occur, partly as a result of your so living. But living in this way will impose huge costs on you: you will become very ill, your standard of living will drop dramatically and your personal relationships will dwindle. If you live in the other way, a history *slightly* less good overall than the A-History will occur, but your own life will be hugely more successful than in the case just discussed. Do you not have a very strong reason to choose the second way of life over the first (see Sidgwick, 1907, p. 498)? Anyone who denies this is probably in the grip of a mistaken theory of the relation between values and reasons.

Self-interested reasons are not the only agent-relative reasons. I have a reason to be loyal to my friends which cannot be stated in a general form without essential reference to me. Thus in some case where I can, by disloyalty to my friends, bring about greater loyalty overall by preventing greater disloyalty between people with whom I am unconnected, my agent-relative reason to be loyal may override my agent-neutral reason to promote loyalty. My reason here cannot plausibly be said to be based solely on the claim that 'People should be loyal to their friends'. Rather the fact that these people are *my* friends gives *me* a special reason to be loyal.

In the self-interest case, the fact that the value I am aiming at will be instantiated in *my* life gives me a strong reason to do what will bring about less than the best state of affairs overall. In the loyalty case, justifications will again refer to relationships *I* have with others. Likewise, in a case where I can save either my mother or some stranger more productive of overall value, I have a very strong reason to save the former because she is *my* mother. To think that this claim requires justification from some impartial principle—in the form of a claim, perhaps, that bringing people up to behave like this will produce most value overall—is to have what Bernard Williams has called 'one thought too many' (Williams, 1981a, p. 18).

XI

Possibility also places limits on maximizing reasons. Someone may describe some way of life, perhaps that of an international states-person, which would bring about vast increases in the value of the overall history of the world. But it is not possible for me to live such a life with my meagre talents. So it cannot be said that I have a reason to live that life.

Someone else may suggest that my reasons are limited not only by circumstances, but also by what I can be motivated to do.[3] If I cannot be motivated by the consideration that some way of life is likely to maximize value, then that consideration cannot count as a reason for my living in that way. But this does not seem correct. Let us imagine that the state would impose huge sanctions on me if I were not to live that life. That consideration, we may assume, may well motivate me to live in the way prescribed. And it still makes sense to claim that one justification, one reason, for my living in that way is that it will maximize value. That, indeed, is the ground for the sanctions.

It does appear that I can have a reason to do X only if I could, *motivated by some consideration or other*, do X. If maximizing calls for very great sacrifices, we can be said to have a reason to maxi-

[3] This person may be influenced by Williams, 1981b. There are two interpretations of what Williams means by 'internalism' about reasons:

Weak internalism: A can have a reason to ϕ iff A has some motive to be served by ϕ-ing.

Strong internalism: A can have a reason to ϕ iff A has some motive to be served by ϕ-ing *for that reason.*

I am accepting weak internalism and would argue that the strong version often seems plausible because it is confused with the weak.

mize to the point where nothing could motivate us to go on. That is the point where motivation does place a limit on the demands of maximization.

XII

The overall value of any world history lies in the degree to which it instantiates certain intrinsic values. Each of us has a reason to live in such a way that these values are maximized overall (that is, when tokens of them are traded off one against the other). But we have also competing reasons, arising out of self-interest and relationships we have with others.

What are the implications of this position for how we should react to the present threat to the environment? First consider what I have called the aesthetic value of the environment—that is, the intrinsically valuable qualities of the environment. Clearly, I have *a* reason to further this value. But not only is it one species of value among others, but any agent-neutral reason to further it will compete with agent-relative reasons to attend to self-interest and considerations grounded in relationships I have with others.

In the present state of the world, purely aesthetic value can safely be ignored for most practical purposes, though this is not to say that it should not come into play in everyday reasoning about, say, how to dispose of one's household rubbish. This is because of competition from other, primarily welfare, values at the agent-neutral level. Individually and collectively, we have the power to improve the world dramatically over the next few decades. The reason we need not allow pure aesthetic value to feature in our decision making arises out of the special weight that welfare values, i.e., referential values, have. This can be illustrated by a thought experiment similar to Moore's, with the added feature that the beautiful world contains one or more people living lives of terrible suffering. Intuition suggests that the beautiful world is then much worse than the ugly world, and, more importantly, that given the sort of choice Moore presents us with we would have a stronger reason to bring about the ugly world.[4] Since we can act to decrease the terrible suffering in the world, this provides us with a

---

[4] It could be that—even if aesthetic values are more weighty here—the referentiality of welfare values somehow gives us an agent-relative reason not to maximize grounded on common humanity. Just as *I* am justified in failing to maximize in order to further *my* self-interest, so *we* might be justified in failing to maximize aesthetic value to further *our* collective welfare.

dominant aim. Deep ecological views are philosophically correct, but of little practical importance.

XIII

But of course the proposal is not that we ignore the environment in most of our decision making, only that we ignore purely aesthetic value. At the agent-neutral level, what matter are primarily fairness and improving welfare by creating permanent conditions in which human and non-human beings can flourish. And in fact advancing these values will anyway turn out to advance the aesthetic value of the environment.

There is a strong case for linking development and the environment (see World Bank, 1992, p. 2 and *passim*). In particular, what are required are so-called 'win-win' policies such as the removal of subsidies on fossil fuels, the clarification of property rights over land, forests and fisheries, the provision of sanitation and water, education (especially for girls), population control, and the empowerment of local communities. Of course, these policies will have to run in tandem with other policies targeted at particular environmental problems, designed, for example, to decrease the influence of vested interests and to develop partnerships between industrial and developing countries.

These policies can be achieved only at the international political level. But politicians can be influenced by individual and group action. Because of the importance of what is at stake—the amount and distribution of human suffering, and the conditions and even the possibility of life for future generations—most of us have a strong reason to sacrifice a great deal of time and money to this cause. And if the cause succeeds, there will be a self-interested payoff for those who have participated in it. Our lives go better for us the more we accomplish. It is hard to imagine a greater accomplishment than preserving decent conditions for life on earth.[5]

[5] I am grateful for comments on previous drafts to Robin Attfield, Nigel Bowles, Robert Frazier, Brad Hooker, Thomas Hurka, Andrew Mason, Mark Nelson, Markku Oksanen and Peter Sandøe.

Awe and Humility: Intrinsic Value in Nature. Beyond an Earthbound Environmental Ethics

KEEKOK LEE

This paper will argue for a conception of intrinsic value which, it is hoped, will do justice to the following issues:

(1) that Nature need not and should not be understood to refer only to what exists on this planet, Earth;

(2) that an environmental ethics informed by features unique to Earth may be misleading and prove inadequate as technology increasingly threatens to invade and colonize other planets in the solar system;

(3) that a comprehensive environmental ethics must encompass not only our attitude to Earth, but to other planets as well—in other words, it must not simply be an Earthbound but virtually an astronomically bounded ethics.

I

What is unique about Earth? That it has water and an atmosphere which supports life. Its atmosphere preserves a constant 0·03% of carbon dioxide, 1·7 ppm of methane, 21% of oxygen, 79% of nitrogen, a surface temperature of 13°C. Water covers roughly two thirds of its surface. By contrast, planets like Venus and Mars which have no life and no water (at least today) have no methane either, but respectively 96·5% and 95% of carbon dioxide, 3·5% and 2·7% of nitrogen, a mere trace and 0·13% of oxygen, and surface temperatures of 459°C and -53°C (see Lovelock, 1988, p. 9).

Looked at from outer space, Earth is a dappled white and blue sphere. On the other hand, Mars is uniformly red. Life on Earth originated in its waters. And today, life is found in them as well as on land.

II

Environmental ethicists are divided along two main axes—anthropocentrism/non-anthropocentrism on the one hand and individualism/holism on the other. Those who argue that not only humans but Nature may have intrinsic value, may be said to reject anthropocentrism, at least in its strong form. But whether these non-anthropocentrists approach the matter *via* the individualist or the holist perspective, they appear to agree that (a) a distinction between biotic (animate) and abiotic (inanimate) Nature is crucial; (b) a conception of intrinsic value in Nature is intelligible only with regard to the former (Taylor, 1986; Attfield, 1991; Johnson, 1991); (c) it is deeply problematic to argue that abiotic Nature could have intrinsic value.[1]

As a result, regarding (c), they tend either to ignore it or to marginalize it by simply acknowledging that, fortunately, because biotic and abiotic Nature are so inextricably involved with each other, as a matter of fact, the former cannot be divorced from the latter. As such, if biotic Nature could be said to have intrinsic value, so may abiotic Nature also be said to possess it. But Johnson, who does grapple with the issue explicitly, is driven to the brink of reintroducing strong anthropocentrism by the back door: 'Perhaps there are some things *it is better for us* that we value for their own sakes' (Johnson, 1991, p. 282, italics added).

The focus on biotic Nature is quite understandable given that organic life is unique to Earth (at least as far as we know today). If environmental ethics were to be confined to this planet alone, there would be no need to agonize too much about the problem of abiotic Nature becoming divorced totally from biotic Nature and/or whether the former thus divorced could be a locus of intrinsic value.[2] But unfortunately, increasingly, such intellectual and ethical *angst* is not an optional extra. To appreciate the urgency of the matter, let us turn to the project of 'terraforming' Mars (see Hawkes, 1993 and Whitehouse, 1993).

III

Mars does not look like a promising alternative habitation for humans. But it is the most promising, nevertheless, of all the planets in the solar system. Technology could eventually make it habit-

[1] One notable exception is Rolston. Although he does not touch on the matter in Rolston, 1988, he has addressed it in Rolston, 1986b. Indeed, all the issues related to environmental ethics and the solar system are given an airing in Hargrove, 1986. (I wish to thank Professor Rolston for kindly drawing my attention to this.)

[2] See Callicott, 1986, for the distinction between the source and locus of values.

able. The programme for transforming Mars into imitation Earth looks somewhat as follows:

(i) First raise the temperature (from -53°C) by pumping greenhouse gases into its atmosphere, releasing chemicals which are already present in the Martian crust by using small nuclear reactors. These gases will then trap the Sun's heat.

(ii) Its frozen polar caps will start to melt as they absorb the heat. Genetically modified plants could be spread over them.

(iii) Positive feedback would next ensure that as the atmosphere gets thicker it gets warmer, and as it gets warmer it gets thicker.

(iv) A century later, nitrogen, carbon dioxide and water would appear. The colour of the sky would change, from pink to pale blue, then to royal blue. Pressure would be half that on Earth. After that, rain would fall. There would be large oceans though not yet salty ones.

(v) Different types of vegetation would take root—first tundra, then evergreens, as soil emerges.

(vi) After another century or so, perhaps the plants together with the atmosphere processors (Mars has abundant iron oxide which could be mined and heated to release oxygen) would generate sufficient oxygen to produce a breathable atmosphere for humans and other animals.

IV

This paper addresses itself to several related issues raised by the 'terraforming' of Mars.

1. Earth has intrinsic value because it has organic life. Its intrinsic value places constraints on human exploitation of Nature to suit our own ends. But Mars has no organic life and, therefore, it follows, no intrinsic value. As such, it has, at the moment, only (potential) instrumental value for humans who can choose to do with it as they please, including 'terraforming' it.

2. As organic life has intrinsic value, although producing further life is not a moral duty (unlike protecting existing life), it may be morally permissible to do so, at least under certain circumstances, such as rehabilitating areas that have become deserts or undergone other forms of degradation. But if such permission obtains on Earth, why not on Mars?

Moreover, given that humans have destroyed so much life on Earth and continue to do so, the moral permission could even become a duty by extending the principle of restitutive justice advocated by Taylor. By 'terraforming' Mars, one would be compensating biotic Nature on Earth for the damage humans have done to it, providing such replication of life on Mars is not meant solely as a further economic resource for humans.

3. But if 'terraformation' is to be rejected out of hand either as moral permission or duty, then one must develop a conception of intrinsic value which is not necessarily tied up solely with the fate of biotic Nature. This means that an environmental ethics, which is not Earthbound but capable of defending other planets against human control and domination, must confront the issue of abiotic or inanimate Nature as a locus of intrinsic value.

How can this task even begin? This paper will attempt to do so by first of all, ironically, outlining a conception of intrinsic value for Earth and extrapolating from it to Mars (or other planets), without being distracted, it is hoped, by the fact that organic life is indeed unique to Earth.

V

Such a conception of intrinsic value for an Earthbound environmental ethics would rest on the following considerations.

1. Earth (Nature) did not come into existence and/or continue to exist to serve human purposes. In this sense there is no teleology. Instead, there are teleomatic processes in abiotic Nature which simply follow physical laws, such as the law of gravity and the second law of thermodynamics (like the cooling of a heated piece of iron). In biotic Nature, teleonomy is at work—organisms display programmed behaviour, the programme being the product of natural selection (Mayr, 1988).

2. Humans, of course, find parts of Nature useful as food, clothing, shelter, etc., just as nonhuman life forms find other parts of Nature of use to them. Plants (autotrophs) can make use of abiotic Nature to sustain their own functioning integrity and in this sense, the carbon dioxide, minerals, water, heat and light from the Sun, etc. have instrumental value for the plants. But it would be misleading to say that abiotic Nature exists for the purpose or goal of keeping plants alive. Similarly, for an insect, the leaves of plants have instrumental value but it would also not be correct to say that plants sustain their own functioning integrity in order to be of use to insects. Neither can it be said that plants and animals exist for the purpose of keeping humans alive and flourishing although they, clearly, have instrumental value for humans. (Call 1 and 2 above the No-Teleology Thesis.)

3. It is obvious that: (a) The genesis of Earth is independent of

humans. It happened 15 eons ago. The genesis of life on Earth is also independent of humans. It happened at least 3·6 eons ago during the Archean period (4·5 to 2·5 eons ago) when the chemistry of the atmosphere was first dominated by oxygen. Humans arrived on the scene only 100,000 years ago. The history of natural evolution is a very long one indeed. (b) Earth and its biosphere would not be extinguished should humans themselves, for some reason, become extinct as a species. As far as the biosphere is concerned, the disappearance of the human species cannot be said to threaten it. Should human extinction happen, the niches formerly filled by humans will be taken over by other existing species as well as very probably provide opportunities for new species to emerge. The continuing existence of Earth and its biosphere is clearly, in this fundamental sense, independent of humans. (c) Moreover, the capacity of the biosphere to function integratively and well is also independent of humans. (d) In other words, the Earth and its extremely complex biosphere are fully autonomous. 'Autonomy' is here used to mean no more and no less than its ability to exist, to function integratively and well without any reference to, assistance from or reliance on humans. (e) From the perspective of biospherical integrity, humans are, therefore, dispensable and could even be redundant. (Call this the Autonomy Thesis.) However, this should not be taken to deny that humans today can damage such integrity.

4. The above shows that there is a distinct asymmetry of causal dependence between humans and Nature. While humans depend on Nature and cannot exist if it were absent or if its functioning integrity were to be upset by humans, Nature's own existence and functioning integrity is independent of human existence. (Call this the Asymmetry Thesis.)

VI

A proper reflection upon the Autonomy and Asymmetry theses would enable one to see that human arrogance and superiority towards Nature are totally misplaced. Humans are, indeed, capable of an exceptionally sophisticated level of abstract thinking, which we have used in the last 250 years or so to develop ever-increasingly powerful technologies to appropriate Nature for our own ends, far exceeding the capacity of any other life-form to do likewise. This gives us the illusion that Nature is entirely under our control, at our disposal and ought to be so. But human superiority lies in another direction—in our cognitive capacity to understand the complex workings of Nature, our critical capacity to construct theories and arguments and to test and assess them, and our ethical capacity for responsibility, for assuming duties towards those which themselves have no conception of the ethical.

From our cognitive engagement with the world, we know that causes and effects in the biosphere are nonlinear, leading to complex interdependence between its parts, and that our increasingly powerful technology produces effects which can and do upset its delicate functioning integrity. Such understanding could be deployed critically to show that a revised ethical attitude to Nature is called for—not one of arrogance and domination but of awe and humility.

Humility is appropriate in view of the Asymmetry Thesis—our absolute dependence on such an intricately complex system whose existence and maintenance are essentially independent and autonomous of us. Humility is the opposite of arrogance. To be arrogant is to behave in a superior dismissive manner towards the Other. Enlightenment philosophy might have encouraged humans to feel superior as it teaches that humans are so clever that they can control Nature through science and technology. But as we have seen, Nature's genesis, its continuing existence, its functioning integrity are fully autonomous of humans. No one can justifiably feel superior to another if the Other is not dependent on oneself.

Through arrogance, humans have assigned themselves a privileged status amongst Nature's species. But as far as evolution is concerned, no one species is privileged. If humans from their mistaken exalted position were to continue to act in ways that would undermine Nature's functioning integrity, the results could be such that the last laugh, so to speak, would be on us, humans. We might find ourselves eliminated, while Nature itself might reach a new and different equilibrium.

From this perspective, humility is justified both from the standpoint that Nature has intrinsic value and from the wider human instrumental standpoint that flows from the asymmetrical relationship. However, in this context, the instrumental consideration does not stem from arrogance or strength, as it does under strong anthropocentrism. Instead, it stems from a position of dependency and hence weakness. It, therefore, highlights the frailty and the limitations of humans before Nature.

In its presence, we humans should be filled with awe, that is, with reverential fear and wonder. Wonder is called for as the thing we behold is so marvellous and remarkable. And reverential fear, because not only is Nature a marvel but also because it has power over us, as on it our very existence depends.

Awe and humility would then dictate that we should maintain a respectful distance from Nature. We should be careful not to make excessive demands of any kind upon it, not only those to sustain ever-increasing consumption but even those which express our 'love' for it. Environmental ethicists often invoke the language of love in their account of our attitude to Nature. But Earth is not necessarily a suitable object for humans to love and to cherish, but a presence before which we should be humble and stand in awe. The concept of love, admittedly, is not totally inappropriate to characterize the human attitude to Nature—for instance, to love something is to care about its well-being even after one's own demise. This aspect is in keeping with Nature possessing intrinsic value. But there are other implications of the concept which are not so congenial to the view of Nature as a locus of intrinsic value—for instance, Nature could be loved to death. To love an object involves wanting to be with the loved object. But too many lovers communing with Nature (or a particular part of it) could damage, indeed, even destroy it.

Similarly with cherishing an object. Cherishing implies the desire to protect the cherished object from damage. But it can also imply mollycoddling it to ensure that it does not deteriorate and decay. In other words, what one cherishes, one wants to remain forever unchanged. But this would be incompatible with the workings of Nature whose processes inherently involve change.

Nature has its own pace and rate of change. Awe and humility would ensure that humans respect its rhythms and not force it to change at a pace dictated solely by our requirements. Otherwise its functioning integrity could be undermined. Subversion of Nature is to be deplored not simply from the instrumental perspective that we cannot survive and flourish without it, or do so less optimally with an impoverished Nature. It is also because Nature is fundamentally independent of us.

VII

To summarize the arguments so far advanced. This conception that intrinsic value exists in Nature, which implies that our appropriate attitude to it should be one of awe and humility, and our appropriate behaviour respectful and cautious, also requires us to acknowledge three fundamental truths:

I. The No-Teleology Thesis—that Nature exists for itself and not for us humans, just as we humans exist for ourselves and not for Nature. If we consider ourselves as a locus of intrinsic value because we are entities who exist for ourselves, then consistency would lead us to conclude (in virtue of our critical capacity) that

Nature as a whole and the various items in it, too, are loci of intrinsic value for they, too, exist for themselves. This, however, is not to deny that what has intrinsic value in this sense may have instrumental value, as a matter of fact, for another.

II. The Autonomy Thesis—if an entity exists for itself, not for us, and if its genesis, its continuing existence and survival, are independent of us, then we ought to recognize that it has a value independent of us. In turn, we ought also to recognize that we have a duty (in virtue of our ethical capacity) not to undermine or destroy such a thing of value.

III. The Asymmetry Thesis—our total dependence on Nature but Nature's independence of us—reinforces the Autonomy Thesis and emphasizes the view that Nature has value which is entirely independent of us.

Such a conception of intrinsic value in Nature highlights the contrast between Nature on the one hand and human artefacts on the other. It has already been observed that the former's genesis, existence and functioning integrity has nothing to do with human purpose or effort. Human artefacts, *ex hypothesi*, are designed and created for our purposes and maintained by us in order to continue serving those purposes. They owe their *raison d'être* and existence to us. In other words, they are our creations. We can do with them as we like. In the ultimate scenario of the the Last Person Argument, there would be nothing morally wrong to arrange for them to be destroyed, as they have been created entirely by humans for humans. Even the most beautiful, exquisite or complicated human artefact, like the Pieta, the Alhambra or a nuclear power station would have no value when there are no humans around, as the totality of its value is generated and determined by us humans. Artefacts exist to be of use to us, to please, amuse or delight us, to elevate or inspire us.

However, one needs to distinguish between true human artefacts and quasi-human ones. The former are made out of inanimate Nature and in any case, even without planned destruction, they would decay, sooner rather than later, in the absence of human maintenance. The latter are fashioned out of animate Nature, like our domesticated animals, plants and ecosystems. Under the Last Person scenario, one should argue that these ought to be left alone. Of those which could survive, *ex hypothesi*, they would have become totally independent and autonomous of humans.

It bears repeating that Nature has not come into existence to be of use to us, to please, amuse or delight, to elevate and inspire us, although as a matter of fact we humans have undoubtedly found Nature useful, pleasing and/or inspiring. In brief, Nature is simply not a human artefact and, therefore, ought not to be treated as such. It is not there at our bidding.

From this standpoint, it would be a mistake for environmental theorists to argue that our attitude to Nature should be like our attitude to art. On this view, Nature is a work of art—we hold it dear and ought to cherish it because, like art, it is a beautiful thing. But art is quintessentially a human artefact. The analogy between Nature and Art may turn out to be fundamentally misleading. It makes Nature out to be like a human artefact, when obviously it is not, but is a distinct contrast to the very idea of Artefact itself. Essentially Nature is beyond human creation and design. It is, therefore, wrong for humans to distort the nature of Nature, to render it into a quasi-, if not a true, artefact.[3]

As hunters and gatherers, humans had appropriated Nature for their own purposes. But they only seriously began to modify Nature and turn it into quasi-artefacts when they became sedentary. The domestication of plants and animals is a supreme instance of such modification. But such attempts have been locally confined and limited, unlike contemporary techniques which can and do have totalising effects in turning the whole of Nature into a quasi-human artefact.

VIII

At the moment, the 'terraforming' of Mars is still very much a blueprint, although institutions like NASA would be more than eager to pump immense sums of money into its R&D, if only they could persuade the politicians to approve the funds. The project embodies the ultimate philosophy of transforming Nature into Artefact. Mars would be designed and moulded by humans to our taste, preferences and requirements. Right now it has no life; but it shall have life. And what sort of life? The sort that we know about, find useful or pleasing or, indeed, even beautiful.

Holmes Rolston is quoted as saying that 'terraforming' Mars would amount to an environmental crime (Hawkes, 1993). One could readily agree with his response. But on what grounds can we resist the project as a morally misplaced one?[4] One way of grounding the resistance would be to argue that Mars has intrinsic value. So let us see if the conception of intrinsic value outlined above for

[3] Other life forms also create artefacts—bees build hives, birds nests, beavers dams, etc. But they make them to fulfil a very specific and limited need. When they have outgrown their creations, they simply leave them to disintegrate on their own.

[4] For Rolston's own arguments, see Rolston, 1986b.

an Earthbound environmental ethics can be applied with modification to do duty for an astronomically bounded one.

As already argued, that conception rests on three strands—the No-Teleology, the Autonomy and the Asymmetry theses. Would these hold in the case of Mars? It is not obvious that they do not. For a start to say that Mars exists to serve human ends is more patently implausible than it is to claim that Earth does. Humans at least exist on Earth and have been evolved to do so. But Mars has no humans. Instead, with our advanced technology we threaten to, and probably could, transform it into an object of use to ourselves. But this possibility of instrumental value does not undermine, in any way, the contention that its *raison d'être* has nothing to do with human ends. It exists for itself, no more and no less. It is both an illusion and a fallacy to hold that whatever we humans happen to find useful, in the light of our technology, must have come into existence just for the purpose of serving our ends—or that its existence is to be justified solely in terms of such a purpose.

The genesis of Mars long antedated the appearance of humans on Earth. Its continuing existence has nothing to do with humans. What happens there is totally independent of us. It might once have had water (as is speculated) but today it is said to be waterless. But neither state of affairs is due either to human effort or design.

Earth's atmosphere, its biosphere upon which human survival and flourishing depends, in turn depend on Mars and other planets in the solar system rotating and exerting gravitational pull on one another in certain ways. So while the existence of humans depends on the existence of Mars, the existence of the latter would not be affected should humans, as a species on Earth, become extinguished.

Awe and humility would then be the appropriate attitude to Mars. Keeping a respectful distance from it is also entailed. However, satellites sent to probe its history, its composition, etc. merely to enlarge our knowledge about the workings of Nature, past and present, would be consonant with such an attitude. But any attempt to go beyond cognitive understanding would constitute a violation of our recognition that it has a value entirely independent of ourselves which ought to constrain any impulse we may have to make it over to our own design, to transform its status as Nature to a status as Artefact.

Looked at in this way, the fact that Mars lacks life—that it is inanimate, abiotic Nature—is irrelevant to the question whether it has intrinsic value. The conception of intrinsic value outlined does not rely on biotic Nature to give abiotic Nature the status of being a locus of intrinsic value. It happens that on Earth abiotic and biotic Nature are inextricably linked. But with Mars and other planets, a divorce between the two has to be directly confronted. In constructing an astronomically bounded environmental ethics, the uniqueness of Earth's biosphere should not make it altogether impossible to lay down a general framework for an account of intrinsic value which in one sense transcends such a feature. At the same time, such a general framework also permits a focussing on this feature when one is merely concentrating on the task of constructing an Earthbound environmental ethics. That general framework turns out to be bounded by the No-Teleology, the Autonomy and the Asymmetry theses.

IX

Potential critics of this conception of intrinsic value which claims to be able to cope with animate and inanimate Nature when both are inextricably intertwined as on Earth, or with the latter when it is divorced from the former as on Mars (and other planets known to us), could complain that it involves a purely verbal manoeuvre.

After all, it is open to anyone to define any term however one likes. But such definitional flexibility is bought at a price as others have no (conceptual) obligation to accept the definition proffered. This paper has advocated a particular definition of the term 'intrinsic value', namely, (a) whatever is autonomous and independent of humans both in its genesis and continuing existence has a value independent of humans; (b) whatever is autonomous and independent of humans is not there primarily to serve human purposes and ends, and therefore exists for itself—although humans may and do, as a matter of fact, find it is of use to them.

It presupposes that the existence of any material entity which is independent of human design and effort has value. Is this so arbitrary an assumption to make? It may look arbitrary but only from a purely homocentric standpoint which assumes that humans are not merely the source but also the locus of all values (see Callicott, 1986). The Last Person Argument may be invoked deploying Callicott's distinction[5] to articulate the possibility that even abiotic

[5] Someone could object that Callicott's distinction cannot be deployed in the context of the Last Person Argument on the grounds that a world without human consciousness is a world without values. But this would not be correct. The last human in contemplating the annihilation of Nature after his or her own demise would be morally prevented from doing so because such a person would recognise that Nature is a locus of intrinsic value.

Nature, divorced from its biotic counterpart, can possess value through the response that it would not be morally permissible for the last human to destroy a lifeless planet should the technology to do so be available.

Is such a response no more than a mere intuition? If not, it must rest on the recognition that Mars has a value which is totally independent of humans. And it seems appropriate to call such a value 'intrinsic value', as it is not bestowed on it by humans and would exist regardless of whether humans exist or not. The issue must not be turned into a verbal matter—if it is felt that the term 'intrinsic value' in this context departs too much from its normal usage, then an alternative term could be used, such as 'human-independent value'. The substantial point can still be made that such a human-independent value could place moral constraint on the human aspiration to transform Mars from Nature into Artefact.

It is assumed that there are only three possibilities as far as abiotic Nature is concerned—(i) that it has (economic) resource value for humans, (ii) that it has psychological or aesthetic value for humans, and (iii) that if neither (i) nor (ii) obtains, then it must be valueless as it cannot have a value independent of humans. But all three views stem from strong anthropocentrism, presupposing that humans are both the source and locus of value. Such a standpoint entails that either Mars has potential instrumental value for humans or it is valueless.

However, we have seen that even a non-anthropocentric perspective which is biocentric does not make it conceptually possible for one to say that abiotic Nature has a value which is independent of biotic Nature itself. Such a perspective allows for only two possibilities—either (i) abiotic Nature has instrumental value for biotic Nature or (ii) it is in danger of being valueless. It follows from it that Mars is valueless since it supports no biota. It is true that organic life has an identity and even a self-identity (in some instances) which it strives to maintain and sustain. But inanimate Nature only has an identity, the persistence or the undermining of which is determined entirely by teleomatic processes, as Mayr has pointed out. There is stability and there is change, but these are not governed by teleonomy as they are in biotic Nature. But it would be 'biocentric chauvinism' to say that abiotic Nature is valueless unless it has instrumental value for biotic Nature.

From the perspective advocated by this paper, it is human and biocentric chauvinism which are arbitrary when they both assume that whatever is of no instrumental value to humans and biota are necessarily valueless. Humans, animals and plants (or the ecosystems they are embedded in) strive to maintain their integrity and hence display end-directed activities. As a result, they may be said to possess interests. *Ex hypothesi*, abiotic Nature does not possess interests at all in the sense just mentioned. To define 'intrinsic value' in terms of interests will entail that abiotic Nature has no intrinsic value whatsoever, and hence is valueless, once any possible instrumental value for humans and biotic Nature has been ruled out. Such a definition could begin to look a shade arbitrary when its anatomy is laid out for examination, so to speak.

If either definition looks suspiciously like a case of special pleading, then perhaps it is proper to concede that the last word has not been said about the matter and that it is time to look seriously at the issue of whether abiotic Nature can be said to be a locus of intrinsic value and in what sense of the term 'intrinsic'.

The End of Anthropocentrism?

MARY MIDGLEY

What is it to be Central?

Are human beings in some sense central to the cosmos? It used to seem obvious that they were. It seems less obvious now. But the idea is still powerful in our thinking, and it may be worth while asking just what it has meant.

There is of course a minor point of view from which we really are central—for our own lives, our own species do provide the natural focus. Our starting-point, the angle from which we look at things, is bound to be our own region. In the same way, if we think about *self*-centredness, each of us does unavoidably see our own self as in some sense the centre of the world.

This parallel is surely helpful. In neither case can we spread our consciousness impartially over the whole scene. We do have powers of sympathy, but since we are finite beings, those powers are necessarily limited. We have no choice but to be specially interested in ourselves and those close to us. As Bishop Butler pointed out, this kind of priority is not necessarily a bad thing. Indeed it is vital that we do love and care for ourselves properly. If we have not enough self-love, if we despise or hate ourselves, we cannot love other people. The trouble with human beings (he said) is not really that they love themselves too much; they ought to love themselves more. The trouble is simply that they don't love others enough (Butler, 1969, p. 24).

In that sense, then, the self *must* be the centre of each person's world and accordingly the word 'self-centred' seems at first to have had quite a good meaning. It was coined to describe the balanced state of heavenly bodies like the sun, spinning securely on their own axes, rather than shooting off at an angle like badly-made tops. Figuratively, then, it was used to describe well-organized, balanced people. Thus the *Oxford English Dictionary* quotes from a novel in 1895: 'He would be fixed at last, swinging steadily on a pivot of happiness . . . . Now at last he would be self-centred'.

Interestingly, however, this image of independence soon began to show a darker side. Thus the Dictionary gives a remark by one Norris, writing *Practical Discourses* in 1693: 'The self-ending, self-centring man does in a very true sense idolise himself'. Again, it

Mary Midgley

quotes from Dr Johnson's letters (1783): 'A stubborn sufficiency self-centred', and from Coleridge (1809): 'They pursue the interests of freedom steadily, but with narrow and self-centring views'. In short, the natural balance of the independent spinning top cannot be relied on for human social life. If there is too much ego in your cosmos, other people are likely to go short. Charity may indeed begin at home, but it had better not end there.

This is now a commonly accepted moral principle, indeed, something of a platitude, not just for individual selves, but also for the various human groups into which they cluster—families, classes, professions, races, nations. Group chauvinism, as well as individual selfishness, is understood to be a serious fault. So far, indeed, we are on ground common to our whole moral tradition.

Species Politics during the Enlightenment

If, however, we turn from self to species, things have not been so simple. Here people have seen themselves as placed, not just at the relative centre of a particular life, but at the absolute, objective centre of everything. The centrality of MAN (sic) has been pretty steadily conceived, both in the West and in many other traditions, not as an illusion of perspective imposed by our starting-point, but as an objective fact, and indeed an essential fact, about the whole universe.

Christian thought grounded this status firmly on creation by a humanoid God who had made man in his (sic) own image in order to mark a quite special status among the ruck of ordinary, non-Godlike creatures. But this Christian account has not stood alone. Enlightenment thinkers who reckoned to be emancipated from such imagery were no less confident on the matter. Thus Kant: 'As the single being upon earth that possesses understanding, [man] is certainly titular lord of nature and, supposing we regard nature as a teleological system, he is born to be its ultimate end' (Kant, 1928, pp. 93–94).

Kant states here three themes which often recur and need a great deal of attention: the claim to dominance, the emphasis on intellect as its ground, and the reference to cosmic teleology. As for dominance, man is 'titular lord'. For beings who think hierarchically, this is no doubt a natural way to interpret centrality. What is alarming about it, however, is how easily the imagery of dominance escalates to that of exploitation and even warfare.

Thus Marx observed that capitalism had been right to reject 'the deification of nature': 'thus nature becomes for the first time simply an object for mankind, purely a matter of utility' (Marx, 1971, p. 94). More sharply still, Freud suggested that the right way to sublimate human aggression was to direct it away from other people against the rest of the biosphere, by 'becoming a member of the human community, and, with the help of a technique guided by science, going over to the attack against nature and subjecting her to the human will' (Freud, 1985, p. 265). William James proposed the same solution to that problem in his famous essay on 'The Moral Equivalent of War'. In fact, the idea that human beings should use the intellectual power of science to conquer nature by war or suppression seems to have looked perfectly normal to many thinkers, at least up till the middle of this century, both in the capitalist world and, if anything, still more so in the communist one. Thus John Passmore quotes (along with many other fascinating examples) M.N. Pokrovskiy, writing in a *Brief History of Russia* in 1931: 'It is easy to foresee that in the future, when science and technique have attained to a perfection which we are as yet unable to visualise, nature will become soft wax in his [man's] hands which he will be able to cast into whatever form he chooses' (Passmore, 1980, p. 25).

Doubt Seeps In

We can understand how people had reached this curious view. Starting from the already ambitious biblical position, human beings had for some centuries been performing many increasingly dazzling technological and scientific feats. At the same time, and partly as a result of these changes, various doctrines of historical progress had been developed, focusing attention still more strongly on the rising curve of human achievement, glorifying humans yet further and making the gap between them and the rest of the biosphere look still wider.

At this same time, however, a whole string of other intellectual developments were moving thought away from this cheerful pattern. The effect has been to leave that pattern now strangely isolated and conceptually unsupported, though still emotionally very strong. I think that a sizeable part of our present confusion may flow from our sense of anomaly here—from the Gestalt-shift between a wildly exaggerated, euphoric idea of human standing and a despairing nihilism about it which may be equally wild ('people are pollution'). Today, though we still often hear very flattering accounts of ourselves, we just as often come across much less flattering ones, and on the whole these are pronounced with more conviction.

Mary Midgley

Thus early in this century William James (writing in the *Atlantic Monthly* in 1904) remarked that 'man, biologically considered, and whatever else he may be into the bargain, is simply the most formidable of all the beasts of prey, and, indeed, the only one that preys systematically on its own species'. Or again, Arthur Koestler observed that 'The most persistent sound that reverberates through man's history is the beating of war-drums .... Man can leave the earth and land on the moon, but cannot cross from East to West Berlin. Prometheus reaches for the stars with an insane grin on his face and a totem-symbol in his hand' (Koestler, 1978, Prologue).

Of course, dark remarks of this sort are not new. There was always an ambivalence within Christian thought that called for humility and penitence and reminded us that our righteousness was as filthy rags. But certain changes in the modern age have given this kind of thinking so much more force that they might, at a glance, be seen as heralding the end of anthropocentrism.

The Paradox of Science

What, then, have been these eroding changes? In the first place, of course, scientific progress itself began to cast doubts on the whole euphoric way of thinking. The universe has turned out to be both so much larger and so much less tidily organized than it used to seem that the idea of its having any centre, in a literal physical sense, no longer makes sense. And though we might think that it should be easy to accept these new factual beliefs without losing what the older ones used to symbolize, it turns out that this imagery is in fact quite hard to shift. Symbols that persist in this way always deserve attention.

Several different sciences have converged to alarm us here. Astronomy now tells us that there is no physical centre and no absolute up and down. There surrounds us, instead, a formless stage so vast, both in time and space, that even the most splendid human actors are almost imperceptible as they move upon it— insects or bacteria, at best. Biology adds that, even among the living things which have lately entered on this scene, human beings are particularly late and perhaps accidental arrivals. Their shape, too, does not appear to be so much a direct imprint from God as a slight variation on an existing primate pattern. Xenophanes, in fact, was right—if horses and cattle had gods, they would make them in the shape of horses and cattle. Man has made God in his own image. Geography adds that the continents which we have usually thought of as at least a firm grounding for our part of the stage are themselves on the move. Most recently, too, ecology has told us that we are by no means securely moulding wax-like nature to suit our needs and are never likely to do so. On the contrary, we are busily sawing off the branches we sit on, and can only cease to do that if we attend respectfully to the internal guiding principles of nature instead of trying to distort it through ones invented by ourselves.

More generally still, however, there is a metaphysical change in the scientific perspective. The teleological assumptions that seemed to hold the symbolic core of 'anthropocentrism' in place are themselves no longer deemed scientific. The idea of a central cosmic purpose is as foreign to modern science as the idea of a central location is. The word 'anthropocentric' itself seems to have been invented to make just this point. Thus the *Oxford English Dictionary* quotes Haeckel (or his translator into English) writing in 1876 of 'the anthropocentric error, that man is the premeditated aim of the creation of the earth'.

The paradox here—comic or tragic, as you choose to look at it—is that science, which has always seemed a particularly bright jewel in the crown of the titular lord, turns out also, paradoxically, to be an axe cutting away the floor under his throne. Nor is science alone in this destructive work; political theory plays an equally double part. After the Enlightenment, what are we doing with the notion of a titular lord anyway? If we are proud of science, we are surely still more proud of discovering that government should always be by consent. Its authority comes from below, from those who accept it, not from an outside ruler, as in the Divine Right of Kings. The idea of being a lord arbitrarily appointed from outside, more particularly a violent lord, liable at the drop of a hat to make war on his disobedient subjects, doesn't suit our self-image at all. Yet, if we keep the traditional reasoning and imagery, that is how we are supposed to see ourselves.

Anthropic Escapism

What is to be done about all this? It is quite interesting that some desperate efforts have been made to extend modern science so as to make it endorse the traditional picture, most strikingly through the Strong Anthropic Principle. This rules that 'The Universe must have those properties which allow life to develop within it at some stage in its history' (Barrow and Tipler, 1986, p. 21). This is considered necessary because matter cannot really function unless it is observed, and observed in the special way in which physicists observe quantum events. (A confused memory of Berkeleian idealism is evidently at work here.) Human perception, and indeed the perception of contemporary scientists, is thus absolutely indispensable to the existence of the cosmos.

Officially, this quasi-idealist approach is not supposed to imply that the cosmos works with the aim of producing the observer who will save it. But it is usually combined with the thought that the constitution of the existing universe is so extraordinarily improbable that the fact of its development can only be accounted for by the need to produce just one of its existing artefacts. And by a remarkable coincidence, this selected artefact turns out to be not a set of giraffes or redwood trees or colonial jellyfish, but the species *Homo sapiens*—especially, of course, in its current manifestation as *Homo sapiens physicus*.

In effect, this can only be an attempt to bring back teleology—to renew the notion of a cosmic drama with a central role for MAN, not in the context of religion, nor with any explicitly defended philosophical assumptions, but nominally as a simple, objective part of physics. This principle teaches that the universe has indeed had the production of MAN as its central business, but that MAN is needed simply as a physicist, able to collapse certain wave-functions by observing quantum events, and thereby to make the universe itself at last fully and properly real. Until then it was not thus real, for, as John Wheeler explains, 'Acts of observer-participancy—via the mechanism of the delayed-choice experiment—in turn give tangible "reality" to the universe not only now but back to the beginning' (Wheeler, 1983, pp. 209, 194; cf. Barrow and Tipler, 1986, p. 464). Professors Barrow and Tipler add that MAN, having performed this feat, will then proceed to computerize himself and to occupy the whole of space by colonization, arriving finally at the Omega Point in possession of all the information that there is, and thereby in some sense apparently becoming God. (Their most startling claims about this may be found at the end of their book, and especially in its concluding sentences.)

I have discussed this amazing project elsewhere (see Midgley, 1992, pp. 21–27 and ch. 17). Here, I can only suggest that this sort of thing is in no sense science, but simply a piece of wild metaphysics, made possible by the weird metaphorical language already in use on the topics of quantum mechanics, time and probability theory. Ignorance about how metaphors work is widespread among modern English-speaking physicists, and is particularly deep among British ones. They very much need to read the chapter on science in Janet Martin Soskice's sharp little book *Metaphor and Religious Language*, and also Graham Richards's *On Psychological Language*.

Why All or Nothing?

What matters here, however, is not the muddles but the point of the project. The Anthropic Principle seems aimed, somewhat desperately, at bridging the gap just mentioned—the gap that yawns in our current thinking between our immense sense of our own importance on the local scene and our apparent total insignificance in the objective universe.

We cannot bridge that gap if we insist on an all-or-nothing solution. The anthropicists are making a desperate effort to keep *all*. They are in fact setting up by far the highest claims ever made for the importance of our species, because they do not even have the background figure of God to moderate our status. While God is present, MAN can be reduced to the figure of a responsible steward, even if he remains, in some sense, central among earthly creatures. But for the anthropicists, MAN replaces God as creator, not just of earth, but of everything. In effect, they are offering us anthropolatry. As Norris puts it: 'The self-ending, self-centring man does in a very true sense idolise himself'.

I suggest that the reason why cosmologists do this is not necessarily that they are more conceited than the rest of us, but that the fear of total insignificance produces a violent reaction, leading people to claim immense, inconceivable kinds of significance. Exactly as happens over individual paranoia, frightened subjects react against being down-graded by grading themselves up—if necessary, indefinitely, and becoming gods. The trouble starts, surely, with the fact that, when our traditional symbols are attacked, we do not stop thinking symbolically, we just change the symbol.

When the cosmic stage on which we used to figure becomes larger, we do not drop the idea of any such stage. Instead, we see ourselves as shrinking puppets, and eventually as ants or bacteria, still performing on this same expanding stage. Because this is unbearable, people look for a counter-symbol, a story which can somehow be taken as scientifically literal, and which yet gives us back our key part in the drama.

What we need to do instead, I suggest, is to change the symbolism in a deeper and more discriminating way. We never needed that vast cosmic stage in the first place, and only very lately have we had it. Our business has never been with anything outside our own planet.

We do indeed need a sense of destiny—a sense of a larger background, a context within which our own lives make sense. We need the idea of a drama in which we are acting. We have to have a sense of the sort of role that is expected of us. We need that sense whether or no we believe in God, whether or no we are important and influential people, whether or no we understand where it comes from. All cultures supply this sort of background framework—indeed, doing so is one of their most basic functions. We need it both for ourselves individually and for all the groups with which we seriously identify. That is what it is for life to have a meaning. But nothing fixes in advance the range of beings that must figure in our drama. Nothing forces us to take the vast extraterrestrial background into our theatre. And certainly nothing commits us to swallowing or conquering all figures in the drama who are outside our own group.

At every level—both for the individual and for various kinds of group—there is a temptation to supply this drama simply by drawing a firm line between ourselves and a range of opponents. That is always the quickest way to give life a meaning. Individuals can set themselves against the whole world; Ajax defies the lightning. Similarly group members can set their group against everybody outside it, and life so organized can go on charmingly for the inside circle. All disasters, even death, are more easily faced in this pugnacious context which so readily gets the adrenalin flowing. This is the tendency which has again and again fixed people in mutually destructive, confrontational groups, and it is surely the one that has accounted for the exclusive, pugnacious glorification of our own species in earlier thinking.

What should we call it?

I do not think Anthropocentrism is the best name for this habit. It is, no doubt, a word that can be used at the everyday level, and at that level I am not trying to get rid of it. But if we try to put much weight on it, it can lead us into trouble. In the first place, as I said at the outset, there is a sense in which it is right for us to feel that we are at the centre of our own lives. Attempts to get rid of that sense would be doomed in the same way as stoical attempts to tell people not to care specially about themselves, or about those dear to them. As Bishop Butler (again) pointed out in his 'Sermon upon Compassion', puritanism of this sort can only be destructive. It may succeed in damaging the particular affections it attacks, but it has no power to produce nobler, more universal affections to replace them. And, in controversy, such unrealistic puritanism is always damaging to one's own cause.

We need, then, to recognize that people do right, not wrong, to have a particular regard for their own kin and their own species. From a practical angle, this recognition does not harm green causes, because the measures needed today to save the human race are, by and large, the same measures that are needed to save the rest of the biosphere. There simply is no lifeboat option by which human beings can save themselves alone, either as a whole or in particular areas. If there were, this issue of emotional centrality might be a serious one, but there isn't. There are indeed local conflicts of interests over things like culling. But in general, in the kind of major emergency we have at present, the interests of different species coincide so widely that really enlightened self-interest would not dictate seriously different policies from species-altruism. I don't, therefore, see much point in disputing hotly about the rightness of 'anthropocentrism' in this very limited sense.

When, however, we leave that intelligible ground—when 'anthropocentrism' is taken to mean an absolute claim to be at the centre of the universe—I simply do not know what this metaphor is supposed to mean at all. The Anthropicists are probably doing us a service by sketching out a possible meaning for it, since that meaning is so ludicrous as to reduce the whole idea to absurdity. What is commonly *meant* by the word 'anthropocentric' today, however, is something much more ordinary and much less intellectually ambitious. It is simple *human chauvinism*, *narrowness of sympathy*, comparable to national or race or gender chauvinism. It could also be called *exclusive humanism*, as opposed to the hospitable, friendly, inclusive kind.

That chauvinism is surely as indefensible rationally as the chauvinism of smaller human groups. Enlightenment thinking has certainly built protective barriers round it by devices like defining the idea of 'rights' in a way that confines it to articulate humans who can speak in law-courts, and ruling that rights can only belong to those who have, in a recognized human sense, duties. These constructions seem to me evidently artificial and unconvincing once the spotlight of attention actually reaches them. (I have discussed them elsewhere (Midgley, 1983, ch. 5).) As tools of admirable campaigning for the Rights of Man, these ideas were originally aimed at extending concern to the whole human race, not at shutting it off from dogs and horses. Some of the major Enlightenment sages, such as Tom Paine, Montaigne and Voltaire, were in fact much concerned about the sufferings of animals, and Bentham surely spoke for the deeper spirit of Enlightenment humanitarianism when he said: 'The question is not, Can they reason? nor Can they talk? but, Can they suffer?'.

Certainly this wider perspective leaves us with some hard problems. We have to arbitrate all sorts of local inter-species conflicts; we do not have a tidy system of Rights and Duties that will always tell us how to do so. But then, did anybody ever suppose that we did have one, even on the human scene? Such a project would be still less plausible if it were applied, as human chauvinists might still like to apply it, to all conflicts of interests between species in the fast-changing, distracted world that we have today.

The kind of anthropolatry that would always set immediate human interests above those of other life-forms is surely no longer defensible. Enlightenment individualism incorporated strong contributions from egoism, which, in their own time, had their uses. But today we need less, not more, ego in our cosmos, both individually and collectively. What we, as philosophers, have to do next is to work hard on forging the ways of thinking that will help to make this need clear and understandable.

Global Religion

STEPHEN R. L. CLARK

Whose Problem?

The social and environmental problems that we face at this tail end of twentieth-century progress require us to identify some cause, some spirit that transcends the petty limits of our time and place.[1] It is easy to believe (or to pretend to ourselves that we believe) that there is no crisis. We have been told too often that the oceans will soon die, the air be poisonous, our energy reserves run dry; that the world will grow warmer, coastlands be flooded and the climate change; that plague, famine and war will be the necessary checks on population growth. But here we are: sufficiently healthy and well-fed, connoisseurs of far-off catastrophe and horror movies, confident that something will turn up or that the prophecies of doom were only dreams. We are the descendants, after all, of creatures who did not despair, who hoped against hope that there would still be life tomorrow. We no more believe in the world's end than we believe that soldiers could break down the door and drag us off to torture and to death: we don't *believe* that they could even when we know that, somewhere altogether elsewhere, they did. Even if we can force ourselves to remember other ages, other lands or other classes, we are content enough.

Our resilience is reinforced by images of seasonal adjustment and return. Such changes as we can make ourselves admit are bound to be temporary. We come to expect heart-warming panics: every few years we are reminded of the abstract possibility of nuclear spasm, poisoned water, global warming, meteor strikes, solar flares and rabid foxes. We shiver, but we know, or firmly believe, that the panic will subside, the threat seem far away, and even if it were to happen, still things would go on. Nature at least is immortal, and our civilization, even though we can give no reason for our confidence, seems to us to be entirely natural. Even to suggest otherwise is at once absurd and impolite: it almost seems that we suspect that speaking makes things so. Of course, we think, such changes are impossible, but talking about them might encourage them to happen. The converse conviction, that talking

[1] Most of the material in this paper is treated at greater length in my Scott Holland lectures (1992), published as Clark, 1993.

about them somehow cures them, is also all too common. 'The mere fact that sometimes appalling developments [have] been displayed in print at all seem[s] to reassure the citizens that they would not happen' (Lessing, 1981, p. 279).

So none of us can quite believe there is a crisis, or cannot believe it long. Nonetheless, I am, in the abstract, fairly sure there is, and that the crisis cannot be resolved without a change more radical than I can quite imagine.

> For generations, we have assumed that the efforts of mankind would leave the fundamental equilibrium of the world's systems and atmosphere stable. But it is possible that with all these enormous changes (population, agricultural, use of fossil fuels) concentrated into such a short period of time, we have unwittingly begun a massive experiment with the system of this planet itself. (Margaret Thatcher, 27 September 1988, cited in Pearce et al., 1989, p. 27)

Maybe the prophets of doom will soon be reduced to Jonah's state, grumpily conscious that the worst will not occur, because enough of us did, after all, 'turn from our wickedness and live'. Or maybe they won't.

Even if we don't believe in total catastrophe, many of us, fortunately for the future, and our children's fortunes, do identify with our posterity, plant woodlands that we shall not see, and seek to save our children's children from disaster. But our willingness to sacrifice our own present interests for the general good of humankind or of the world is feeble: advising others not to cut down rain forests or pollute the seas is easy enough; preserving our own wetlands or cutting back on burgers or not travelling to conferences on conservation by convenient means is another matter. Only a 'religious spirit', a willed and eager commitment to a larger whole, can easily sustain us through adversity, let alone through prosperity. The question is: what spirit shall that be?

And Who's to Blame?

In 1967 Lynn White gave forceful expression to the common judgment that 'we shall continue to have a worsening ecological crisis until we reject the Christian axiom that nature has no reason for existence save to serve man' (White, 1967). The theme has been repeated with variations ever since. Arnold Toynbee, conversing with Daisaku Ikeda in the early 1970s, declared a right religion is one that teaches respect for the dignity and sanctity of all nature. The wrong religion is one that licenses the indulgence of human greed at the expense of non-human nature. I conclude that the religion we need to embrace now is pantheism, as exemplified in Shinto, and that the religion we now need to discard is Judaic monotheism and the post-Christian non-theistic faith in scientific progress, which has inherited from Christianity the belief that mankind is morally entitled to exploit the rest of the universe for the indulgence of human greed. (Toynbee and Ikeda, 1976, p. 324)

As long as we think that there are no proper limits on what we may individually and collectively do with the world, we shall do what looks like bringing the best advantage. Even if, other things being equal, we would genuinely prefer to live among established woodlands and breath clean air, we also have other wants, and know that other people have them too. What our religion lets us use, we will. So 'the Christian axiom', if such it is, gets in the way of crisis-resolution.

It is easy enough to devise an answer to what White suggested (see Barr, 1972, pp. 7–32). It certainly can't be *only* Christians that pollute the world. White himself acknowledged that the Pleistocene extinctions might well have been caused by human fire-drives. An American eco-feminist, by the way, is romantically inclined to speak of those animals 'giving themselves for food' (Starhawk, 1984, p. 17): I doubt that they did. Human beings, turning from such bloody acts to agriculture (perhaps because there were too few prey left to kill), drained the land of its fertility and seasoned it with salt. Human beings cut down forests and let the soil dry out and blow away. We did all this without being Christians, and in doing so behaved, most probably, like any successful species.

But though Christians cannot be exclusively to blame, and plenty of non-Christian countries have done as badly or still worse, it may still be true that 'the Christian axiom' prevents a resolution. The argument in the literature of environmentalism is not well conducted. The evidence for the existence of the axiom (which appears in no creed known to me) seems at times to consist of Ronald Reagan's throw-away remark that 'when you've seen one redwood tree you've seen them all', uncritical quotation of the biblical injunction to have 'dominion', and an equally uncritical conviction that Christianity, being dualist, anti-materialist, and founded on the idea of a transcendent, male deity, must be opposed to nature, animals and women. The speech attributed to

115

Chief Seattle in 1854—but mostly composed in 1970 (Seed *et al.*, 1988, pp. 67–73; see also Callicott, 1989, p. 204)—suggests that Christians place their ancestors in Heaven, not in earth, and so feel no identity with the material world (without being in the least ascetic in their use of it). Many commentators, by way of reply, have pointed out that biblical theists are usually powerfully convinced of the real and sacramental importance of the material universe. The God of the Bible—and also the Koran—is present in the world, and so far from licensing our exploitation of it, places limits on it with a threat of judgment.

Nor is it any easier to convict mediaeval Christianity of any contempt for 'Mother Nature'. As Carolyn Merchant's study, *The Death of Nature*, makes clear, the dominant morality of that time was opposed to mining in that it literally devastated land, and metaphorically or mystically raped the earth (Merchant, 1982, pp. 29ff). When Callenbach's rather irritating Ecotopians remark 'who would use an earth-mover on his own mother?'[2] they are reviving mediaeval rhetoric. That same rhetoric is commonly attributed to 'aboriginals' and 'native peoples'; thus Warwick Fox quotes an Amerindian response to the offer of a more effective plough: 'shall I tear my mother's breast?' (Fox, 1986, p. 76; cited by Dobson, 1990, p. 59). It is alarmingly easy to locate such notions among 'aboriginals'. Alarmingly so, because it is simply the product of the same racist imperialism as regularly assimilates conquered tribes, and women, to 'nature' rather than 'culture'. The environmentalists who do this may think they are revaluing 'nature' (and the conquered), but it is more likely to serve their own cultural ends.

As Merchant also says, earth-respecting rhetoric was undermined by commercial needs that were long resisted by the church authorities. Nor were those authorities merely 'spiritual'. On the contrary, as Boulding has observed, in the Benedictines 'for almost the first time in history we had intellectuals who worked with their hands, and belonged to a religion which regarded the physical world as in some sense sacred and capable of enshrining goodness' (Foricy, 1982, p. 75, quoting Boulding, 1964, p. 6). Doubtless those Benedictines acted in ways I might myself think wrong, but it is just not true that their creed licensed either literal or symbolic rape. Bahro may even be right to suspect that we need a new 'Benedictine' Order (Bahro, 1986, p. 90).

Even the Enlightenment, which those not busy blaming Christians tend to excoriate, was clear about our duties. People

[2] Callenbach, 1978, p. 29, a fairly conventional post-Morris utopia.

who do not care what happens to our children and grandchildren are recognizably rogues. 'As we feel it wicked and inhuman for men to declare that they care not if when they themselves are dead, the universal conflagration ensues, it is undoubtedly true that we are bound to study the interest of posterity also for its own sake' (Cicero, *De Finibus*, 3.64). We should not live in ways that would make our descendants' lives enormously difficult, should not use up or destroy what they will need. As Thomas Jefferson insisted, in line with the common law of England, we have no claim upon the land itself, but only on its lawful fruits (White, 1978, p. 223): we do not inherit the land from our ancestors, but rather hold it in trust for our descendants. Nothing, said Locke, was given to man to spoil or destroy (*Second Treatise*, 31: Locke, 1963, p. 332). The point preceded Locke: 'this is what an early Muslim legal scholar, Abu al-Faraj, says: People do not in fact own things, for the real owner is their Creator; they only enjoy the usufruct of things, subject to the Divine Law' (Mazri, 1992, p. 7). The dictum goes back to Leviticus. It has recently been remembered even by British Ministers, quoting Ruskin:

> Over a hundred years ago John Ruskin wrote 'God has lent us the earth for our life. It is a great entail. It belongs as much to those who follow us as it does to us, and we have no right by anything we do, or neglect to do, to involve them in unnecessary penalties, or to deprive them of the benefit we have it in our power to bequeath'. This has a very contemporary ring to it. Nothing that I recall being said in Rio quite matched Ruskin's elegance and economy of expression . . . . The task before us now is to give practical expression to Ruskin's admonition, that is, to put sustainable development into practice.[3]

It does not follow that we should never use up non-renewable resources on the plea that this would leave no such resources for our descendants to use: if they may use them, so may we. But ordinary counsels of prudence (which include concern for those of our kind that come after us) suggest that we should not use things up without good reason, and without any effort to locate alternative resources. 'To plant a tree, to cultivate a field, to beget children; meritorious acts, according to the religion of Zoroaster' (*Enquiry Concerning the Principles of Morals*, 2.2: Hume, 1962, p. 180). Even Descartes, who was certainly rather a bad influence on our

---

[3] Michael Howard, Secretary of State for the Environment, to the Royal Society for the Protection of Birds/Green Alliance Conference, 30 October 1992. Quite what 'sustainable development' actually means in practice is another question.

view of animals (though Spinoza, who is sometimes hailed as 'deeply ecological', was actually far worse), knew where and what we were: 'though each of us is a person distinct from others whose interests are accordingly in some way different from those of the rest of the world, we must still think that none of us could subsist alone and each one of us is really one of the many parts of the universe, and more particularly a part of the earth, the State, the society, the family to which we belong by our domicile, our oath of allegiance and our birth' (Descartes, 1970, p. 172). Descartes actually attacked both individualism and solipsism: so far from elevating his own will and reason, or that of each rational individual, above the truth, his whole effort was to bring to our attention something not ourselves that merited our worship. A true Cartesian recognizes herself as a dependent, confronted and contained by a world not of her making, the one true substance (see Clark, 1992a). According to Matthew Fox, a Catholic figure roughly (but maybe rightly) silenced by the Vatican, 'creation spirituality takes opposite positions on just about all of Descartes' principles' (Fox, 1991, p. 102). If this is true, it shouldn't be.

Pace such environmentalist rhetoric, neither our Hebrew nor our Greek inheritance can sensibly be held at fault. The Torah ruled long since that we should not take everything as if it were ours alone, but leave resources for the wild things of the world, who also seek their food from God (see Leviticus, 26.6ff). We hold the land in trust for our descendants, maybe: but we also hold it in company with God's other creatures. From this it follows that it is not enough to plant such trees as our descendants may find useful: we must also weigh up the interests of other animals who also need trees (and their sustaining habitat). So also Plato, whom too many environmentalists traduce: 'the land is [our] ancestral home and [we] must cherish it even more than children cherish their mother; furthermore, the Earth is a goddess and mistress of mortal men, and the gods and spirits already established in the locality must be treated with the same respect' (Plato, *Laws*, 5.740; see also 6.761).

The impulse to blame our situation on Christians, Hebrews, Greeks, the Eighteenth Century or, generally, patriarchs is one that most serious environmentalists would normally seek to curb. Selecting villains, and identifying ourselves with their historical victim, is just the sort of 'dualism' we should avoid. Supposing that events have simple, linear causes is to forget how complex history is. Supposing that human beings do things because of their beliefs, and not because their material situation determines that result, is perhaps a little too idealist. These failings are compounded by romantic fantasies of some place long ago or far away when people lived in 'harmony with nature'. Perhaps they did, or do. But the suspicion must be that this was because they lacked the power to do much else. 'Modern environmentalists may wish to insist, for example, that "it is not *our* ecology, we are *its*", that we belong to the land that shaped us, that "we are the rocks dancing"' (Seed *et al.*, 1988, p. 36). There is something to be said for this, as there is certainly something to be said for ancient virtues of thrift and moderation, and against the vicious desire for *more*. The fact remains that people given the opportunity *do* leave the land. 'City air makes free' the proverb says, and thousands of our ancestors, escaping from serfdom as *part of the land*, were glad it did. We may now be confident that industrial civilization has its costs, that we need to recover some less bourgeois virtues. But let us not pretend that life on the land or on the sea was romantically suffused with meaning; let us recall instead that even the horrors of Britain's Industrial Revolution were considered better than the life people left, and that another name for being 'one with the land' is serfdom. I admit that I am here ignoring certain other pressures, of usury and enclosure. But I doubt if even a less usurious, genuinely 'peasant economy' was without its trials (see Harrison, 1982, p. 96).

So perhaps the successive changes in our history owe less to religious feeling or theological doctrine or even the Enlightenment than to the ordinary need of people to make a better life somewhere. In our beginnings we had simply to endure the cycles of glut and shortage, gorging ourselves when we had the chance. When it became possible to store our surplus, we could avoid a sharp collapse, perhaps at the price, Rabbinic thought suggests, of enslaving ourselves to the one who had secured the store.[4] The possibility of 'borrowing upon our expectations', either literally or in the extended sense of deferring the environmental problems we create, ensures that our riches are so much greater than our past imaginings that we cannot now imagine they will one day be exhausted. At each stage of our history people made what seemed to them good choices: that the bills are falling due does not make our forebears fools or knaves.

Geometry and Geomancy

Our forebears were not fools, maybe, nor can we sensibly blame 'the Christians', 'the Europeans', the military-industrial complex

---

[4] Joseph, in this interpretation, is the villain, who sold the Egyptian people into slavery to Pharoah, and whose own people paid the price of it.

or the man in the moon. Nor is Christian doctrine wholly inhospitable even to the very 'deepest' of ecological concerns. But it is still worth asking if there are assumptions, adopted for whatever reason, that get in our way. In Wendell Berry's words: 'I believe that until fairly recently our destructions of nature were more or less unwitting—the by-products, so to speak, of our ignorance or weakness or depravity. It is our present principled and elaborately rationalized rape and plunder of the natural world that is a new thing under the sun' (Berry, 1990, p. 108).

If people think, or feel, that the world is made 'for them', or that there is nothing valuable but people, or that only rational order, imposed from without, makes chaos bearable, or that the rational intellect forbids emotional involvement in the lower orders, or that the material world is what we must abandon, they may not be restrained from actions liable to have bad consequences, even if they think those consequences bad. If those are the actual axioms of folk-Christianity—as they are certainly not of the dogmatic creed—perhaps we do need a new religion. It would be absurd to blame Aristotle for the existence of slavery, an institution that long outlasted and preceded him, but it may still be important to refute the Aristotelian arguments that slave-owners sometimes used, even if we know that they would willingly use any arguments, and never showed any sign of accepting Aristotle's other, and more deeply felt, beliefs (see Pagden, 1982). It is correspondingly important for environmentalists to deflate such reasons as are offered for not minding much about the situation, and for Christians, if they do care, to show that their Christianity is not an obstacle.

So far I have suggested that something like a religion is required. If there is indeed a crisis, as I think, we shall not cope with it unless we are woken to a real assent, unless we can do our acts 'as worship' without hope or fear of consequences, unless we can recognize a 'sacred' limit on our actions, unless these features are or could be widely shared in the world community. One of the many problems is that even if we prove to need a 'new religion', a new religion is a thing we emphatically don't need. The crisis would be far worse if wars of religion spread—a point on which I agree with born-again atheists, while noting that they do not notice that their own conviction is just such another begetter of holy wars. We need a radical change of life which yet, somehow, confirms and can be endorsed by all the old religions. It is not, I repeat, a *new* religion that we need, but the revival of an ancient and wide-spread *pietas*. I don't say this is possible.

What modern environmentalists are often objecting to is

humanism, which is a significant strand in all 'great religions' (that is why they are called great). Humanists of whatever style require us to believe in individuals, in individual human worth, in the reliability of human reason and the hope of progress. In particular, they dichotomize, dividing 'us' from 'our (or even *the*) environment'. Is that the doctrine we should seek to excise?

Long ago or far away, romantics tell us, people were unself-consciously united with their world. Nineteenth-century romantics liked to think 'the Greeks' were like that; late twentieth-century ones locate the fantasy in Old Europe or among native Americans (see Craig, 1987). People did not think of themselves as independent individuals, we are told, but as members of a shining congregation of gods, spirits, dryad-infested trees and families. They did not distinguish culture or art or custom from natural happenings. They did not imagine an 'objective world' behind or apart from the world experienced by them. They had no reason to distinguish thought and matter, *res cogitans* and *res extensa*, nor did they think that the truth was to be discovered by a resolute attention to physical geometry. The real world and the world of our experience were one, and to know it better was to know its values. Nothing was available to us as mere material, for to be at all is to embody value. The names of things dictated what their values and their natures were. That archaic unity was broken by the dichotomizing intellect, and our spiritual crisis is mirrored in the ecological.

There is, perhaps, some truth in this. We have constructed our idea of the 'real world', the world as it is apart from sentient and human experience, by a careful inattention to what usually matters most to us. Moral and aesthetic values as well as secondary qualities, historical associations and, in the end, identities depend on us, not on the things themselves: the truth of things is modelled by detachment, non-involvement. Having decided that no really true proposition can have moral implications, we are disingenuously surprised to realize that moral propositions can't be true, that values can only be projections of our values, as dryads are only representations of an older imaginative involvement in the world of trees. Because our idea of the real world is of a world without values, we conclude that the real world has no value, that it is available for any use we please.

The position is, in the end, grotesque. A hypothesis originally formed to explain our experience turns out to be so incapable of explaining it that some of its admirers now deny that we experience things at all. Once upon a time, ghosts, memories and secondary qualities were only projections of the human mind; now that mind turns out to be a projection too. 'But how can any philosopher think this suggestion has even the semblance of making sense? . . . The very notion of "projection" *presupposes* intentionality' (Putnam, 1987, p. 15). Some commentators have responded by insisting on the primacy and inescapability of the life-world, the undivided world of experience. The world of physical geometry, by this account, is not the causal origin of experience: it has, after all, been defined as a world without *qualia*, and therefore provides no intelligible explanation of their existence. It is often beautiful, precisely because we have constructed it to suit our ideas of beauty. It often has a certain usefulness: to predict the path of a projectile we need only study the geometry, and not its colour, aesthetic values or familiar name. The conviction that geometry will one day help us to explain human or animal behaviour is as blind and unreasonable a faith as any. Ordinarily academic anti-realists (which is to say: philosophers who have come to doubt that it even makes sense to suppose that we could uncover a reality that was not *our* reality) rarely draw the obvious conclusion that dryads are, after all, 'real' or 'quasi-real' inhabitants of the human world, not to be denied existence in favour of mere lumber. Nor do they explain how they can continue to pay lip-service to the notion that the world existed for many thousand million years before human or sentient experience.

Romantics of a less conventional kind do draw something like the obvious conclusions, and often with an eye to the environmental consequences. Perhaps we would treat the land better if we allowed ourselves to be conscious of it as a land suffused with memories, symbolism, values. Considered geometrically, a hill, a lake, a spinney is one shape out of many, with no particular call on our attention. It may still have a claim on us when considered as a historical entity, the name of remembered ancestors and earth-spirits. Instead of geometry, geomancy.

The land is a mnemonic. By this I mean, at its crudest, that we are reminded of personal, tribal memories by features of the landscape, whether 'built' or 'natural'. Those memories are living realities for us, confronting us when we confront the landmarks. They are what our forebears called dead heroes, spirits, godlets, and are (for all of us) as real as the images and meanings we convey through literal texts like this one. Those who would burn books do not burn merely paper: they (foolishly, no doubt) attempt to destroy spirits. Those who remodel landscapes do the like, most often to fill them up again with *their* own spirits. The kind of religious enterprise described by would-be Celts or Native Americans (sometimes, it must be feared, without much respect for people who actually are Native Americans or Celts or what you will) takes these spirits seriously. If we meditate upon imagined landmarks (whether these be ancient trees, or battle sites, or large-scale fictions like the zodiacal figures around Glastonbury Tor) we will find our old self stretched and changed to accommodate the godlets. Maybe (who knows) such imagined figures are more than helpful fictions. It is certainly true that make-believe like this facilitates the construction of new arguments, helps us to see things differently. Some 'New Age' writers have apparently convinced themselves that they can be the mediums for godlets that exist beyond, as well as in, their own imagining. Those who imagine what the land, the tree, the stream would say, perhaps succeed in hearing what it does.

But although the attempt to resurrect or slip back into the old world may be well-intentioned, I am doubtful that it serves our ecological needs. Many of the gods and godlets people have imagined have been demons, and those crude missionaries who took it on themselves to cut down sacred groves may have had a point. If the grove were gone, the memory might fade, and have less influence in the waking day. Maybe Chesterton was right, that the past had to be purged and purified. Gardens, woods and the stars themselves were polluted (that is, the world of nature as it features in our imaginative experience was polluted) by the perversions of late paganism (Chesterton, 1923, pp. 29ff). Only when four centuries of ascetic practice had purified the imagination could St Francis rededicate the natural world. Those are not the only possible corruptions. There have been many life-worlds, after all, and some of them have identified the creatures with whom we share the land as walking larders, prey, vermin, pets and sacrificial victims. Returning to an innocent, unself-conscious identification with the world in which we find ourselves would be to surround ourselves with loyal dogs, proud peacocks, horridly half-human apes, self-sacrificial lambs, and human beings themselves identified by their social roles and imagined histories. It was no small achievement to discover that people, animals, the land have their own being outside the names we put on them. There really is something 'outside the text'. It would be no advance at all to forego our real engagement with a really Other being: it would, instead of waking-up, be sinking back to sleep.

Despite the rhetoric of romantics, there is little evidence that 'spirit-haunted glades' are treated better than mere timber: the spirits that haunt them, after all, are created by our needs and imagination, and perhaps especially by our need to evade guilt. There is little enough to choose between the butcher who thinks the animal is meat, and the priest (or eco-feminist) who thinks it goes consenting to its death: maybe the sacrificial beast is allowed a little dignity, but it still ends in pieces. Those Christian environmentalists who, from a different metaphysical background, speak of man (sic) as 'the world's high priest' should likewise remember what priests, in Greece and Israel, actually did.

If the only reality we need consider is the life-world of our innocent experience, we may as well solve the crisis by calling it something different. Pollution and environmental degradation are no more than evolution in action, or artistry. Romantic eco-feminists will sometimes admit that stories about peace-loving neolithic matriarchies, 'in harmony with nature', with undichotomized life-worlds, are not historical, but only helpful fables. They may add that academic histories are no more. But in that case we can as easily invent a past to evade the pain of loss. Big Brother, in Orwell's *Nineteen Eighty-Four*, need only claim to have *raised* the chocolate ration instead of lowering it for this to be 'true' (see Clark, 1992b). If what's 'true' is what the Party said, we need fear no crisis from external nature. But it is just that willed evasion of real consequences, that reliance on the magic of making words, that has been our curse. Kipling's characterization of those who 'rose to suppose themselves kings over all things created—to decree a new earth at a birth without labour or sorrow' applies as well to romantics as to technophiles:

> They denied what they dared not abide if it came to the trial;
> But the sword that was forged while they lied did not heed their denial.
>
> ('The City of Brass': Kipling, 1927, pp. 313ff)

Accustomed language governs thought: what is needed is the sudden realization of something that transcends such custom. 'In nothing is the modern German more modern, or more mad, than in his dream of finding a German word for everything; eating his language, or in other words biting his tongue. And in nothing were the mediaevals more free and sane than in their acceptance of names and emblems from outside their most beloved limits'.[5]

> There is at the back of all our lives an abyss of light, more blinding and unfathomable than any abyss of darkness; and it is the abyss of actuality, of existence, of the fact that things truly are, and that we ourselves are incredibly and sometimes almost incredulously real. It is the fundamental fact of being, as against not being; it is unthinkable, yet we cannot unthink it, though we

[5] Chesterton, 1917, p. 59. Chesterton might now find it more appropriate to castigate certain once-fashionable French ideologues.

may sometimes be unthinking about it; unthinking and especially unthanking. For he who has realized this reality knows that it
does outweigh, literally to infinity, all lesser regrets or arguments for negation, and that under all our grumblings there is a
subconscious substance of gratitude. (Chesterton, 1933, p. 36)

'I would maintain', Chesterton had said fifteen years before, 'that
thanks are the highest form of thought' (Chesterton, 1917, p. 59).

We cannot and must not retreat to an imagined innocence when
we did not distinguish between our fables and reality. But neither
need we accept a pure objectivism, defining the 'real' world as
what does not matter. Pure objectivism was always silly: if no true
proposition carries any moral implication then it is not true of any
that it ought to be believed. The contemplation of truth, through
the recognition of a kind of beauty, is a duty only if there are such
duties; if there aren't we can have no notion of a truth we should
not deny. When we wake up to a real assent, to a deep recognition
of real existences beyond the purposes we dreamily endorsed for
them, we are in the same instant recognizing something worthy of
respect. Physical geometry reveals a truth, and so do other disci-
plines. Romantics who rightly reject the fable that reality is *only*
geometric but fall back on geomancy are making exactly the wrong
move.

Conclusion

So what are the roots of our crisis, and what spiritual changes do
we need to cope with them? By my account the crisis is the unin-
tended outcome of a general wish to live a little better. We have
devised all manner of excuses for not troubling ourselves too much
about what we do. We pretend that animals give themselves, or are
given to us, or are merely meat or matter in motion. We pretend
that the airs and waters are indefatigably purifying, that the land
need not lie fallow, that Nature or the Lord will surely keep us
going because we are so nice. We don't act as we do because we
believe these things, but believe, or pretend to believe them,
because we want to go on acting just like that. If we are to have
any chance of stopping, we must wake up to a real appreciation of
a genuine Otherness, a world not limited by what we make of it.
So far from giving up rational realism and the dichotomizing intellect we must exert our intellectual powers, must make distinctions,
must seek to see things as they are, whether we will or no. We
must not retreat to a romantic paganism, pantheism or animism,

even though we should acknowledge the truths that such romantics have discerned.

The world we inhabit, and should revere, is not just our environment. There are indeed good reasons to deny that there is any such thing as *the* environment at all. Every creature or every kind of creature has its own *Umwelt*, its structure of marks and favoured routes, its own needs and delights. The whole that contains and includes us all has its own wholeness, and we should indeed remember that we are not divided from it, that it is not 'outside over there', in far-off wilderness or in the country. If we are to cope with our crisis, we must both recognize the World as other than the human world, and recognize ourselves as inextricably dependent on that World. It is both our Other and our Origin, something unconstrained by our projected values and recognized as something by which we should be constrained. 'Honour your father and your mother that your days may be long in the land the Lord your God has given you': honour, in fact, the land, which is to say the complexity of earth, air and water and their living denizens (Kohák, 1984, p. 80; see Clark, 1989, p. 138). This recognition of the Other as something which we should respect exactly as *not* being ourselves, nor even very much like ourselves, is recognized by Murdoch in the Anglophone tradition, and by Levinas in the 'Continental' (see Murdoch, 1970; Hand, 1989). This is what makes some recent moral argument rather suspect. Moralists have tended to suggest that it is insofar as things are like 'us' that they are deserving of respect: but the better way is to respect them as *not* being like ourselves, and so to allow them to *be*. The world emphatically *does* 'exist in itself over against human beings' (see Cobb, 1982, p. 6). Of course it is also true that, insofar as we are aware of the world at all, it becomes part of the story we tell. Of course, since we are are utterly dependent on the world (and so a minor part of it) there can be no gap between Us and It. But what It is does not depend on what we say it is. All attempts to evade this fact, like similar attempts to evade the laws of logic, seem to me appallingly misguided.

Sacramental theism, involving reverence for the created cosmos of which we are simultaneously parts and partial observers, can easily degenerate into mere magic: the weird, unspoken assumption that if we speak as though we reverenced the earth, we shall be spared the pain of doing so. The one further gloss that might best be recalled from Christian and Jewish thought is that there is a real need of atonement. 'Woe to those who add house to house, and join field to field until everywhere belongs to them and they are the sole inhabitants of the land' (Isaiah, 5.1ff). And not just woe to them. According to a Talmudic story:

In a boat at sea, someone began to bore a hole in the bottom of the boat. On being remonstrated with he answered 'I am only boring under my own seat'. 'Yes', said his comrades, 'but when the sea rushes in we shall be drowned with you'. So it is with Israel. Its weal or woe is in the hands of every individual Israelite.

Sacramental theism declares that we do not own the world, but only enjoy its fruits on the condition that we leave as good for others. It declares that Beauty and Justice are not different at different times and places, although their detailed manifestations may (or even must) be, and that there is a true description of the world and of its denizens which denies us any right to redescribe our victims and our sins. It declares, almost above all, that although 'nature' is to be respected, it is not now exactly as it should be (and if it were, we need not trouble ourselves about a crisis). Rabbinic Judaism, Islam and Christianity can all agree that there is one God, one source of life and light. They can even agree that there is one true religion, which is to do justice and love mercy and walk humbly with that God. No true believer can reckon things 'fair game', made solely for our pleasure. We receive all things as gift; we are ourselves a gift. If we intercept and deny the gift to others we should not expect to keep it.

The day of Yahweh is coming, merciless, with wrath and fierce anger, to reduce the earth to desert and root out the sinners from it . . . . Babylon, that pearl of kingdoms, the jewel and boast of Chaldaeans, like Sodom and Gomorrah shall be overthrown by God. Never more will anyone live there or be born there from generation to generation. No Arab will pitch his tent there, nor shepherds feed their flocks, but beasts of the desert will lie there, and owls fill its houses. Ostriches will make their homes there and satyrs have their dances there. Hyenas will call to each other in its keeps, jackals in the luxury of its palaces . . . . Its time is almost up, its day will not last long. (Isaiah, 32.15ff)

Or in Berry's words: '[Nature] is plainly saying to us: "if you put the fates of whole communities or cities or regions or ecosystems at risk in single ships or factories or powerplants, then I will furnish the drunk or fool or imbecile who will make the necessary small mistake"' (Berry, 1990, p. 203). That should be enough.

There was no need of a steed nor a lance to pursue them;
It was decreed their own deed, and not chance, should undo them.

('The City of Brass': Kipling, 1927, p. 314)

127

We do not even need to wait for accidents: the cruelty and indifference we display in breeding cattle for our gastronomic pleasure has played a part in bringing about the 'greenhouse effect'. The more cattle there are, the greater the output of greenhouse gases and the fewer trees to mop them up.

We still need hope. At the far side of tribulation, God will restore the land, Isaiah said.

> Once more there will be poured on us the spirit from above; then shall the wilderness be fertile land and fertile land become forest. In the wilderness justice will come to live and integrity in the fertile land. My people will live in a peaceful home, in safe houses in quiet dwellings . . . . Happy will you be, sowing by every stream, letting ox and donkey roam free. (Isaiah, 35.9)

God will restore the land for those who will obey his laws (to allow all things their place): 'the redeemed will walk there, for those Yahweh has ransomed shall return'. If we forget our danger, or brood on it as inescapable and final, we shall be lost. If we can believe that there is a better way, on the far side of imaginable disaster, maybe we shall, beyond all reasonable hope, discomfort Jonah.[6]

---

[6] It is noteworthy that the one Biblical prophet to have clearly succeeded in reforming anyone is the one most obviously a fiction!

Kant and the Moral Considerability of Non-Rational Beings

TIM HAYWARD

Kant's ethics is widely viewed as inimical to environmental values, as arbitrary and morally impoverished, because, while exalting the value of human, rational, beings, it denies moral consideration to non-human, or non-rational, beings. In this paper I seek to show how, when specific statements of this general view are examined, they turn out to involve some significant inaccuracies or confusions. This will lead me to suggest that Kant might have more to offer to environmental ethics than has hitherto been acknowledged.

In the first place, then, the general claim to be investigated is that Kant denies, or at least fails to accord, moral standing or considerability to non-rational beings (e.g., other animals). This claim has been advanced on various grounds, which will need to be separated out and examined. It has to be said that writers on environmental ethics have offered little explicit reflection on this question—usually focusing on the question of which beings *have* standing, rather than on what it is. The first section examines the claim that Kant denies moral standing to any beings other than moral agents—or, in other words, that he subscribes to the 'patient-agent parity thesis'—and shows that this objection resolves into the 'no direct duties thesis'. In the second section, two formulations of this thesis are distinguished. On a narrower one, direct duties are understood as duties which correlate with rights, so the objection would be that Kant denies non-rational beings rights-bearing status. This has to be granted, but given that most of Kant's critics would not consider rights-bearing a necessary condition of moral standing, this objection does not suffice to make the case. Turning to the other, broader, interpretation of the 'no direct duties thesis', the objection to Kant is identified as this: a direct duty towards a being is one that is owed to that being *for its own sake*—and in denying such duties to non-rational beings, Kant denies them moral consideration. In the third section I enquire further into exactly what Kant is denying here—namely that the good of a being is a ground of obligation on a moral agent to pursue that being's good. The issue comes down to the gap between a being's 'having a good' and that good's being a ground of obligation: the

129

possession of moral standing or considerability is the idea which is supposed to bridge that gap. However, by indicating how the various ways of attempting it fail to span the gap, it appears that scepticism on that score is not unjustified. Certainly the case against Kant has not been sustained, since he has not been shown to deny anything that anyone else can consistently maintain.

Finally I seek to draw out some constructive conclusions. Firstly I diagnose as a general problem that the various charges against Kant resolve into claims either that he accords insufficient moral *significance* to non-rational beings, or that the standing he accords them is for the wrong *reasons*—different claims that actually presuppose that standing has been granted. Once analysed out in these terms, moreover, the critics' own positions appear vulnerable to counter-attacks on similar grounds. The second suggestion in the conclusion is that some terminological conventions might be agreed to reduce potential equivocations over terms like 'standing' and 'considerability'. Thirdly I indicate, very sketchily, some reasons for thinking that Kant's ethics may make more of a contribution to the development of environmental ethics than generally thought hitherto.

'Patient-Agent Parity'

One point to mention at the outset is that moral standing needs to be distinguished from moral agency. The claim to be investigated here is whether Kant denies moral *standing* to non-rational beings; it is not a matter of dispute that he denies that non-rational beings can be moral agents—since moral agency is precisely defined as a rational capacity. Although there is little risk of misunderstanding on this score, it is worth making explicit that denying to non-rational beings a capacity of making or acting on moral judgments—as Kant does—is not in itself to deny them moral standing. For, indeed, if a capacity for moral agency were a necessary condition of moral standing, then, not only Kant but anyone who recognizes the capacity for moral obligation as a peculiarly human (or more precisely, rational) characteristic would equally deny moral consideration to non-rational beings.

With this clarification made, however, the most direct line of attack on Kant would be to argue that, even though standing and agency are in principle distinct, he precisely does restrict moral consideration to moral agents. This is a line taken, for example, by Christina Hoff, when she attributes to Kant what she calls the 'patient-agent parity thesis'—that is, the view that all and only moral agents can be moral patients (Hoff, 1983). Hoff glosses the idea that for Kant the domain of moral agents coincides with the domain of moral patients with these words: 'we can only wrong those who can wrong us'. Now this proposition, which I think Kant would affirm, does assert a certain 'parity' between moral agents and possible moral patients. What looks objectionable about it is the idea that rational beings can *only* wrong other rational beings, and therefore that they cannot wrong those who cannot wrong them. This point may be illustrated by considering the kinds of moral relation which can and cannot obtain between a moral agent—say a human—and a being which is not a moral agent—say a lion. A lion is able to hurt a human being, but if we cannot ascribe moral agency to the lion then it makes no sense to say that the lion, in doing so, 'wrongs' the human being. The parity then lies in the corollary, namely, that a human being is able to hurt a lion, but, in doing so, cannot wrong it. This way of putting it enables us to appreciate Hoff's charge against Kant inasmuch as the parity—which lies in its being the case that neither the lion nor the human can wrong the other—seems to be misplaced: the lion cannot wrong the human being just because, *ex hypothesi*, the lion cannot *do wrong* at all; the human being, on the other hand, *can* do wrong. So it makes sense to ask, as Hoff does, whether the human being can wrong the lion, or, more generally, whether a rational being can ever wrong a non-rational being. To this question Kant would reply in the negative, because moral agents can only wrong other moral agents, and I take it to be this that seems to Hoff to exhibit an arbitrary bias in favour of humans.

Nevertheless, this needs some unpacking, since the negative reply is liable to be misunderstood, as I think it is by Hoff. She writes: 'Can one wrong an animal? Kant, who thinks not, accounts for our felt duties to animals as indirect duties to mankind. When we beat a horse, or allow a dog to starve, humanity, and not the horse or dog, is the victim' (Hoff, 1983, p. 63).

This report of Kant's views is noteworthy because it contains elements of both truth and absurdity—due, it seems, to an equivocation on the meaning of the transitive verb 'to wrong': for while 'to (do) wrong (to) someone' most usually means 'to do someone an injustice', it can also be used to mean 'to do harm to'—a quite distinct idea. Hoff takes advantage of both senses: on the one hand to record—the element of truth—that Kant denies that humans can do an injustice to animals; and on the other to suggest—the element of absurdity—that Kant thinks that if one beats a horse then the horse is not the victim, as if one cannot do harm to animals. Kant's views are not as implausible as this last suggestion.

131

Nor, I think, are they so callous. Yet Hoff is not alone in attributing such views to Kant. Thus Passmore, for instance, has interpreted Kant as saying that cruelty to animals is wrong if it induces callousness towards human suffering, but that there is nothing intrinsically wrong with cruelty to animals (Passmore, 1980, p. 210). However, I believe this interpretation is misleading. In the passage as a whole it is quite clear that for Kant cruelty to animals is cruelty; that it does not become cruelty merely if it affects some human; and that cruelty to animals, for Kant, is *wrong*. In the absence of an explanation of the supposed difference between 'wrong' and 'intrinsically wrong', I would propose that Kant took a simpler view: cruelty which can be the matter of moral consideration is always and only manifested in human actions; and actions which are cruel are always wrong. Since cruelty to animals can be identified without reference to human suffering, but not without reference to the animal's suffering, the case cannot therefore be made on this ground that Kant denies animals moral consideration. So the objection must focus on his denial that humans can do wrong, in the other sense of doing an injustice, to non-rational beings. The next section investigates how this case might be made.

'No Direct Duties'

To see why Kant believes it is not possible to wrong an animal in the sense of doing it an injustice, we can focus on Kant's statement, in the *Lectures on Ethics*, that 'so far as animals are concerned, we have no direct duties'. Thus, because to wrong, or to do wrong to, someone is to fail in one's duty to them, and since Kant does not believe it possible to have duties to non-rational beings, he does not think it possible to wrong them. The question then is whether that amounts to denying them moral standing or moral consideration. Some of Kant's environmentalist critics believe it does, and can cite in support the idea expressed in the *Lectures on Ethics* that 'Our duties toward animals are merely indirect duties toward humanity' (Kant, 1963, p. 239). These are not direct duties toward animals, and, in fact, are more accurately described as duties *'with regard to'* them (cf. Kant, 1964, p. 108). Thus Kant explicitly states: 'If a man shoots his dog . . . he does not fail in his duty to the dog, for the dog cannot judge, but his act is inhuman and damages in himself that humanity which it is his duty to show toward mankind' (Kant, 1963, p. 240). This is seen as evidence of the invidiously human-centred bias of Kant's ethics: it does not really matter about the dog, it seems, only about other humans.

But is Kant really saying this? In Kant's ethics there are no 'direct duties' towards animals, but this is not self-evidently invidious, since he does admit duties from which non-rational beings may benefit. Thus, in the example, even if the duty is 'owed to' humanity, the dog stands to benefit from its performance. In order to make the case, therefore, it has to be shown either (1) that to deny the possibility of direct duties to non-rational beings is, in itself and quite generally, also to deny them moral consideration—which implies that direct duties are a necessary condition of moral consideration; or (2) that, at least on Kant's particular formulation of them, duties 'with regard to' non-rational beings do not suffice as moral consideration of those beings. I shall briefly consider these two arguments in turn.

(1) In the example we have been discussing, Kant affirms a duty not to shoot the dog: what he does not suggest is that the man has a duty owed directly *to the dog* not to shoot the dog. So the question is why a duty not to shoot it would not suffice, or what would be added by asserting a duty *to the dog*. Now one way of marking the difference between having a duty to do something, and having a duty *to* someone to do something, is to say that the latter duty gives rise to a right, whereas the former need not. The latter yields a right because if you have a duty *to* someone, that someone has a *right* that you perform it (cf. Hohfeld, 1919)—in speaking of the logic of the relation, it does not matter if the source of the right would be legal, moral or customary. One thing Kant quite evidently denies, then, is that the dog has a *right* that his master not shoot him. But the basic question remains: if the man has a duty not to shoot the dog, how would the dog's situation be altered by having a right not to be shot? The kind of right which correlates with a duty can be characterized as a *claim*-right (as distinguished by Hohfeld (1919) from other relations, loosely referred to as rights, which are better described as privileges, powers or immunities). Could a dog exercise such a right? On the most plausible accounts of it, claiming is the kind of thing that persons (*qua* legal or moral agents) do among themselves, and that only they can do. For claiming rights involves, in Kant's terminology, 'moral necessitation' exercised by the will of one subject over another—something which is only possible between beings who have this kind of intersubjective relation. Such beings are defined as 'persons', a category Kant takes over from Roman Law. To present claims on the part of animals would normally involve relaxing precisely the requirement that the relation between duty-bearer and right-bearer be a *direct* one. So although the existence of direct duties would be a sufficient condition of the corresponding right-bearer's moral

standing, it would be difficult if not impossible to fulfil in cases other than between moral agents. Furthermore, it would anyway not seem to be a *necessary* criterion of moral standing. Indeed, if it were, then the objection against Kant would also apply to a considerable part of environmental ethics in general, and to consequentialist alternatives in particular, for they not only do not seek to attribute rights to non-humans, but actively deny the need to do so in order to grant standing (cf. Attfield, 1991). In fact, to deny a human can 'wrong' an animal, on this interpretation, is not to deny moral standing to non-rational beings, but only to deny the possibility of a specific relation of justice between moral agents and other beings. All this tells us is that humans cannot have reciprocal rights-duties relations with animals—not that they cannot consider animals as moral patients.

There is a widely held intuition that animals can be exploited, and thus treated unjustly: the questions discussed here are not intended to deny this intuition but to highlight some of the problems with conceptualizing it. There are parallels between this discussion and that of Habermas (1982, pp. 238–250); but even a less sceptical commentator like Benton (1993) has also found, in his sustained attempt to conceptualize the exploitation of animals, that there are practical and epistemic limits to the degree that these matters can be couched in terms of rights.

(2) There is, though, a more far-reaching objection that can be made. The defence of Kant so far has turned on showing that beings can benefit from duties even if those duties are not directly 'owed' them—for although Kant maintains that humans can have duties *to* humans only, they can nevertheless have duties *with regard to* beings other than humans. But it can be objected that the 'regard' involved here does not amount to moral consideration. If a being is to be considered *morally*, not just incidentally, and especially not just instrumentally, then it must be considered 'for its own sake': that is, reference must be made to 'its good'. Moreover, 'its good' must be the end to be realised by the duty in question, it must be the determining *ground* of the obligation. And with this we are at last able to formulate a definition of moral considerability such as Kant does indeed deny can be applied to non-rational beings.

'Consideration not for their Own Sake'

The objection we have arrived at is that Kant denies moral consideration to non-rational beings *'for their own sake'*. But we need to be clear what this does and does not mean. It does not mean that Kant *refuses* moral consideration of non-rational beings altogether: the range of beings considered is not restricted to agents, as the 'patient-agent parity' thesis would have it, because, for Kant, the treatment of non-rational beings is not a matter of moral indifference. He also does not deny that appropriate treatment of those beings would make reference to their good or welfare. What he would deny is something more specific: namely, that their welfare is the determining *ground* of moral obligation. This means that Kant's implicit challenge to environmental ethics is to show how a non-rational being might have an independent claim on a moral agent such that its good determines which duties a moral agent has. For it needs to be established whether Kant is actually denying anything that anyone could consistently maintain.

Now I see no reason for Kant to deny that non-human living beings *have* their own good. However, two further questions follow where a degree of scepticism may be more appropriate. One is to specify *what* that good consists in; the other is to explain why that good may also be recognized as a ground of obligation for moral agents. Theorists who want to adopt the moral stance in question do not appear to think that the first challenge presents much of a problem—or, at least, that too much of a problem can be made by those who wish to resist giving any moral consideration to non-humans, when in fact some basic criteria of harm and advantage can quite straightforwardly be applied (e.g., Attfield, 1981, pp. 38ff). So I shall grant this for the moment, and focus on the question, to which they devote more attention, of how the good of a being can be the ground of an obligation for moral agents. The answer turns on its good having *intrinsic value*. In what follows I shall distinguish between two kinds of approach which are, respectively, 'qualified' and 'unqualified' in their commitment to the intrinsic value of the good of non-rational beings.

A representative of the qualified view is Robin Attfield. For him, whatever has a good of its own has moral standing—that is, merits moral consideration (Attfield, 1987, ch. 1). Attfield's position is that if we grant consideration to humans then we cannot consistently deny it to other living beings: the onus is on a would-be opponent of this view to name some morally-relevant difference between humans and other living beings (something which proves hard to do) which would justify considering humans as moral patients and non-humans not. However, standing is granted with such ease because it is intended only to establish an undemanding interpretation of considerability which need bear little weight: 'there might well be a preponderant need most of the time to treat plants, and, perhaps, some other creatures, as resources, valuable though their lives are in themselves' (Attfield, 1987, p. 18). For Attfield, the moral standing of a being is established separately and prior to any judgments as to its moral *significance*. All beings which have standing have intrinsic value, but some of them will have very little of it—indeed, too little to be a determinant of any obligation of a moral agent. It therefore does not appear that the qualified approach will necessarily lay the ground for claiming anything that Kant denies—at least as regards the principle that the good of a non-rational being, when known, should figure in moral consideration; Kant would, though, be less ready to affirm particular claims about significance—since the suggestion that we can rank quantities of intrinsic value, in terms, for instance, of more and less morally-pressing needs, places demands on *knowledge* which may not be redeemable. Moreover, if some beings gain on the basis of such a calculus, what of the moral considerability of those who, perhaps through defective human knowledge, lose?

On the unqualified approach, all beings are supposed to be of *equal* worth. This approach can be illustrated by reference to Paul Taylor's idea of 'inherent worth'. For Taylor, to say that a being possesses inherent worth is to say *both* that its good is deserving of the consideration of all moral agents, *and* 'that the realization of its good has intrinsic value, to be pursued as an end in itself and for the sake of the entity whose good it is' (Taylor, 1981, p. 201). In this way, granting standing is not a prelude to deliberating about moral significance, it is already to take up a specific moral attitude which has definite normative implications: 'Living things are now viewed as *the appropriate objects of the attitude of respect*' (Taylor, 1981, p. 206)—and 'respect' is not a formal preliminary but is itself a moral commitment. Yet if this commitment applies equally to all living beings it raises very awkward questions about how it can lead to any determinate judgments about values (Attfield, 1991, p. 208); there may also be a further problem of arbitrariness and indeterminacy regarding the kinds of beings to consider (Thompson, 1990). A major question, therefore, is why the attitude should be assumed in the first place. Taylor accepts that this does not automatically follow from granting that non-human beings can have their own good. Rather, he says, it depends on a *belief system*—the biocentric outlook. For Taylor, biocentrism means, in particular, seeing individual organisms as teleological centres of life. Along with the beliefs, according to Taylor, comes an ability: '*Conceiving of it as a centre of life, one is able to look at the world from its perspective*' (Taylor, 1981, p. 210). In looking at the world from that perspective, Taylor says, we recognize objects and events occurring in its life as being beneficent, maleficent, or indifferent. We can take their point of view just because we can recognize what does them harm and what benefits them. But can we? Some very strong knowledge claims are implicit here, which I think Kant would deny. It is worth noting, though, that Kant would not take issue with the biocentric belief system as described: in fact, the judgment that individual organisms are teleological centres of life is one which Kant quite explicitly grants in his *Critique of Judgment* when explaining that an organism is 'an organised natural product in which every part is reciprocally both end and means' (Kant, 1949, pp. 310–324). It is the ability Taylor claims to come with it that Kant would deny. For Kant, rational beings can know their own ends subjectively, but cannot know other beings' ends in this way. On the one hand, such natural ends as are posited or inferred by biological sciences are known, if at all, *objectively*; on the other hand, positing subjective ends in nature, on analogy with our own, not only proceeds without any assurance that the analogy holds, but, furthermore, may introduce a more insidious anthropomorphism through the projecting of human characteristics, needs and interests on to other beings which may in fact be radically different from what humans imagine (cf. Hayward, 1992). This applies to the qualified view too. In both cases it is the epistemic claims that Kant would deny, not the moral considerability of other beings.

Where there *is* the ability to know another being's good, however, Kant would have no reason to disagree that it should be taken account of. It is easy enough to see how Kant's ethics would generate maxims of humaneness; I cannot envisage it generating inhumane ones. So where we know what the good of a being is— and presumably, in practice, and notwithstanding the above caveats, standards of knowledge could be agreed—Kant would be able to grant that, other things being equal, it should be pursued. To do otherwise would be to diminish one's humanity.

It may now be objected, however, that when other things are not equal, this particular reason for promoting the good of other beings is not going to be sufficiently compelling. The final claim to be considered, therefore, is not that Kant *denies* moral consideration to non-rational beings, but that there is something deficient with his *reasons* for allowing such consideration. The basic objection to Kant's reasons is that they ultimately depend on human interests. Thus, as was seen in the passage discussed earlier, if the man fails in his duty not to shoot the dog, his act 'damages in himself that humanity which it is his duty to show toward mankind'. In giving reasons for the duty here, there is no mention of the *dog's* own good—the concern is for the good of *humanity*. The dog appears to be merely a fortuitous beneficiary of humanity's self-improvement programme, but with no independent claim to moral consideration. Still, we need to be clear exactly what the problem might be here: the lack of such a claim will presumably be significant if such guarantees as Kant's reasons might provide for the welfare of non-rational beings are either insufficiently secure or insufficiently deep or generalizable.

It may be argued they are insecure when Kant's reasons are interpreted as involving a contingent psychological proposition. Kant wrote: 'If he is not to stifle his human feelings, he must practise kindness towards animals, for he who is cruel to animals becomes hard also in his treatment of men' (Kant, 1963, p. 240). This sort of statement has been understood by some critics as a debatable psychological prediction with doubtful ethical implications (Broadie and Pybus, 1974; Midgley, 1978, pp. 44ff; Regan, 1983, ch. 5.5). For even if there were evidence that being habitually cruel to animals leads to treating humans badly, they suggest, it would seem to leave insufficient reason for avoiding occasional ill-treatment of them.

However, I do not believe this interpretation does justice to what Kant intended—which was not an empirical claim, but one more tightly bound by the logic of his ethics: any action is wrong, whether repeated or not, witnessed or not, which goes against a maxim to avoid hurting beings capable of suffering when hurting can be avoided.[1] The 'humanity' it damages is the moral quality which one is to *show* to other humans—as an *example*; the 'humanity' is that ideal whose possible realization is anticipated in moral action as such. In short, what we have here is not primarily a physical, or psychological, but a *moral* offence—and hence it is not contingent in the way these critics suggest. To say this is to reaffirm that there is a genuine and secure duty here.

The other line of objection is that this sort of duty will not work well enough to meet the ends of non-rational beings. Such duties might not go wide enough or deep enough. Thus, on the one hand, it may be suggested that the dog in Kant's illustration is something of a special case, an 'honorary human' whose favourable treatment has been earned through faithful service—other animals

---

[1] This has been questioned by Broadie and Pybus (1974, p. 376) who claim 'there is no contradiction involved either in the universalisation, or in the willing of the universalisation, of the maxim that I will always treat animals as if they have no capacity for suffering'. There *is* a contradiction, though, in saying 'I will always treat beings with a capacity for suffering as if they have no capacity for suffering'.

in other circumstances will not be so lucky. It should be noted, though, that Kant is in fact thinking of animals more generally: 'The more we come in contact with animals and observe their behaviour, the more we love them. . . . It is then difficult to be cruel in thought even to a wolf' (Kant, 1963, p. 240). Still, the thrust of the objection might be maintained by arguing that 'even wolves', in being not unprepossessing mammals, may benefit simply thanks to their relative proximity to humans—while other species will not. Then again, it might be argued that although it is wrong, for Kant, to shoot a dog, or perhaps even a wolf, it is *more* wrong to shoot a human; or, to take another example Kant gives, while it is wrong to be wantonly cruel, it might not be wrong to use animals in experiments where vital human interests are at stake. Now as regards these last objections—that moral consideration of other beings increases with the proximity of their own interests to those of humans, and that Kant places greater value, other things being equal, on human than non-human interests—I envisage no real reply that Kant could meet them with. The point I would argue, though, is that these objections imply exacting standards which no plausible version of environmental ethics has yet come up to. Hence I should emphasize, what I hope is obvious, that the intention here is not to offer a gratuitous defence of Kant. Certainly he never gave attention, as environmental ethicists do, to highly pertinent questions such as whether or how the assumption that human interests take precedence over non-human ones stands up when 'other things are not equal'. Attfield shows that a number of different versions of the 'greater value assumption' can be distinguished (Attfield, 1994b). My point here is simply that if Kant is to be criticized for subscribing to the 'greater value assumption' in any form at all, it has to be acknowledged that he is in the company of virtually all environmental ethicists—with the possible exception of those 'biospheric egalitarians', who, in fact, may be claimed to void ethics of any content (cf. Attfield, 1993).

Conclusion

A number of formulations of the charge that Kant denies moral considerability to non-rational beings have now been examined, and it has been seen how each attempt to state the case against Kant raises important questions about the meaning of moral standing or considerability itself.

With regard to these questions I now seek to offer some con-

Tim Hayward

structive conclusions. I want to suggest: firstly, a diagnosis of the problem; then, elements of a makeshift remedy, in the form of some terminological clarifications; and, finally, with the aim of a fuller solution in mind, some indications of the constructive role Kant may play in the future development of environmental ethics.

We have seen how the idea of moral standing or considerability is packed with different contents depending on its particular place in a particular argument. The weight of criticism against Kant, accordingly, gets shifted. But I have sought to show that, for each line of criticism, what is at stake is actually not Kant's alleged denial of standing or considerability to non-rational beings, but something else. In the case of the first 'no direct duties' objection what Kant denies is the possibility of a specific type of moral relation between agents and non-agents—namely, a rights-duty relation. In the case of the objection that Kant allows 'no duties for the sake of non-rational beings' what is objected to is the *reason* for the consideration of non-rational beings—but this very objection acknowledges that Kant does at least allow them consideration. This only leaves it to the critics to argue that the consideration is in some way insufficient—but this is actually a claim concerning their moral *significance*.

It might help avoid the equivocations noted if the terminology were tightened up. To this end I would offer the following remarks. 'Considerability' is a generic term which, as has been demonstrated, can be analysed out in various ways. My own view, though, is that 'considerability' will almost inevitably be used equivocally in any but the most undemanding sense where the nature of consideration may even be instrumental or incidental. 'Bare considerability' is a term that might be used to mark a contrast with something more 'vested'. I have in mind here an analogy with the 'bare' and 'vested' liberties discussed by Hart (1973, pp. 175–182), who points out that the idea of a bare liberty may be useful in analysis, but real liberties will always be constituted by a perimeter of protecting duties: I think much the same point can be made regarding the idea of considerability. 'Bare considerability' alone would imply nothing about what consideration, if any, may actually prove to be due. Something more vested, though, would necessarily involve an anticipation of actual *consideration*—i.e., once degrees of considerability are admitted, one is already committed to according it some specific *significance*. This raises the question whether the notion of moral considerability which does not already imply some determinant significance is a useful or coherent one. I have noted that for Attfield the idea of moral *standing* is distinct from significance, although it implies more than my notion of 'bare considerability': the difficulty I have sought to highlight is getting a conceptual grasp of the 'more' here. My own preference would be to restrict the use of *standing* to mean a capacity to bear rights. The need for a term univocally to mark off this meaning has been shown, and the appropriateness of this choice is supported both by its provenance—in legal discourse—and the continuing aptness of its connotations.[2]

Finally, I should like to offer some very brief remarks concerning Kant's own potential contribution to environmental ethics. Kant is largely silent about non-rational beings. According to his own lights, he has good reason to be since his ethics is not focused on moral patients, as opposed to agents, at all. This does not mean, though, that he has nothing to say of relevance to environmental ethics. For there may be other ways for environmental ethics to proceed than by occupying itself with identifying bearers of moral considerability—this, incidentally, is a point also made by Goodpaster (1979), which is significant given his own earlier attempt to do just that (Goodpaster, 1978). Kant's ethics is addressed to rational agents; its subject matter is their actions and motivations; its prescriptions apply to the principles and maxims guiding their actions. The ultimate objective it anticipates is a world in which rational beings realize the ends of their own rational nature. For the rational beings we are acquainted with—human beings—this ultimate aim can be couched in terms of realising human dignity. The pursuit of this aim is not inconsistent with, and may prove to have advantages for, environmental ethics. I believe it could be shown that the imperatives of human dignity are incompatible with inhumane treatment of other living beings or irresponsible treatment of our common environment. By speaking of inhumaneness and irresponsibility we are speaking of attributes of moral agents—and also precisely of the beings who cause all the problems environmental ethics seeks to redress. This is a highly appropriate asymmetry, therefore.

We may never know what exactly we owe to non-human nature—any more than we can know, according to Kant, what we might owe to God. In this intellectual humility Kant has allies among deep ecologists who refrain from attributing values to

---

[2] 'A right is something a man can *stand* on, something that can be demanded or insisted upon without embarrassment or shame. . . . No amount of love and compassion . . . can substitute for those values' (Feinberg, 1973, pp. 58–59). Given that it may not always be possible to separate the metaphor of 'standing' from the (masculine) values of the courtroom, it might be better to restrict its use so as to leave other spaces for other values.

nature, and those like Albert Schweitzer who advocates reverence for life, asking: 'Who among us knows what significance any other kind of life has in itself, and as part of the universe?' (quoted in Birch and Cobb, 1981, p. 149). What Kant believes we do know, though, is that we owe certain things to ourselves, things that go under the name of dignity. To speak about environmental ethics in terms of what we owe ourselves is of course 'anthropocentric', but one needs to be clear about what is *wrong* with anthropocentrism. It is arguable that *meta*-ethics cannot but be anthropocentric[3]—but this does not mean one's normative maxims must be. The pursuit of human dignity need not—I believe it *does* not—imply the crude selfishness of 'human chauvinism' or the arbitrary prejudice of 'speciesism'. It only would do so on a restricted conception of human selves, or in small-minded humans. If *these* are the problem for environmental ethics to solve, then environmental ethics will find a ready ally in Kant.[4]

[3] See also the contributions of Elliot and Midgley in this volume.

[4] Thanks especially to Robin Attfield, Angelika Krebs and John O'Neill for their helpful and probing responses to an earlier version of this paper.

The Idea of the Environment

NIGEL DOWER

This is in part a reflection on issues raised by David Cooper in his paper entitled 'The Idea of Environment' (Cooper, 1992), a paper that I have an ambiguous attitude towards. On the one hand it has opened my eyes to a way of thinking about the environment, namely as a field of significance, but on the other hand it seems to be unfortunate in its tone of negative criticism of much of the thinking of deep environmentalists, and wrong in its dismissal of the idea that the environment as a whole should be a field of significance.

Much of my paper will be an attempt to defend the latter possibility, not only as intellectually intelligible but also as morally imperative, given the environmental predicament we are in. But the paper also has a more theoretical aim, namely to argue that the idea of having an environment involves both the aspect of an environment as a field of significance and the aspect of an objective environment out there, independent of our field of significance. The paper is also somewhat programmatic in that if this way of thinking about the environment is fruitful, there is *much* more to be said.

Cooper's Account

First let me sketch out some of the ideas in Cooper's paper. He criticizes the new environmental ethic as hollow, vague and full of tensions as follows:

> The source of the problems, I think, is the distended notion of environment which imbues the new ethic . . . . Put crudely, [this] notion of environment is of something much too *big* . . . . The expression 'the global environment' makes this largeness of scope explicit; but even when the adjective is omitted, the definite article and singular noun indicate that there is just one big environment—the biosphere, the order of things . . . 'The Environment'. (Cooper, 1992, p. 167)

He contrasts this with what he sees as the older concept of an environment, which like *milieu*, or *ambiente*, indicates a field of

143

significance, something a person (or indeed an animal like a badger) might be familiar with and be 'at home in'. In a passing but significant observation about the predicament of today's intellectuals who flit around the world (which no doubt includes me), he says: 'At home everywhere, today's intellectual is at home nowhere in particular. It would be no surprise if his idea of an environment should be The Environment' (Cooper, 1992, pp. 171–172). This, incidentally, is remarkably similar in tone to Alasdair MacIntyre's criticism of cosmopolitanism in that in making people citizens of everywhere it makes them rootless citizens of nowhere (see Almond, 1990, p. 102). This parallel is I believe instructive since, although it is not mentioned, I suspect that a communitarian suspicion of the idea of global community and global ethics is part of what underlies Cooper's position.

Cooper accepts that one cannot object to an understanding of a concept just because it is different from an earlier one, but argues that this idea of the environment contributes to three errors. First it fails to give adequate weight in the right ways to concerns about animal welfare and about economic justice for the Third World, by subsuming them under one umbrella concern; second it encourages an inappropriate idea of nature as a whole as an object of reverence; and third it tells us to develop a sense of oneness and unity with nature, which at the same time is seen as alien from us.

Cooper is not against action to protect the environment, but he thinks that all that is realistically possible (though he is not sure it is adequate) can be achieved through the application of familiar ethical principles (e.g., the 'no-harm' principle) as applied to animals and future generations, and the resurrection of the older idea of caring for one's own environment as a field of significance (generally local), and through the recognition that morally, 'if I appreciate the importance for my life of a place I know my way around I must appreciate the importance this has for others as well, and I will want to defend their efforts to preserve such places' (Cooper, 1992, p. 179).

Some Remarks on Cooper's Position

Before developing my own account, let me first make a few critical remarks about the above line of thought. My general position would be to say that Cooper seems to be throwing out the baby with the bath water. It is true that what some deep environmentalists say is unclear, fuzzy, or wrong—in any case they do not all say the same things. But that does not mean that what is at fault is the idea of 'the environment' as 'the whole of the world'. It is true that some environmentalists do not give adequate or the right kind of defence of animal rights or the demand for economic justice. However, the fault does not lie in talk of 'the environment', but in not having the right normative principles for acting within the framework of the environment, i.e., as the total backcloth to the range of our ethical concerns. No doubt some ideas of oneness and reverence do not stand up to careful examination, but it is difficult to see why one cannot accept some kinds of relationship—cognitive, aesthetic, ethical—to the environment as a whole, and indeed there seems every reason to say that we need to.

At one point Cooper criticizes the demand that we should feel part of the environment because we all already have a relationship to our environment—our field of significance. But unless one accepts an implicitly conservative assumption that it is inappropriate for people to *change* their environments as fields of significance, the remark does nothing to undermine arguments for making the environment as a whole part of our field of significance.

Indeed, there is within Cooper's analysis an implicit acceptance of the idea of 'the environment'. First, Cooper criticizes the deep ecologists for their anti-scientism on the grounds that ecology itself is part of our scientific worldview, according to which the world is to be described in terms which are as free as possible from those terms which register 'subjective' attitudes and feelings—ideally the only relations being those of 'time, space and causality'. But Cooper is not here denying that the world *is* a system of causes and effects, ecological as well as physical, chemical, etc. Furthermore when at the end he develops the idea of the need to appreciate the importance each person attaches to their own environment as a field of significance, the idea of 'the environment' is really coming in through the backdoor. For if I am to take appropriate action to protect the various fields of significance of other people, my action will be directed to sustaining the common basis—the quality of the physical and more generally the public environment—which underlies the sustaining of all the various fields of significance—and what is this but *the* environment and the common objective world.

Indeed one way of thinking about the environment (which would make it partly a function of the idea of a field of significance) is to think of it as that which sustains or underlies the set of different and variable fields of significance of those who have them. But if the latter (those who have fields of significance) include all people, what we have is in effect one common entity called the environment. So my point is that if we are to make sense of moral concern for the quality of the perceived environment for other people, our concern cannot help but be mediated by what we do for this *one common* publicly shared environment which causally underpins all those perceived environments. That is, if each person has their *own* environment, there is nevertheless a public common environment as well. What else could this be, at least in many contexts, but the 'global environment'?

Some Distinctions

But it is now time to turn to a more careful analysis of the some of the distinctions which I have been suggesting in the above discussion.

Field of Significance versus Objective System of Causes and Effects

First and foremost there is the distinction between what I shall call an environment as a field of significance (broadly along the lines which Cooper suggests but later to be modified) and an environment as an objective system of causes and effects or, to be more precise, the continuing existence of a number of entities which together exert a significant causal influence on the state of the subject for whom it is an environment.

Thus the difference between the two senses of environment which I am suggesting is not a difference between an environment as a relational concept and an environment as a non-relational concept. Both senses bring out the fact (which is expressed in equivalent words like *milieu* and *ambiente*) that an environment is 'around' some entity for whom or even for which it is an environment. What is different is the nature of the relation involved. An environment as a field of significance essentially stands in an intentional relation as an intentional object (in the sense emphasized by phenomenologists which of course includes Cooper). It is an environment for the subject who perceives it in some way and meaningfully acts within it (as home, as familiar or friendly, but also of course possibly as hostile, dangerous, harsh, such as the social environment of someone economically very poor). Thus environments as fields of significance will vary considerably from person to person, from one group to another.

An environment as that which objectively exerts causal influences on the state of an entity is still something to be explained in relational terms, viz. causal terms, but it is something that surrounds an entity and significantly determines how that entity continues its existence, without that entity necessarily having an awareness of what that environment is. A tree may wither because of lack of water or because of strong cold prevailing winds, which are key elements of its environment, i.e., what determines how it fares, but it does not know of it. Children who die of leukaemia from radiation from a nearby nuclear power station may know nothing of the significant feature of their environment which is in fact causing them to die early, and likewise the poor living in a suburb of a Third World city may have no idea of the causal role that the terms of global economic trade or IMF structural adjustment have on their plight.

Two further notes of clarification are necessary, though they only highlight the need for further discussion. First, the 'environment out there' is *not* merely the physical world, as the last example indicates. It may also for example be, as the deep ecologists suggest, the repository of intrinsic value or objective beauty; for a religious person it may well have a spiritual character. Second, the idea of an environment as a field of significance does not indirectly favour a human-centred as opposed to a nature-centred approach to environmental ethics; it is neutral between them.

Physical versus Social

The last example points to the second distinction which needs to be made, and which cuts across the first distinction. Namely, the distinction between an environment as a physical environment and an environment as a social environment (where I am using 'social' broadly to include economic, political, cultural dimensions, etc.). The latter would be made up of laws, customs, contractual obligations and the like.

Natural versus Artificial

The previous distinction is similar to but not identical to the distinction between 'natural' and 'artificial' environments, where artifice is taken to imply the intervention of human intelligence in some act of modification or creation. In this sense a natural environment would be one where naturally occurring objects exist which have not been significantly modified by past human intervention either in internal structure or external arrangements. Wilderness areas would still just count as pure examples of this, whereas ornamental gardens and the Houses of Parliament would not, though the latter two would count as part of the physical environment as well as being in other ways parts of our social environment.

It is not my intention here to explore these two sets of contrasts and their relationships, which are complex. The general point I wish to make is merely that all these kinds of environments, or perhaps to be more accurate, our environment in all these aspects, may both feature as part of a person's field of significance, but at the same time also contribute part of the objective causal network which, *vis-à-vis* any individual or group of individuals, may exert influences on them beyond their level of comprehension or knowledge. Consider the effect of lead piping on the Romans.

Local versus Non-local/Global

The fourth kind of distinction I wish to bring in is more relevant to my central theme—it is the distinction between an environment as a local environment and an environment as something more extensive. The local/global distinction has become something of a cliché in environmental circles, so one wants to use it cautiously. More accurately, 'local' and 'global' represent poles on a continuum from the very local (a stinking drain in my backyard) to the whole world (ozone layer depletion), with many other levels (community, valley, country, region, etc.) in between. What will determine the size of an environment for a level of discourse will be either how the objective system of causes and effects is understood (the scale of the impacts of human activity, the scale of the modification in human behaviour needed to change the impacts, etc.), or how people and groups perceive their significant milieus (which depends on many factors such as travel, interests in other parts of the world, the accidents of relatives' marriages, etc.).

My Central Practical Concern

With this small amount of conceptual mapping behind us, let me now try and state one significant way in which it may be used to identify the nature of our environmental predicament (though no doubt there are others). Put very crudely, my contention is that, given the nature of the objective system of causes and effects within the world as a whole, and given the effects which it is already having on human life (and that of other living things) and is likely to have in the future, *there is an essential mismatch between the levels and kinds of environments as fields of significance for most people and the actual levels at which and ways in which our environments, including especially the global environment as a whole, are exerting causal influences of a detrimental kind.* This mismatch can be identified in two ways.

First, putting the point more negatively, people in the pursuit of quality of life within the fields of significance which they currently value are participating in practices which are contributing to the deterioration of the physical environment as an objective reality, in such ways that the continuation of those valued fields of significance is being undermined by the causal system (whether most of us are aware of it or not). Of course, sooner or later these causal impacts will break into and cause disarray for people's perceived environments, but by the time that has happened, things will have got much worse.

Second, to look at the point more positively, our being able collectively to get into a changed relationship with the global environment, i.e., to change our practices in such a way that the system of causes and effects will not produce major large-scale changes in the future, depends precisely on our being able to transform our environments as fields of significance into something large enough to match the scale of the impacts of the global environment as a whole. Unlike Cooper, I believe the great challenge is precisely to render 'the environment' as a very large thing into a field of significance, charged with sufficient motivating power to get us off our backsides. To adapt a perceptive remark made by the poet Piet Hein, since we are global citizens, we need to acquire global souls.[1]

Perhaps the word 'mismatch' is misleadingly simple, both because it suggests that what is needed is a one-to-one correlation between how people perceive their environment and the objective environment, and because it suggests that we need to embrace the whole world as the field a significance correlative to the world out there.

First, with regard to any objective environment, extensive such as a country or the world, or local such as a city or valley, there will be considerable differences between the common, single environment (or the common set of environmental impacts that are of concern) and the wide variety of ways in which people will perceive and value the environment they live in. This variety in life-style may indeed be significant (like biodiversity in other ecological contexts) but what is here important is the need for the range of 'perceived environments as fields of significance' to be sufficiently *adjusted* as to bring about sustaining, or returning to, the objective environmental base needed.

Second, it is not being suggested that in order for the global objective environment to be properly sustained, everyone should

[1] Piet Hein said 'We are global citizens with tribal souls' (quoted in Barnaby, 1988, p. 192). Perhaps 'local' would be better than 'tribal'.

adopt a uniform, homogenized love of, or cherishing of, planet earth in place of all their diverse and localized fields of significance. Far from it. Most of the adjustments in behaviour needed to sustain the overall environment will come from adjustments in local perceptions and priorities. But insofar as a dimension of our changed perceptions will be the global dimension, the ways in which people will value the world they live in may take many forms.

Third, it is not sufficient that some adopt a global attitude, though it is necessary. It is important that the right global approach is adopted. The executive director of a transnational company who surveys the whole world as a pool of resources to be exploited no doubt sees the global environment as a field of significance—but it is hardly what is needed!

What I think is important about Cooper's approach is that unless we do see the environment as a field of significance we are unlikely to do much about it. One fault perhaps with much environmental ethics (including my own attempts at it) is the assumption that if we can articulate moral arguments (to do with the future, other life-forms, etc.) then people who cannot fault the logic of them will be motivated to do what is needed. (Hare's account (e.g., Hare, 1963, ch. 5) about the problematic nature of backsliding is a significant example of what might be seen as a common philosopher's blind spot about ethics.) The truth is that the extent to which people generally act on these arguments is a function of how they 'perceive' the environment—with all the richer connotations which the word 'perceive' has compared with 'intellectually accept'. Part of what is at stake is how one perceives one's 'moral environment', as discussed further later.

Further Conceptual Observations

We need to look a little more closely at the idea of a field of significance and its relation to the environment as existing independently of our perceptions. First, it must immediately be conceded that in one sense the environment as a system of causes and effects is also a field of significance—namely cognitive significance. It is only because human beings, or at least some of them—scientists, politicians, informed citizens and so on—have an understanding of the physical world (and indeed social world) as something which has an existence and causality over and above what is perceived in ordinary lived life, which can have effects, some later understood, some perhaps not, on those lived lives, that the issues I am raising can be articulated at all. Intellectually 'the environment' constitutes itself a field of significance.

We could perhaps imagine people who lived in relation to their natural environment, were at home with it, accepted its ways, benign and hostile, but had no conception of it other than at its phenomenal level, for whom therefore the distinction between the environment as lived in and something out there was not available. Though all societies we know about have probably operated with some kind of distinction between appearance and reality, perhaps the above imagined situation applies to higher animals insofar as they live in a perceived environment. On the other hand one can see the rise of modern science, and its development of ideas of primary and secondary qualities and of a world of physics significantly different from the phenomenal world, as giving most starkly the contrast between them. One might say, slightly paradoxically, that our environment includes the perspective in which we see the difference between a lived environment and an environment out there, and see the need to view them in some kind of relationship.

The idea of the environment as a field of significance is itself rather a vague one. Cooper's characterization of it as something in which we are at home, one we know our way around, is helpful but in a sense one-sided. It gives the impression that each of us has an environment with which we are happy, i.e., one which we positively value. Now I take it that for any person to *have* an environment of some kind, is a *necessary* condition of their well-being. But it by no means follows that it is sufficient. If people are not familiar with their environment, and do not 'know their way about', they will be disoriented, fragmented, not perhaps able to lead a fully human life.

On the other hand there are many environments (physical, social, economic) which one may be familiar with but which one dislikes and wishes were different. Part of what it is for human beings to have an environment is to have an idea of alternative possibilities, some seen as realistic, some maybe as ideal dreams. *Environments are meaningful partly in respect of our power of choice whether to accept them, modify them or change them.* Environments as fields of significance are not necessarily good things—though it is a good thing that anyone has some environment in this sense. To have an environment is to stand in a dynamic relationship to it, not just a passive relationship of acceptance of it. ('Dynamic' here does not imply an attitude of manipulating, exploiting or controlling the environment. It simply signals the point that human agents *act* and *choose* in their environment—including deliberate 'letting be'—as well as accepting it, intellectually and emotionally.)

Although the main motivation for this paper was the identification, for practical purposes, of the *distinction* between an environment as a field of significance and an environment out there, a secondary thesis is to argue that there is a *duality* within a *single concept* of what it is to 'have an environment' (for self-conscious agents such as human beings). Though it is *not* part of the concept of the environment that human agents have a concept of their environment as the 'global environment' or the whole world, there does seem to be a duality at the core, namely the environment both as something 'out there' and at the same time that which one acts in, values and finds significant. In other words, it is not the case that the same word 'environment' *happens* to be used in two quite distinct senses (e.g., that of a phenomenologist and that of an ecologist). It is no accident that this word and others like it (e.g., 'world') have both aspects.[2]

The Idea of Changing an Environment

Given that we act and choose in our environments, there may be a number of reasons to change a person's environment as a field of significance; first, because that person may wish to live in a different perceived environment—one of less poverty, more knowledge, more beauty, less subjection to injustice or humiliation, etc.; second, because it may become apparent to those with a greater knowledge of the wider causal impacts of human practices based on their associated perceived environments, that, if those causal impacts are to be stopped, it is necessary for people to change the nature of their environments as fields of significance.

This raises the question: what is involved in 'changing' an environment? There are three different ways in which agents can be said to change their environment:

(1) to change the place/space (i.e., physical location) in which they live or operate;

(2) to change the character of their current space or the moveable objects/artefacts in the place/space they currently occupy;

(3) to change their environment as a field of significance by changing their perspective.

Traditionally, (1)—changing place or space—was resorted to when people moved on to virgin lands. Likewise on a smaller scale a family may move house to a new more congenial neighbourhood.

Changes under (2)—namely changing the character of one's cur-

---

[2] These ideas are explored further in Nigel Dower, 'Technology as Environment', a paper delivered at a conference in Aberdeen in September 1993 (copies available from the author).

rent space—are common nowadays. This may be done of course for a variety of reasons:

(i) The changes in the environment are made so as to improve the quality of the environment as lived in. Decorating a dowdy living room is a case in point, and illustrates the point that such actions may have nothing to do with 'protecting the environment' (as normally understood nowadays) at all.

(ii) Changing the environment is done because one thinks that these changes will contribute to benefits elsewhere and/or in the future. There are really three ways of doing this:

(a) By trying to alter the objective conditions through technological innovation, etc., in such a way as to preserve (by and large) the currently preferred fields of significance. (This approach reflects the 'technological fix' mentality and the 'growth' conception of sustainable development.)[3]

(b) By making changes to our activities as well (i.e., life-style changes) which are seen as both causing an improvement in the objective physical (and socio-economic) environment, and involving some changes in the way one lives one's life in the perceived environment.

(c) By doing what is involved in (3), namely changing one's whole way of valuing one's world. That is, *as a means* to changing the objective environment, one changes the way one values the environment.

However, a change under (3)—namely changing one's environment as a field of significance by changing the perceiver's perspective—is not merely important (practically) because it is (arguably) the most significant way of changing the objective environment. It is also important in its own right, and as casting light on the whole idea of what it is to have an environment.

To put the point in a more formalized way: if E is an environment for a subject S, then E stands in a relation R to S such that E may change either because of a change in S or because of a change in E independent of a change in S. What is distinctive (and maybe counter-intuitive at first) is the first feature, namely that, in virtue of changes in S (of attitude, perception, value, priorities, etc.), E itself is said to change.

This is not a claim that there is some kind of illusion (based on the supposition that 'really' E has not changed) or, parallel to what is claimed in ethics sometimes, some kind of error theory (e.g., Mackie, 1977). It is part of the dynamics of the idea of an environ-

[3] It involves changing the 'T' element rather than the 'P' or 'A' elements in Ehrlich's IPAT formula (Impact = Population x Affluence x Technology) (see Ehrlich *et al.*, 1977, p. 720).

ment that the environment *qua* field of significance really has changed. It would be a mistake to say, 'No, your environment has not changed, only the way you think about it', precisely because the way you think about it is constitutive of what makes you have an environment at all! But of course it is not entirely constitutive, since the environment is not just what you make of it. 'Environment' seems to have this duality at its very conceptual core, as I noted earlier and as is illustrated here by what is involved in changing one's environment.

Some examples will illustrate this. A teenager whose sexuality is developing looks at the same person one day without interest and again a year later with interest. The teenager's 'world', as we say, is changing. A person who once regarded classical music with indifference now hears the same opening bars of Mozart's 40th Symphony with emotional electrification. Culturally the person is now in a different environment. Another person, who once scarcely noticed birds when they were around, is now fascinated by their colours, flight, song, etc. The natural world is becoming part of this engaged perceiver's environment in a way it was not before.

Suppose again that someone at one time gave not a second thought about jumping into a car for any trip however short, using and throwing away tins, paper, glass, etc., and was not even aware of the ecological aspects of these practices. One can imagine a transformation, through various stages of intellectual, moral and social awareness, whereby our hitherto thoughtless motorist becomes committed to protecting the environment, comes to enjoy doing this, joins organizations so as to feel part of a wider social commitment, and no longer thinks of the natural world as something there to exploit. The environment (as perceived as the physical world around us) is no longer something in the background, just taken for granted; it is now charged with importance. The person's environment has changed.

The Moral Environment

I now want finally to turn to the question: how does morality come into this changing of one's valued environment? A key question is this: is morality part of the environment? Or is it part of what agents-as-subjects bring to bear on the environment in the light of which they act on or in the environment as they perceive it? The answer, I suggest, is that it is both, or rather that the 'either/or/both' approach is misleading and needs transcending.

On the one hand, morality is clearly part of our *social* environment, part of the social matrix in which agents act. They have an awareness of moral norms and practices, types of moral discourse, ranges of behaviours permitted, etc., which are part of the back-cloth of their society. Thus morality is part of the environment which confronts them and in relation to which they have to act. As such it affects people's lives both (primarily) as part of their field of significance, but also as something out there, which, whether they realize it or not, has effects on their life (such as career advancement, social acceptability, etc.).

On the other hand, morality is often seen as part of what the valuing subject brings towards the environment perceived as something objective. In the 'subject-object' relation morality belongs to the subject, not the object. (In this way of thinking the 'morality *qua* social environment' is just another 'fact' to which one reacts, but distinct from the principles or values one personal-ly accepts in one's decision-making.) Thus people as agents may see themselves as having certain obligations in respect of the envi-ronment, to maintain it, improve it (where it has been damaged), to modify it. But the moral relations they have with it indicate how they, the subjects, ought to act in relation to it as something exist-ing outside them, and are *quite different from* the relations they actually do have with the environment (either in the field of signif-icance sense or the objective sense). The environment they have is there, as a matter of fact—either scientific fact or psychological fact about how they perceive it. Since (on this argument) how things are is quite separate from how they ought to be, the envi-ronment itself is not imbued with moral character. (This could be true whether the environment is seen as having merely instrumen-tal value or is seen as having intrinsic but non-moral value.)

My suggestion is that we need to go beyond this polarity. It is true that a person *can* regard morality merely as part of the social environment—something to be reckoned with in one's egoist cal-culations. It is equally true that moral agents *can* have a mere acceptance that they ought to act *without an engaged valuing* of the environment (social or natural) in which they act. But characteris-tically, and as a manifestation of a more developed moral sensibili-ty, people go beyond this. For them the environment is itself charged with moral character. Having a morality is partly a matter of standing in moral relations with what surrounds them. That is, the environment which they have is one informed by moral 'relat-edness'—it is not just that they can make or accept moral judg-ments about what they ought to do in relation to it.

The idea of an environment *qua* field of significance is some-thing in which I act and which I find important in virtue of my projects and interests. In other words my relation to my environment, what makes it the environment it is for me, depends as much on how I actively relate to it, as on how I perceive it or feel about it in other ways; and my forms of action are expressions of moral concerns. There is a parallel to be drawn here with the concept of peace, which is arguably not just a neutral object of moral obligation, as Hobbes (*Leviathan*, chs. 13–14) thought of it, but is to be understood itself as constituted by activities informed by certain moral values. Indeed peace itself is a dimension of the environment in this broader sense.

From the point of view of environmental ethics, the nature of this 'ethical' dimension to our environment (both at the level of the perceived and at the level of entities which exert influences not always perceived) cannot be underestimated. For it makes a large difference to the extent to which individuals will act on the principles which their theories may lead them to endorse, whether or not these practices are already part of the accepted culture. I am not just making the point that people are more likely to act when there is (perceived to be) general compliance or reciprocity in action or the possibility of reciprocity. It is also the more theoretical point about the reality of ethics depending on its public embodiment as well as the private commitments of individuals. I recall what Bradley (1876, pp. 177–181) had to say about the body and soul of morality (but stripping it of his conservative tendencies!). Morality then is part of our environment, and anyone seriously concerned with the state of the environment must attend to the state of our moral environment as part of it.

No doubt much of this paper will be seen as working over familiar issues in a somewhat different guise, but I hope at least to have shown that for any one at all concerned with environmental protection, the concept of the environment is not at all straightforward and is worth careful attention.

Chaos and Order, Environment and Anarchy

ANDREW BELSEY

Chaos and Order

The distinction between chaos and order has been central to western philosophy, both in metaphysics and politics. At the beginning, it was intrinsic to presocratic natural philosophy, and shortly after that to the cosmology and social philosophy of Plato. Even in the pre-presocratic period there were important intimations of it. Thus Hesiod tells us that 'first of all did Chaos come into being' (*Theogony*, line 116, in Kirk *et al.*, 1983, p. 35)—although exactly what is meant by 'chaos' in this context is not clear. (It could be some sort of undifferentiated, primordial mass, or just the separation (the gap) between earth and sky (Kirk *et al.*, 1983, pp. 38–41). Nor does Hesiod concern himself with what Chaos came from (Barnes, 1987, p. 57).) The myth of origin in the *Theogony*, though, can be seen in contrast to the underlying theme of *Works and Days*, namely, Zeus's eternal rule over the world in accordance with Justice or Order (Kirk *et al.*, 1983, pp. 34, 72). This point will become centrally important in what follows.

What distinguishes the presocratics from their predecessors, according to the modern commentators, is that the ideas of the former depend on and exemplify a definite shift from a mythopoeic to a rationalistic, philosophical, proto-scientific mode of thought. Whereas Hesiod's cosmogony is a theogony, that of the presocratics is anything but: both their cosmogony and cosmology are natural philosophy. Hesiod's world was one in which the distinction between the natural and the supernatural had no application because of the predominance of the supernatural. The presocratic natural philosophers quietly reversed this upside-down cosmology so that its feet were back on the ground. They abandoned the supernatural, but did so without making a song and dance about it. The supernatural disappeared into silence (Vlastos, 1975, p. 20). (But it must be remembered that the older outlook persisted for the majority. Among their contemporaries the natural philosophers were a small minority, and not always a very popular one.)

In a manner of speaking, the cosmos too appeared in silence.

There was no fanfare to introduce it to the world. The presocratics did not make an explicit distinction between chaos and cosmos: they just saw the world as orderly and explicable in rational terms, and constructed their theories accordingly, with a minimum of methodological fuss. This is just as true for Thales, Anaximander and Xenophanes, who did not use the word 'cosmos', as for Heraclitus, who (about a century after Hesiod) did, and who provides the earliest surviving use of the word in the sense of general world-order: 'This cosmos, the same for all, no god or man has made, but it was, is, and will be for ever: ever-living fire, kindling according to measure and being extinguished according to measure' (fr. B30, as in Vlastos, 1975, pp. 4–5). (Though there is a tradition that Pythagoras had first used the term (Diamandopoulos, 1967, p. 80).)

What then is this cosmos of the presocratic natural philosophers? First, 'the cosmos is the universe, the totality of things' (Barnes, 1987, p. 18). Second, it is an ordered totality. So it is not just order but that which has this order, 'the world in its aspect of order' (Vlastos, 1975, p. 6). Order is expressed in high-level regularities (what would later be called laws of nature or scientific laws), knowledge of which provides explanation of all natural phenomena (Vlastos, 1975, p. 10). The cosmos, then, is (among other things) the rational, intelligible, regular universe. What else it is will appear shortly.

The cosmos is regular because there is no possibility of supernatural intervention, for the supernatural has been abolished. There is just nature. It is the nature of the cosmos to be regular because it is nature. 'Regardless of many disagreements among themselves, the *physiologoi* are united in the assumption that the order which makes our world a cosmos is natural . . . is immanent in nature' (Vlastos, 1975, p. 24). Even Anaximenes, Heraclitus and Diogenes of Apollonia (who might otherwise be considered the most theological of the presocratics) 'assume that order is inherent in nature and does not need to be imposed on it by a supernatural ordering mind' (Vlastos, 1975, p. 25). As for the attempts by Anaxagoras to find a role for 'Mind' in his cosmos, consider with what disappointment they were received by Plato (*Phaedo*, 97c–99c).

Plato was disturbed by what he diagnosed as the failure of Anaxagoras to rise above the typical mechanistic, soulless cosmology of the presocratic tradition, and he set out to destroy that tradition, with some success. In the *Timaeus* he not only disinterred an explicit chaos/cosmos distinction but also reintroduced the supernatural in the shape of the Demiurge, the craftsperson-artist-god who 'takes over matter in a chaotic state and moulds it in the likeness of an ideal model', who is 'the imposer of pre-existing form on an as yet formless material' (Vlastos, 1975, pp. 25, 27).

Vlastos is unable to conceal his distaste for the reactionary supernatural conceptual framework which Plato (re)introduced, nor his admiration for the fertility of the research programme which Plato initiated within it. For by a twist of irony, Plato's supernaturalism turns out to be scientifically redundant: by a self-denying ordinance Plato offers a guarantee that the supernatural power 'will never be exercised to disturb the regularities of nature' (Vlastos, 1975, p. 61). So Plato's universe turns out to be as regular as any put forward by his presocratic predecessors, or even more regular, for it became possible to translate Plato's astronomical insights in the *Timaeus* into mathematical form. Thus began the tradition of mathematical astronomy which can be traced— with many transformations, admittedly—through Eudoxus, Hipparchus, Ptolemy, Copernicus, Galileo, Kepler, Newton, Laplace, Poincaré, down to the astronomers of today who are bringing to order the 'chaotic' tumblings of Hyperion in its orbit around Saturn (Stewart, 1990, pp. 243–253).

But Plato's appropriation and reconceptualization of the presocratic cosmos, involving as it does a sleight-of-hand whereby it is made supernatural in its origin but simultaneously thoroughly regular in its operation, is not surprising. In the view of Vlastos, it is indeed necessary for anyone who wants a rational understanding of things, for 'the conception of the cosmos . . . is *presupposed* by the idea of natural science and by its practice' (Vlastos, 1975, p. xii). This view has become a commonplace ('All science is founded on the assumption that the physical world is ordered' (Davies and Gribbin, 1992, p. 24)), although a philosopher might hope for some attempt at a justification for an assumption of such enormity. But leaving this aside, the fact remains that whatever his motivation or his argument Plato placed the cosmos deep in the heart of the tradition of rational enquiry.

The cosmos, as discussed earlier, was (among other things) the rational, intelligible, regular universe. But in addition it had an aesthetic component: 'it is a beautiful arrangement: the word *kosmos* in ordinary Greek meant not only an ordering but also an adornment (hence the English word "cosmetic"), something which beautifies and is pleasant to contemplate' (Barnes, 1987, p. 18). By the time of the atomists, with their rigorously mechanistic, deterministic universe, this aspect of cosmos had largely disappeared, but Plato had no difficulty in accepting the cosmos as an aesthetically-designed and created order—his creator was after all an artist. So in Plato's universe there was an identity of aesthetic harmony and mathematical elegance, exemplified in, for example, his insistence on uniform circular motion for the celestial bodies.

But further, originally aesthetic values were not sharply separated from moral values. Cosmos, then, is also moral order, or justice (Vlastos, 1975, pp. 3–4). This feature again disappears by the time of the atomists, but the earlier presocratics still described the universe in moral terms (showing, perhaps, traces of Hesiod-type views on Zeus and justice (Kirk *et al.*, 1983, p. 34)). Thus 'Anaximander and Heraclitus . . . projected into the physical cosmos their faith in justice' (Vlastos, 1975, p. 29). What this means is that physical transformations, processes and cycles are seen in terms of justice, but this in no way disturbs the commitment to the naturalistic principles of the presocratics. Rather, it can be seen as a way of expressing in simple, though by no means unsophisticated, terms a conservation principle: given that the world is a cosmos (in all senses), any change would threaten to unbalance it and thus create injustice; therefore there must be an opposite change by way of reparation to restore the balance of justice. The underlying sense of 'natural justice' here could be understood as equivalent to 'the principle of the conservation of cosmos'. This is quite different from the teleology of Plato, according to which things happen for the best, uniform circular motion again being an example, and one that demonstrates the inseparability for Plato of the physical, mathematical, aesthetic and moral orders.

Environment

What, though, have all these ancient ideas to do with the environment? Plenty. The cosmos is the environment, in the widest possible sense. It is not just the universe, but the universe as order, not under the sway of the supernatural, but as the workings of nature, according to regularity, or law. But the cosmos, though definitely not supernatural, is not necessarily value-free, at least according to some of the presocratics. The later presocratics, such as the atomists, with their proto-Laplacean determinism, could find no place for values in nature. Nevertheless, the overall presocratic view of the cosmos, a view shared by Plato, is one of balance and long-term harmony, and although these are attained through the operation of law, I have argued that the conservation of balance (the 'conservation of nature') can also be seen in terms of 'natural justice'.

Most environmental problems are concerned with only a small

part of the cosmos, the biosphere of the earth. (But not all, if the sending of space-probes into deepest space is a form of pollution.[1]) The biosphere is nature in a more restricted sense. Yet it is part of the totality of nature, and the way in which it is thought about, assessed and appraised, will depend on how the universe is theorized. Environmental philosophy, therefore, is part of cosmology, not cosmology as part of mathematical physics (though this might be relevant) but cosmology as metaphysics, and perhaps ethics. This last point depends on the existence or otherwise of values in nature.

But before proceeding with this line of thought, it is necessary to consider an objection. Such a universal notion of environment might be considered too grandiose. It would certainly not go down well with David E. Cooper, who in his paper 'The Idea of Environment' criticizes the notion of environment which 'includes everything from the street corner to the stratosphere' (Cooper, 1992, pp. 167, 179), which is considerably less than is being included here.

Cooper rejects any environmentalism based on an ecophilosophy or global ethics within which the environment (all of it) is held to be a unity to be approached with respect, awe and reverence. Such a notion of environment (Cooper calls it 'The Environment')—the global environment, the whole of the natural order, the order of things, the biosphere—this 'notion of environment is of something much too big' (Cooper, 1992, p. 167).

Instead Cooper offers a notion of environment as something local, though this involves locality defined neither in terms of yards or miles, nor causal impact. Rather, it is a matter of symbolic significance. A creature's environment is its surroundings considered as a network of meanings within which it both lives and belongs: a milieu, an ambience, a neighbourhood, with which the creature is familiar in a practical, unreflective way.

What is wrong with The Environment, according to Cooper, is that it is (1) an incorrect account of the environment, and (2) incapable of doing the work that is required of it: it fails to provide a basis for the solution of environmental problems. However, it is possible to share Cooper's scepticism about the religious tinges of environmental holism without rejecting its metaphysical and ethical components, and without accepting Cooper's two objections to The Environment.

The objections are connected: it is the wrong idea of the envi-

[1] On this and other extra-terrestrial issues see Hargrove, 1986; Marshall, 1993; and Keekok Lee's contribution to this volume.

ronment (partly) because it doesn't work. To this it is possible to reply with a *tu quoque*. Cooper is playing the old (but not unrespectable) philosophical game of offering a definition that is both stipulative and persuasive. But why should anyone accept it, especially since it is in fact Cooper's idea of the environment which does not work. But before coming to that, it should be asked what is so special about locality. The local/global contrast is political (in a wide sense): the difference between a parochial and a cosmopolitan outlook. Furthermore, Cooper's claim that the environment (rather than The Environment) is the 'earlier and once prevalent concept' (Cooper, 1992, p. 167) could be challenged on historical grounds: for example, Genesis 1 gives an account of The Environment; Genesis 2 of the environment of Adam and Eve, the Garden of Eden. I am not claiming that the first chapter of Genesis is chronologically earlier than the second chapter, but merely that both accounts are very ancient (see also Porter, 1981, and Williams, 1983).

However, the main objection to Cooper's version of environmentalism is that it is impractical: it cannot do what is required of it. Rejecting the call for a new environmental ethics, Cooper suggests that 'It can be argued that the real need is for intelligent and robust application of some perfectly familiar moral injunctions. Especially important would be the one discussed at some length by Passmore: duty towards our children and grandchildren requiring that they be bequeathed a world no less clean and healthy than the one we are willing to tolerate for ourselves' (Cooper, 1992, p. 178). But who are 'we'? One of Cooper's objections to The Environment is that the concept can lead to 'tensions, hollowness and vagueness' (Cooper, 1992, p. 172), but exactly the same can be said about the trivial, familiar pronouns in the last-but-one quotation. Not everyone has children or grandchildren. Do such persons have no environmental duties? And why stop at grandchildren? Are not the interests of great-grandchildren of equal concern? Furthermore, why assume that our children and grandchildren would (or should) be satisfied with our own low standards of environmental cleanliness and healthiness?

However, the main problem for Cooper is that his position is contradictory (or perhaps just self-refuting) because of his use of the word 'world' in his statement about our children etc. The point is fairly obvious, surely, but the argument might as well be followed through in detail. Suppose I desire for my children a clean and healthy environment. I am powerless to provide this for them if my neighbour insists on polluting my garden with bonfire smoke and drift from a chemical spray. Perhaps Cooper would say that all this shows is that we *do* need a neighbourhood concept of the environment. But this is still no good. Even if everyone in my neighbourhood, in my country, agrees to provide a decent environment for their next generation, they cannot do this if other countries continue to pollute the atmosphere with nuclear waste or refuse to reduce their use of CFCs. It is, as Cooper really knows, a world problem, a global problem.

This is shown by the fact that Cooper has to find a stratagem for raising environmental concern to a world-wide level but without abandoning his local version of environment. His scheme is that we start with concern for our own local environment, but recognize that other communities will have a like concern for their local environments. The result would be environmental concern with a global coverage but on a local basis, through a 'mutually supporting league of little, local pockets of resistance' (Cooper, 1992, p. 179).

It won't work. It is significant that Cooper's examples in this context are indeed local—the factory farm or the motorway that threaten the locality. There is certainly nothing wrong with such local environmental concern. But what about the rest of the world? The major environmental problems, the ones that threaten everyone's children and grandchildren and all future generations, are global: the greenhouse effect, the loss of the ozone layer, the destruction of the rainforests, the growth of deserts, the pollution of the oceans, the disposal of nuclear waste, etc. Cooper might not like it, but we are no longer just parishioners, we are cosmopolitans, global citizens facing global problems. We need to cultivate at least a planetary outlook, and we must not abandon, therefore, what Cooper calls 'The Environment'.

But, furthermore, there is reason to believe that our outlook should be even wider. We are not creatures that become familiar with our own local environment in an 'unreflective' way. Cooper is right to claim that this environment is 'meaningful', but we might ask how it becomes so. Human beings are reflective: they are theorizers, scientifically or speculatively inclined, able to locate their neighbourhood within a larger whole, 'The Environment' or even the cosmos. Indeed, it could be argued that it is at least partly through cosmology that we are able to give meanings to our locally-lived lives.[2]

[2] I owe this point to Professor Jan J. Boersema of the University of Groningen. I am grateful to Professor Boersema for showing me some of his work in progress, which also draws attention to the evaluative content of cosmology.

Andrew Belsey

Order and Anarchy

Plato, however, in addition to his physical, mathematical, aesthetic and moral harmonies, had yet another trick up his sleeve: he integrated the serious Greek interest in politics into philosophy, into natural philosophy, one might say. So the cosmos, the once-created but now natural order, sets the boundary conditions not just for physics but also for politics. In the *Republic* Plato sets off on the quest for justice, and he discovers it within the just constitution of the state, founded on a tripartite division of labour and function for the population: 'when each of our three classes (workers, auxiliaries, and guardians) does its own job and minds its own business, that . . . is justice and makes our state just' (*Republic*, 434c). And it is *nature* that determines an individual's class position (374b-c).

Plato was concerned with the maintenance of social order and the avoidance of what is often, and wrongly, called 'anarchy', that is, social disorder or chaos. Plato's political philosophy could not be further from the principles of anarchism. There is something disreputable about Plato's politics, as has been pointed out by many critics. It is not just the anti-democratic, authoritarian intolerance, nor just the need for strong rule to impose order on and maintain it within the state, and not even simply the need of the ruling class to resort to lies and propaganda about nature and the nature of the state. It is the impudence of claiming that order is natural while knowing that it has to be imposed. It is possible that Plato was relying on an analogy: just as the Demiurge imposes order on the universe, so the philosopher-rulers impose it on the state. In both cases the implicit claim is that loss of order would lead to chaos. But this is a poor analogy for numerous reasons. For example, there is no suggestion that the philosopher-rulers create order and then withdraw. No, they must be continuously interventionist, to ensure the continuation of their own class rule.

No theory of social order which involves the imposition of order can legitimately claim that the order is natural—though Plato's propaganda and myth has been enormously influential and successful right down to the present day, since most people continue to regard lack of rule as lack of order in society, and see lack of social order as unnatural.

It is the anarchist tradition that has stood against the idea that order imposed by rule is natural. This involves rejecting and reversing Plato's political philosophy and his cosmology, both of which involve imposed order. As one spokesperson for anarchism puts it: 'order for the anarchist is not something imposed from above. It is a natural order' (Woodcock, 1977, p. 12). However, it is important to recognize that the anarchist is not concerned solely with political philosophy, with order in human society. Anarchist thought is cosmological in the sense mentioned earlier, not a branch of astrophysics but a combination of metaphysics and ethics.

This anarchist approach to cosmology has ancient roots. Thus Zeno of Citium, the founder of Stoicism, held that 'the end may be defined as life in accordance with nature, or in other words, in accordance with our own human nature as well as that of the universe, a life in which we refrain from every action forbidden by the law common to all things' (quoted in Marshall, 1992, p. 77). Zeno, however, is too anthropocentric to be a totally suitable guide for today. Nevertheless, the combination of metaphysics and ethics has had a powerful and long-standing appeal.

Consider the view of Herbert Read (not perhaps a typical anarchist—but then who could be?): 'The most general law in nature is *equity*—the principle of balance and symmetry which guides the growth of forms along the lines of greatest structural efficiency. It is the law which gives . . . the universe itself, an harmonious and functional shape, which is at the same time objective beauty'. And again: 'there exist principles of justice . . . principles of equality and fairness inherent in the natural order of the universe' (Read, 1940, p. 16).

These views might seem to hark back to Plato, and perhaps they do a bit, with their aesthetic outlook, but they are totally opposed to Plato's theory of order, and they recall, in fact, not just Zeno but the early presocratics. But such views also anticipated an alliance with the ecologists, as Woodcock saw: 'Everything . . . has its place in the order of being, and if it followed its own nature, all would be well. But let any species break the chain by departing from its nature, and disaster would ensue. It was a doctrine that would appeal to the modern ecologist' (Woodcock, 1977, pp. 16–17).

What the anarchists have in common with the early presocratics, and what makes them the natural allies of the ecologists, is the tendency to read justice into nature. But is it allowable to suppose in a literal sense that there are values in nature, or is it either metaphorical or just fantastical? Perhaps *justice* is too anthropomorphic, but the idea of nature as balance, as harmony, makes sense, provided the presocratic version is updated in two ways. First, assuming the universe is a closed entropic system, it is heading irreversibly towards heat-death. Second, within the biosphere evolutionary processes are also irreversible, but in ways which are quite different from though not incompatible with thermodynamic irreversibility. (Furthermore, evolution could be interrupted if the earth were to undergo its own local version of 'heat-death'.)

Allowing for these long-term processes within the biosphere and the cosmos, there are short- and medium-term balances on which life depends, and which have value. But there is an important proviso to the claim that there are values in nature. Even if there are, they do not tell us how to live. There is no looking into the 'Mind' of 'Nature' and reading off a set of moral injunctions. There needs to be considerable scepticism, therefore, about suggestions such as: 'The only necessity is to discover the true laws of nature and conduct our lives in accordance with them' (Read, 1940, p. 16).

In an obvious sense there is no option but to live in accordance with the laws of nature. But there is some further sense that can be extracted from Read's claim if it is taken as an example of the common tendency to over-emphasize the role of laws in science and to under-estimate the importance of initial conditions. Given the laws of nature and the present state of the environment, the continued pollution of (especially) the atmosphere will bring about conditions which, again in conjunction with the laws of nature, will make life (as we know it on earth) impossible. Pollution disrupts the natural harmonies from which the song of life is composed. In this sense, given knowledge of the present state of the environment, and granted a set of desires and objectives, the laws of nature are determining of conduct.

The anarchist outlook on the universe, with its recapitulation of presocratic cosmology, offers assistance to ecologists concerned with environmental problems. It provides a framework for thinking about nature, on a pretty grand (or grandiose) scale, to be sure, but this has advantages, given the nature of the problems. But do anarchist politics and practice provide any guidance to environmentalists? For it is noteworthy that the practical consequences of Cooper's idea of the environment appear somewhat anarchist. There is the emphasis on the small-scale neighbourhood, and the suggestion of a federation of neighbourhoods to take account of the required larger scale. Both of these ideas point towards anarchist practices.

But a lot more is needed for (and from) an alliance of anarchism and ecology. There needs to be a way of life with minimum environmental impact. Here there is much to be said for the anarchist emphasis on the small-scale community. But for reasons already discussed, a local approach to environmental problems could solve at most only local problems, and many of the major problems cannot be tackled on this basis. But it is not yet clear how to combine the required global outlook and action with the desirable political principles of democracy, devolution and local autonomy.

But in the end I wish to claim that two things are clear: saving the earth cannot be accomplished without transforming society, and neither can be achieved without a proper appreciation of the cosmos. We need liberatory environmentalism and liberatory politics—or, in other words, liberatory cosmology.

Natural Capital

ALAN HOLLAND

Interest in the concept of natural capital stems from the key role which this concept plays in certain attempts to elucidate the goal of sustainable development—a goal which currently preoccupies environmental policy-makers. My purpose in this paper is to examine the viability of what, adapting an expression of Bryan Norton's, may be termed the 'social scientific approach' to natural capital (Norton, 1992, p. 97). This approach largely determines the way in which environmental concern is currently being represented in the environmental policy community.

I

On any account of sustainability—and these are now legion—something or other is supposed to be kept going, or at any rate not allowed to decline, over time. In *Blueprint for a Green Economy* (Pearce *et al.*, 1989), which I shall treat as epitomizing the social scientific approach, sustainable development (or sustainability—I shall not trouble over the distinction) is construed as requiring that each generation leave its successor a stock of capital assets no less than it receives. In other words, the requirement is that capital—explained also as capital wealth or productive potential—be constant, or at any rate not decline, over time. A distinction is drawn between natural and human-made capital, generating two possible versions of the sustainability requirement, each with variations:

(i) that overall capital—the total comprising both natural and human-made capital—should not decline, or

(ii) that natural capital in particular should not decline (Pearce *et al.*, 1989, p. 34).

Included under human-made capital are physical items such as machines, roads and buildings, but also 'human capital' such as knowledge, skills and capabilities. Included under natural capital are naturally occurring organic and inorganic resources construed in the widest possible sense to cover not just physical items but also genetic information, biodiversity, ecosystemic functions and waste assimilation capacity. Natural resources can be further

169

divided into renewables and non-renewables. If one continues to use non-renewables (e.g., fossil fuels) one will eventually use them up; renewables (e.g., forests), on the other hand, can be used indefinitely, although they can also be used up if they are over-exploited. A class of 'cultivated natural capital', or 'agricultural capital' is sometimes recognized, which straddles the categories of natural and human-made capital (Pearce *et al.*, 1989, p. 3; see also Pearce, 1991, pp. 22–23). This chiefly comprises cultivated plants and domesticated animals, but also associated soils, landscapes, etc. Despite its appearing almost as an afterthought in the conceptual scheme outlined, this category is, of course, of enormous importance.

As the references to 'genetic information', 'waste assimilation capacity' and the like reveal, this approach to sustainability is centred firmly on the needs of human society—which is why we are referring to it as the 'social scientific' approach. Indeed, in the very first sentence of *Blueprint 2*, in a passage outlining the 'central messages of *Blueprint 1*' we see this clearly acknowledged: 'sustainable development is readily interpretable as non-declining human welfare over time' (Pearce, 1991, p. 1). In taking this view the authors are following the well-known prescription of the Brundtland Report, which stipulates that sustainability allows for present people's needs to be satisfied subject only to the constraint that this does not compromise the ability of future people to meet their needs (World Commission on Environment and Development, 1987, p. 43).

II

A leading variation which is offered of the first version of the sustainability requirement ((i) above) is that, while not allowing total capital to decline, one should also avoid—so far as possible—instigating any irreversible developments (Pearce *et al.*, 1989, p. 36). It must be said at once that the thinking behind this constraint is a little curious. It is suggested that the effect of introducing the constraint will be to protect natural capital, since it is this, rather than human-made capital, which is most susceptible to irreversible loss: we can recreate the bronze axe, but not the Irish elk. But no explanation is given of why this is important in the context of a theory dedicated to maintaining the level of human well-being. *If*, despite an irreversible loss, overall capital does not decline then why, from the point of view of the theory, should this matter? *Critical* irreversibilities will no doubt inevitably affect total capital adversely—

indeed, this might constitute a definition of 'critical' in this context—but, in that case, they will not be allowed under the basic requirement, and should not need to be singled out for separate mention. What we seem to have here is the first inkling of a failure of nerve—a failure to stick by the declared interpretation of the principle of sustainability, and perhaps a recognition that there is something of importance which it fails to capture.

As regards the second version of the sustainability requirement ((ii) above), which stipulates that natural capital in particular should not decline, two variations are offered. One variation stipulates that natural capital in the simple physical sense—physical stock—should not decline. Among preliminary difficulties with this suggestion (to which we shall return), three might be noticed at this point. One is that working out a criterion for non-declining physical stock turns out to be a less simple matter than might first appear, particularly where living things are involved, because of the constantly changing relations between them. A second is that, whatever criterion is used, it would seem *prima facie* to rule out the use of non-renewable resources, unless their use can be compensated for by an increase in renewable resources. A third is that the criterion of constant physical stock does not seem to answer too well to the needs of the theory under consideration, because not all physical capital is equally useful to humans, and some perhaps is of no use at all. So the reason for attempting to maintain the level of physical stocks, in an undiscriminating sense, remains somewhat obscure.

The other variation stipulates that what should be held (at least) constant is not the natural assets themselves but their economic value: it requires, in other words, that there should be no reduction in the flow of services yielded by the stock of natural capital. This variation immediately allows for more flexibility: it would seem, for example, to sanction some use of non-renewables, provided that technology was at the same time opening up new possibilities for exploitation. It also restores the rationale for preserving natural capital, which now refers to those aspects of nature which are used or usable in human social and economic systems (Clayton, 1991, p. 14). This would appear to be the approach favoured by Pearce and his colleagues: 'in the rest of this report we tend to adopt the "constant natural capital" approach to sustainable development' (Pearce *et al.*, 1989, p. 48). At the same time they appear to contemplate combining this with a vestige of the purely physical criterion so as not to permit certain physical stocks to fall below some 'critical minimum' (Pearce *et al.*, 1989, p. 44).

Alan Holland

III

A first point to notice about the preferred interpretation of sustainable development is the 'fickleness' which it introduces into the attempt to describe what counts as maintaining the *constancy* of natural capital, understood as constancy of economic value. There are two aspects to this, both of which stem from the fact that the ability of a given generation to meet its needs or, in Pearce's terms, the flow of services yielded by a given stock of natural capital, is a function, first, of the technology, second, of the social arrangements and, third, of the human needs which pertain at the time.

In the first place, while the authors of *Blueprint for a Green Economy* claim that *knowledge* is rarely lost (Pearce *et al.*, 1989, p. 43), this is already a questionable and ambiguous claim. For example, the ancient Cretan script known as 'Linear B' has not been lost, but the Linear B language itself, although it has as a matter of fact been recovered, might well not have been. In that event, would we or would we not count this as a case of lost knowledge? But the more important point is that technology, which is the *understanding* of how to apply knowledge, together with the social arrangements which enable such applications to be carried into effect, certainly can be lost. Recent events in the former Soviet Union, for example, illustrate how both these institutions might begin to unravel, with respect, say, to the capacity of a society to sustain its nuclear installations. Thus, the economic value of natural capital is only as secure as the technology, social conditions and cultural needs which enable that value to be realized, and these can be quite fragile.

In the second place, technology and social arrangements in particular are aspects of human-made capital. To point to the dependency of the economic value of natural assets on technology and social arrangements is to draw attention to the symbiotic relationship between natural and human-made capital. To a profound extent, the relation between them is a *complementary* one (Daly, 1991, p. 258). What this means, for example, is that an explosion in technology coupled with a relatively static physical stock of natural assets must be judged, on this view, to constitute a dramatic rise in natural capital, i.e., in the economic value of the natural assets. Some would say that this is precisely what has been happening in human societies over the past 6000 or so years since settled agriculture took hold. Somewhat counter-intuitively, then, the period of human civilization must be judged to coincide not with a *decline* in natural capital, as the usual scenario would have it, but with an *increase*. Which raises the further question of the *level* at which we should seek to maintain natural capital, understood in the social scientific sense. For on this understanding, it becomes fairly arbitrary where we set the level at which natural capital should be maintained. Why, for example, should we seek to maintain current and no doubt ephemeral levels of natural capital, rather than simply sit back and enjoy the windfall which 'civilization' has brought about? Equally counter-intuitively, we may well be obliged to judge that driving a road through a wilderness area is justified, not simply on the grounds of the social benefits which might accrue, but on the grounds that it actually constitutes an *increase* in natural capital, because it renders an otherwise indifferent portion of nature serviceable to human needs. Conversely, because of technological progress, constant levels of natural capital could be maintained despite rapidly dwindling stocks of natural assets. Thus the criterion of constant economic value does little to protect natural assets. Indeed, so fickle does the social scientific concept of natural capital prove to be that, in the last analysis, it is hard to see how there can any longer be any difference between the two versions of sustainability introduced at the start, one in terms of total capital, the other in terms of natural capital; for the criterion of the constancy of natural capital effectively dissolves into the criterion of the constancy of total capital.

Alongside the fickleness in its application, the other point which arises in connection with the social scientific account of sustainability concerns the question of motivation: what has the thinking behind sustainability to do with the thinking behind environmentalism? It cannot be denied that the notion of sustainability under discussion is the generally prevailing notion. Moreover, the prescription to pursue sustainability, understood in this way, can both readily and plausibly be derived from just two premises. The first premise is a statement prescribing the extension of the general obligation of justice to future peoples. The second premise is a statement describing the actions which must be undertaken in order to discharge that obligation. It turns out that respect for the environment is the instrument—no more—by which we are to secure justice for all peoples, including future ones. Now it is unlikely that environmentalists will have any quarrel with justice, and they would no doubt think that the more of it there was, the better. But I also venture to say that the ideal of justice, however worthy, fails to capture, and even misrepresents, what it is that many environmentalists thought they were about.

To this reflection there is a natural rejoinder: if the planet is saved, what does it matter how? In particular, what does it matter if this was the purpose of our actions, or if it was simply the means to some further purpose, such as securing the human future?

IV

But is it in fact true that the actions required to secure justice for future people coincide with those which are required to secure the environmental interest in nature? As we have seen, the *Blueprint* authors fight shy of endorsing the 'total capital' version of sustainability which permits indefinite trade-offs between natural and human-made capital. In attempting to do justice to the environmental interest, they endorse instead the version which requires the constancy of *natural* capital. But the question which then arises is whether this restriction can plausibly be represented as the logical outcome of a theory of sustainability based exclusively on the aim of securing justice for future generations. And it is far from obvious that it can. The point is that if it cannot, then the focus of the social scientific interpretation upon the constancy of *natural* capital in particular is being driven at least in some small measure by considerations which the authors of the *Blueprints*, at any rate, are refusing to acknowledge.

An attempt is indeed made in *Blueprint 1* to show that the focus on natural capital *is* a logical outcome of considerations internal to a theory of justice (Pearce *et al.*, 1989, p. 37); but the attempt seems to me unsuccessful. Four such considerations are cited: non-substitutability; uncertainty; irreversibility, and equity (Pearce *et al.*, 1989, pp. 37–38). We shall best pursue the cause of justice across generations, it is argued, if we take care to preserve assets for which no substitute can be found, if in circumstances of uncertainty we adopt a policy of minimizing risks, if we avoid irreversible losses and if, in general, we work to decrease inequities. Pursuing each of these causes is thought, in turn, to point towards a policy of preserving natural capital in particular.

Of these considerations the last is perhaps the most persuasive. The livelihoods of the poor tend especially to be directly dependent on the availability of natural resources (Pearce *et al.*, 1989, pp. 38, 40). So, measures to conserve these resources will tend to benefit the poor in particular and thus serve the cause of increasing equity between peoples. None of the other considerations, however, seems to draw a line at the required spot.

Taking the case of non-substitutability, it is generally agreed that some *human-made* capital is non-substitutable and some natural capital is substitutable. This is indeed openly—if questionably—acknowledged by the *Blueprint* authors: 'torn up hedgerows [given as an example of *natural* capital] can just as easily be replanted'; 'Built "heritage" cannot, of course, be reconstructed' (Pearce *et al.*, 1989, p. 36). However, the appropriate conclusion is not drawn, which is that operating with a prescription to save the non-substitutable will simply not deliver the preservation of natural capital, *specifically*. What is more, some non-substitutable natural items may be a matter of complete indifference so far as human interests are concerned; and there are by now familiar examples of natural items which are actually inimical to those interests— notably the AIDS and smallpox viruses, but also athlete's foot and sundry other life-forms. Not being serviceable from the point of view of human interests, we have to suppose that these items do not count as natural capital; yet they will merit protection under the prescription to save the non-substitutable. Exactly the same points apply in the case of irreversibility which, as Pearce and his fellow authors say, is but an extreme form of non-substitutability (Pearce *et al.*, 1989, p. 38).

So far as the consideration of uncertainty is concerned, it is no doubt true that uncertainty as to the importance of various features of our natural environment and about whether we shall ever find human-made substitutes for them points to the wisdom of preserving them intact. But at the same time there *are* natural substances whose properties are perfectly understood and for which we do have human-made substitutes. From the point of view of a theory aimed at securing justice across generations, their fate should be a matter of complete indifference.

In general, since all human-made capital has to derive ultimately from natural capital, it has to be true that from the point of view of human needs and welfare human-made capital is relatively more dispensable than natural capital. But not all and only natural capital is indispensable, and in any case, dispensability is a matter of degree and so, once again, does not provide a reason why natural capital specifically should be held constant.

In similar vein it is worth mentioning briefly the discussion in *Blueprint 1* of resilience, or the ability of a system—whether natural or human-managed—to maintain its structure and patterns of behaviour in the face of external disturbance. It seems to be assumed that a resilient system in which humans are involved is one which delivers non-declining human welfare. It is then argued that since resilience is enhanced by diversity which in turn requires the avoidance of irreversible effects, and since natural capital is particularly vulnerable to irreversible effects which also carry a very high risk because essential life-support systems are involved, then resilience requires the protection of natural capital. However, even if a connection between resilience and natural capital is established it does not follow that a connection between sustainability (in the sense of justice for all peoples) and natural capital is established. The reason is that it is hard to see what grounds there are for supposing that resilience and justice for humans will necessarily go hand in hand. Perhaps the most resilient system will require that some humans go to the wall; alternatively, perhaps a system slanted towards securing non-declining human welfare will lack resilience as, arguably, many existing agricultural systems seem to do.

A possible response to this line of argument is to say that if it proves to be true that the criterion of sustainability understood in terms of justice across generations fails to match up to the criterion of constant natural capital, then (a) it is arguably a preferable criterion and (b) it in fact answers to the environmental interest in nature better than does the criterion of constant natural capital. For, how many environmentalists does one hear defending the AIDS virus? I want to suggest that both these claims are false, but also to air the suspicion that this view is in fact shared by Pearce and his colleagues.

V

It has been argued that an account of sustainability in terms of non-declining human welfare will not necessarily yield a defence of natural capital. Conversely, in so far as the latter notion figures prominently in the working out of the notion of sustainability in *Blueprints 1* and *2*, it would seem to be an accretion to the 'pure' theory of those works and to represent on the part of the authors the interpolation of other considerations and values than the ones which are explicitly avowed—perhaps, even, some recognition of the 'value in things' which is anathema to the official position of those works. If so, there would be some irony in the situation. Referring to claims to detect intrinsic value in the natural world, *Blueprint 2* declares: 'As yet, no operational rules for decision-makers seem to have emerged from the "value in things" literature' (Pearce, 1991, p. 4). The irony is that, on my reading, that is exactly what the *Blueprints have* provided.

A similar conclusion is suggested by the strategy with which the authors officially seek to incorporate the 'value in things' point of view into their social scientific framework. This they do through the device of 'existence value', which amounts to recognizing a 'disinterested interest' in nature, failure to satisfy which will detract from the aggregate of human welfare. Nature thus secures a vicarious representation—*vicarious*, but also *precarious*, since its representation depends entirely upon the vicissitudes of human interest. However that may be, in a more recent article Kerry Turner and David Pearce develop their position further by giving 'loss aversion' as a reason, of equal standing with, for example, considerations about irreversibility, for protecting natural capital. In explanation they refer to 'strong evidence in economics and psychology that people are highly averse to environmental losses, i.e., they feel a natural right to their existing endowment of natural assets' (Turner and Pearce, 1993, p. 181). Now it may well be that in taking such interests seriously and counting them in as components of human welfare, a more adequate level of environmental protection will result. But the idea that these results will have been achieved without getting involved in 'debatable ethical implications' (Turner and Pearce, 1993, p. 182) is an illusion. The authors affect a position aloof from the debate about values, but such a stance is simply untenable. In the first place, their very advocacy of a version of preference utilitarianism as a method of addressing environmental issues involves a quite contentious evaluative commitment. In the second place, their proposal to set some store by people's aversion to environmental loss implies a fairly particular evaluative commitment. For it cannot plausibly be supposed that they would, or should, count in *any* aversion (or preference), whatever its nature, since some aversions and preferences might be quite disgraceful. The decision to 'count in' this particular aversion suggests an evaluative endorsement of its content. There is, I am suggesting, an implicit commitment by the *Blueprint* authors to the protection of natural capital in something other than the purely social scientific sense which they explicitly avow. But what sense is that?

VI

In a further attempt to accommodate the environmental interest in nature, Bryan Norton purports to strike out in a new direction by proposing what he terms a 'scientific contextual' approach to sustainability. While still firmly centred on human welfare and the recognition of an obligation to 'perpetuate the conditions necessary for the continuation of the human species and of its culture' (Norton, 1992, p. 103), this approach involves a shared rather than an individualistic value system and, above all, recognizes how deeply embedded is human culture in larger natural systems and therefore how necessary is a scientific understanding of the impact of human activities on these larger systems. Such an approach, Norton believes, will result in the recognition of *non-negotiable obligations* regarding our use of certain resources. This is said to represent a departure from the social scientific approach; but only, however, because Norton characterizes the latter as committed to a belief in the unlimited substitutability of resources—i.e., as roughly equivalent to the total capital version of sustainability identified by Pearce. In effect, Norton's position turns out to be very close to that of Pearce, with critical natural capital equating to the sphere of non-negotiable obligations.

However, there is one departure from that position which is highly significant. This emerges when Norton turns to clarifying the Leopoldian notions of 'health' and 'integrity' as applied to ecosystems. Here he makes the interesting suggestion that we should understand 'integrity' as the stronger term, to denote not simply the capacity of the system to maintain autonomous functioning (its health) but also the retention of 'total diversity . . . *the sum total of the species and associations that have held sway, historically*' (Norton, 1992, p. 107, italics added). I propose to build on this suggestion.

The more constrained social scientific interpretation of sustainable development, which requires the maintenance of natural capital specifically, or the recognition of non-negotiable obligations, was supposed to secure the environmental interest in nature. But this, in its 'pure' form, I have argued, it does not do. Maintaining equivalence of function, flow of services or ecosystem health is not enough. What is as important, I now suggest, is maintaining enough of the historically particular forms of association and their historically particular components—all the better if they have the marks of nature upon them. Admittedly there are difficulties in giving effect to such a suggestion, because of the immense flexibility in our descriptions of nature, but a useful approach to this problem is to recognize that what is handed down and maintained does need to retain in the process something of its original form and something of its identity: there need to be continuities of form, which constitute what may be called 'units of significance' for us, as well as continuities of matter. The ashes of one's dear ones, for example, are not enough. A more pertinent example, perhaps, is that gene banks are not enough to constitute the preservation of biological diversity. And here, no doubt, a human *perspective* shows through in identifying the units of significance, even if the human *interest* is muted. What is missing from the social scientific approach is the recognition that nature, and all its various component events and processes, is a particular historical phenomenon and to be valued as such. What this means, in turn, is that the simple 'physical stock' interpretation of natural capital is not some crude interpretation which we have to transcend, but actually captures something at the heart of environmental concern.

VII

It is implied, however, in *Blueprint 1* that a pure 'physical stock' interpretation of natural capital is unworkable because it would be incompatible with any use whatsoever of non-renewable resources. But how does the social scientific approach handle this type of natural capital?

One suggestion is that the use of non-renewables does not impinge upon the policy of sustainable development at all. The reasoning is that, by their nature, non-renewables can only be used once and might as well be used now as at any time—whenever 'now' may be (Bowers, 1990, p. 10). Moreover, if the rationale for sustainable development rests on considerations of intergenerational justice, and we assume a Rawlsian account of justice, then using up non-renewables will seem not to be unjust. For, saving the fact that the use of exhaustible resources will create waste products, which may, however, be compensated for by the artificial capital deriving from the use of those resources, no generation will be worse off; and at least one generation will be better off.

But this suggestion seems counter-intuitive and would probably be unwelcome to most environmentalists. A more plausible position to take is that, even if substitute resources can be found for some given resource which is used up, in the sense that they render the same service, to exhaust any resource is still to affect subsequent generations adversely by virtue of narrowing the options which are open to them. If this is accepted, then the social scientific approach to natural capital, as much as the 'physical stock' approach, will be committed to an 'unworkable' embargo on the use of non-renewables. This cannot then be cited as a specific objection to the physical stock approach.

In arguing that conserving nature 'cannot be a simple matter of conserving what currently exists', Michael Jacobs seems to have somewhat different considerations in mind. Nature, he argues, has evolved not simply of its own accord but in conjunction with human development. The natural environment is 'as much "produced" as the more obviously human-made structures of our towns and cities' (Jacobs, 1990, p. 63). Therefore, we have no clear idea what constitutes nature any more and 'the environment cannot provide its own answers'. These remarks, however, seem to express a one-dimensional view of the distinction between what is natural and what is not. Conservationists, for example, would not agree that there is nothing to choose between an ancient hay meadow and a weed-free field of wheat, in view of the prevalence of native species in the former (Nature Conservancy Council, 1989, p. 11). Probably no very sensible answers are forthcoming to the general and context-free question: What constitutes the natural? But ask: What is natural to *this* place?, and answers are usually forthcoming, determined partially by climate and geophysical factors. Even global answers are not as hard to come by as Jacobs makes out. We know that there has naturally come to be an ozone layer around the earth and that the notorious 'hole' is a debit so far as natural capital is concerned. Moreover, he himself seems to provide the answer to his own question, 'What is the natural rate of methane emission?', when observing that although it is naturally emitted by animals, such emissions are significantly boosted by concentrations of domestic livestock. His point that carcinogenic hydrocarbons are emitted naturally from vegetation and microbial decomposition reveals not that there is any difficulty in deciding what counts as the conservation of nature in the physical sense, but only that what is natural is not always good for humans.

VIII

Clearly, much more remains to be said concerning the workability of a 'physical stock' interpretation of natural capital; but probably the biggest obstacle to its acceptance concerns the *desirability* of conserving natural capital understood in this sense. Whereas the social scientific account provides an obvious incentive for not allowing natural capital to decline, namely, justice and the welfare of future generations, such an incentive is notably absent from the 'physical stock' account. Even friends of the natural seem to feel obliged to concede that: 'It will not do to argue that what is natural is necessarily of value' (Elliot, 1982, p. 86).

Let us take the claim under discussion to be the simple claim that 'nature is good'. This claim may be interpreted in two ways. First, it may be interpreted as a conceptual claim—as the claim that *whatever* is natural is good, by virtue of the meaning of the term 'natural'. Second, it may be interpreted as a moral claim—as a simple ascription of value to nature. Taken in the first way, the claim is indefensible. For if we assume as a possibility that nature might have been otherwise, we would be committed to the view that all possible (natural) worlds are good. But some possible (natural) worlds might be indistinguishable from, say, the more hideous medieval depictions of hell, which we would shrink from describing as good. Moreover, the claim commits the most obvious form of 'naturalistic fallacy', of deducing a value judgement from a factual judgement.

But the claim may also be construed as a straightforward value judgement—a simple and unqualified affirmation of the goodness of nature. Rather than construe the term 'nature' in this context as an implicit universal—as designating any nature that might possibly exist, we may construe it instead as a 'rigid designator'—as designating the real and unique historical nature of which we form a part. Taken in this way, the claim is, I believe, defensible. For, returning, first, to the objection raised by Robert Elliot, he continues the passage cited by averring: 'Sickness and disease are natural . . . and are certainly not good'. Such examples are indeed commonly thought to present a problem for the claim that nature is good. This objection faces a simple dilemma. Either he is using 'good' in an unqualified sense, or he is using it in a qualified sense. If he is using it in an unqualified sense, then he is not producing an objection to the original claim, but simply issuing a counter-claim. If, on the other hand, he is using it in a qualified sense, i.e., as claiming that sickness and disease are not good for those whom they afflict, then he has not produced an objection at all, since this claim is perfectly compatible with the truth of the original claim.

As has been suggested, there are possible (natural) worlds which one might judge to be bad. There are also possible (natural) worlds which one might judge to be better than the actual natural world.[1] Both of these possibilities are compatible with, and should not inhibit, the simple affirmation that the actual natural world as we know it is good.[2] It should be observed, and sometimes is not, that this affirmation, in turn, does not imply that human modification of nature is bad, or that natural processes are always and everywhere to be preferred to humanly modified ones; nor is it incompatible with the recognition that many naturally occurring processes are bad for humans. Construed in the simple and basic way which I have described, it seems to me eminently defensible.

[1] Hence I am not simply reiterating the theological defence against the problem of evil, which claims that this is the best of all possible worlds.

[2] The judgement is simple. The reasons for making it are complex, and nowhere more eloquently elaborated than in Holmes Rolston's *Environmental Ethics* (Rolston, 1988).

Its justification lies mainly in the manifest perversity of complaining about the conditions which have made one's life possible, and in supposing that there might have been a choice about which bits of nature should have existed. But the claim is not only defensible. It also seems to me true that no defence of the environment is ultimately secure which does not embody such an affirmation.

Some Philosophical Assessments of Environmental Disobedience

PETER LIST

Since the late 1970s there has been within the world-wide environmental movement increasing dissatisfaction with moderate or reform environmentalism, and more radical tactics have been advocated and used to respond to the human destruction of nature. These range from typical kinds of political protest, such as rallies and marches, to environmental civil disobedience and the more militant environmental actions known as 'monkey-wrenching', 'ecotage', or 'ecosabotage'.[1] The use of these 'ecotactics' has led inevitably to controversy in the environmental movement itself and in public discussions of environmentalism in North America and elsewhere. The same cannot be said, however, about academic philosophy, where it is rare to find assessments of these actions or of their connections to the wealth of philosophical ideas in environmental ethics and ecophilosophy.[2] At the same time there are many traditional philosophical theories that have implications for these kinds of behaviour even though the theories were constructed originally without examples of ecotactics in mind. In particular, theories about the nature and justifications of civil disobedience provide yardsticks by which some forms of environmental disobedience can be assessed, and I will turn to two widely known philosophical accounts, those of John Rawls and Carl Cohen, to consider how well they accomplish this task.

The issue I will consider is as follows: what do these accounts imply about the ethical reasoning underlying the use of the more uncompromising ecotactics? Since this is a question about the applicability of philosophy, I shall match up the assessments of Rawls and Cohen against specific examples of environmental disobedience. In the process I will argue that these philosophical theories are only partially illuminating as evaluations of the justifications behind these cases. One of them fails to take adequately into

[1] For historical accounts of radical environmental protest, especially in the United States, see Scarce, 1990 and the introduction to List, 1993.

[2] Recent exceptions include Michael Martin's careful evaluation of ecosabotage (1990) and, to a lesser degree, Bill Devall and George Sessions on 'ecological resisting' (1985) and Arne Naess on 'direct action' (1989).

consideration the environmental ethics of the disobedients in generating conclusions about the political morality of their actions. The other establishes a rather strict intellectual standard for that reasoning, a standard that it cannot meet. But it is a standard that it need not meet, I will suggest.

Although it is impossible, in a short compass, to give examples of the many kinds of ecotactics that generate controversy, I will describe two cases that are relevant to the analyses of Rawls and Cohen. These will be abstracted from real examples to facilitate an understanding of their features and the force of the reasoning behind them.

Case #1: Logging Protests in an Old-Growth Forest

The members of a forest action group decide to participate in several acts of disobedience against the clear-cutting of old-growth Douglas fir forests in one of the national forests of Oregon, in the American Pacific Northwest, that is managed by the United States Forest Service. Their aim is to halt logging throughout the summer in an area of the forest called the 'Cathedral Grove' by blockading logging roads so that log trucks will not be able to gain access to the grove. One morning in June, twenty-six of them drive to a logging road near the grove that is officially closed to the public while logging is proceeding. Under the eyes of the local sheriff, several of his deputies, and some newspaper reporters, they calmly walk up the road to a small bridge and 'occupy it'. They form lines across the bridge, sitting down so as to completely block the path of any log trucks or other vehicles. Several log trucks drive up to the bridge, on their way to the grove, and pull very close to the protesters, but stop when it is clear that they will not move.

The sheriff's deputies ask the protesters to disperse, claiming that they are breaking the law. About half of them get up and leave voluntarily, but the other half refuse to budge, saying that they are there to protect and defend the forest wilderness and are not leaving until the clear-cutting ceases. The deputies then announce that the remaining protesters are under arrest. The protesters go limp, so the deputies must carry them off the bridge, one by one, to some waiting vehicles. Once the protesters are loaded up, they are driven to a mobile booking station on a public highway nearby for legal processing. But they refuse to give their names or any other information, and hence are charged with the misdemeanour of disorderly conduct and driven to a county jail, some fifty miles away.

On arriving at the jail, they are again processed and put in cells to spend the night. The next morning they are brought to court and, over objections from the district attorney, are asked to sign release agreements on condition that they remain law-abiding citizens. Most of them do and are released, but a few do not because it means that they cannot return to the logging site, so they are placed back in their cells to await trial. The blockade succeeds in stopping log trucks for several hours, but once the protesters are carted away, the log trucks continue their work, and the clear-cutting of the grove continues.

During the next two months, other groups of protesters carry on with this campaign by conducting additional blockades of the same logging road. One of the blockades lasts for a day; several are shorter than this. More protesters are arrested and charged with disorderly conduct. Some are released on their own recognizance; others remain in jail because they refuse to give their names or other information to the authorities.[3]

A Rawlsian Analysis of Case #1

This is a very typical kind of case of environmental civil disobedience, and there is certainly nothing unusual in the tactics. The protesters follow the nonviolent methods used by many other groups in the United States to protest against such things as nuclear weapons testing on inland sites. How then does Rawls's theory of civil disobedience apply to the case?

In his well-known and highly acclaimed book, *A Theory of Justice*, Rawls defines civil disobedience in a fairly standard way; he says that it is 'a public, nonviolent, conscientious yet political act contrary to law usually done with the aim of bringing about a change in the law or policies of the government' (Rawls, 1971, p. 364). He also states that it 'addresses the sense of justice of the majority of the community' and asserts that the 'principles of social cooperation among free and equal men are not being respected' (Rawls, 1971, p. 364). The idea is that civil disobedience must be guided and justified by political principles, which to Rawls means 'the principles of justice which regulate the constitu-

---

[3] This case is based on a series of actions that were undertaken by the Cathedral Forest Action Group and some members of the radical environmental group Earth First! in the summer of 1984, in the western Oregon Cascades. They were reported in local newspapers and in the *Earth First!* journal, excerpts from which are reprinted in List, 1993, pp. 195–201.

tion and social institutions generally' in an ideal political democracy (Rawls, 1971, p. 365). The point is that it 'does not appeal to principles of personal morality or to religious doctrines', though these may 'coincide with and support' the claims of the disobedients. Moreover the act must be public which means that it must be addressed to 'public principles' of justice and be done in public. That is, it must be engaged in openly with fair and advance notice, cannot be covert or secretive (Rawls, 1971, p. 366). It is nonviolent for two reasons: first because it is a mode of address and gives voice to 'conscientious and deeply held convictions'; thus 'while it may warn and admonish, it is not itself a threat'. But second because it 'expresses disobedience to law within the limits of fidelity to law'. This is shown both in the character of the act and in the willingness of practitioners to accept the consequences of their actions.

Notice that in many respects, the logging protests conform to these definitional conditions. For the sake of argument, one can assume that the protests occur in a democratic regime that is nearly just and backed by a constitution that is accepted by the protesters. These acts are obviously public, nonviolent ones that involve law breaking and are aimed at changing the environmental policies of the government. They are conscientiously motivated and addressed to a sense of justice in the public at large and perhaps in those who legislate, create, and administer these policies in the national government.

Rawlsian Requirements and the Protesters' Reasons

But there are some crucial respects in which Rawls's account does not fit the situation of the protesters very well, and this can be seen by looking more closely at the reasoning behind their actions. Rawls argues that, for acts of civil disobedience to be justified acts, they must conform to certain additional conditions. Most importantly, they must be limited to 'substantial and clear' injustices in the society and 'preferably to those which block . . . the way to removing other injustices' (Rawls, 1971, p. 372). This means that they must be directed at violations not of just any principles of social justice but of those that Rawls outlines in his theory of justice. The injustices must thus be 'serious infringements of the first principle of justice, the principle of equal liberty, and . . . blatant violations of the second part of the second principle, the principle of fair equality of opportunity' (Rawls, 1971, p. 372). Rawls's first principle refers to the equal right of all citizens to certain equal basic liberties, such as the right to vote, to hold public office, to freedom of speech and assembly, to possess and hold property, and to be free from arbitrary arrest and seizure. The second part of the second principle states that social and economic inequalities are to be arranged so that they are attached to offices and positions open to all, backed up by fair equality of opportunity. In light of these Rawlsian requirements, what reasons do the protesters give for their actions? Interviews with the protesters reveal that they were following their consciences in participating in these block-ades and were trying to protect valuable life on earth. They argue that logging the Cathedral Grove poses an imminent threat to the forest environment of the western Oregon Cascade Mountains because a rare Douglas fir, low-elevation forest wilderness ecosys-tem will be endangered. The area contains one of the last and best examples of such an ecosystem left in the Cascades, and the grove is one part of that system. It is an important genetic reservoir for scientific research and education and provides invaluable habitat for a variety of birds and animals, some unique to old-growth forests. The amount of wildlife in the area will diminish drastically if logging continues, and other wild animals will be pushed out of their local habitats. Logging will also cause soil erosion, landslides next to logging roads, pollution of streams with logging debris, rechannelization of forest streams, and serious alterations to the food chains in the area.

The protesters state that they see the grove as a 'spiritual' haven because of its cathedral-like trees and inspirational natural quali-ties, and personally have deep reverence for it as a result. It pro-vides a place for humans to commune with nature in peace and to understand nature's secrets. They and other members of the pub-lic will thus in the future be deprived of spiritual nourishment if the grove is cut.

Additionally, they argue that they had no other choice but to commit disobedience because they exhausted all other means of halting logging in the grove and have been attempting to have the surrounding area legally designated as wilderness. Once the clear-cutting is completed, it will be impossible to redo what nature has built up over more than five centuries because the grove will be turned into a tree farm and any chance for preserving it as a wilderness will be lost. They have tried for years to get federal protection for more forest wilderness, including the Grove, unsuc-cessfully. They have filed many lawsuits, with little effect, and no longer have the money to bring further legal actions against the government. They have written letters to politicians and testified at the relevant public hearings held by the Forest Service on the area, all to no avail. Court rulings have leaned away from protection of this particular forested wilderness and thus they had to blockade the road. One reason they started their disobedience campaign was to arouse the public into calling for new legislation from the United States Congress that would preserve the area. They also claim that the Forest Service is determined to road and harvest the area as soon as possible so that it will be unsuitable for any subsequent designation. The area had been opened up for logging earlier in the year following passage of the federal Wilderness Protection Act, which protects some of the forests near the Grove, but less than ten per cent of the amount the protesters would like to have set aside. In the meantime the Forest Service has contracted out the logging to a private company, in accordance with legal requirements, and the logging has begun.

Now it is clear that, to a degree, these reasons correspond with Rawlsian conditions. Thus the protesters imply that they are addressing the sense of justice of the public about preserving the grove, and are attempting to move the public to action. They also argue that they have exhausted their routes of appeal; that this is truly a last resort for saving this particular wilderness. On the other hand, the other reasons they cite are different: they refer to such important matters as the irreversible harm and damage that will be done to natural systems, the destruction of wild and precious habitat for wild animals, the violation of their own needs for spiritual and religious experience in nature, the possibilities of utilizing the grove for other human benefits, and the uniqueness of the place. Are these reasons relevant in a Rawlsian political justification?

A Response to the Rawlsian Account

If one combines Rawls's special justice condition with his condition that the reasoning of disobedients cannot refer to principles of personal morality or religious conviction, then many of the reasons that the protesters take to be really important and to substantively justify their behaviour, as they see it, are directly irrelevant in a Rawlsian political justification of their actions. The protesters cite no infringements of their fundamental human liberties in the political system and no violations of equality of opportunity or of justice in the distribution of wealth or income. Thus their political argument cannot completely succeed, logically speaking. In effect, the deepest matters of personal morality and environmental ethics have no bearing on their political appeal except as noted, and that appeal is not otherwise a strong one by Rawlsian criteria. Yet, on the face of it, this is surely an odd result.

To make this conclusion even more evident, suppose we add some details about the relationship between their ethical and political reasoning: suppose that the protesters profess to follow deep ecology principles. They believe that humans need to institute deep changes in their attitudes towards nature; they need a new biocentred philosophy that emphasizes such ideas as the intrinsic value of all natural objects and systems, the biocentric equality of all species, the submergence of the human self in a larger, natural self, and the importance of biodiversity. In agreement with this, they insist that political philosophies be jettisoned that focus only on human political arrangements and associations, on human liberties and rights, on human opportunities and requirements, and on human-centred justice. They ask that philosophies be substituted that are oriented around these deep ecology ideas, and that consequently regard trees, animals, and natural systems not as ancillary background to political thinking but as the very core of political reality and reflection. The protesters also believe that the Rawlsian theory of social justice is hopelessly human-centred or anthropocentric; it puts nature second to human interests and concerns, and is thus outmoded. According to the protesters' logic, a Rawlsian account only makes limited sense in this situation, for it does not allow that ecological ideas could serve as part of the primary intellectual basis for a political system.

Given the force and content of this reasoning, I suggest that this should lead one to question the relevance of Rawlsian principles and conditions in justifying these forms of environmental civil disobedience. Rawls's account tells us very little that we need to know to understand or assess the ethical bases of the reasoning, and the same could be said of numerous other common cases of environmental civil disobedience where this kind of thinking prevails.

Rawls sees civil disobedience as a means of appeal to the 'moral basis of civic life' and thus as a particular kind of political appeal, an appeal to principles of human justice that regulate the political system in a constitutional democracy, in a nearly ideal case. Given his description of the nature of justice, it has very little to do then with that vast class of relationships and that significant area of morality that ecophilosophers have been pointing to for some twenty years or so, namely, with the primary relationships between humans and natural objects and natural systems, and with the ecological moralities that are constructed out of these bases. Rawls's theory has nothing directly to say about injustices or harms committed by humans against non-humans or non-human systems, nothing much to say about ecological injustice. It is thus not a theory that could account for these kinds of environmental civil disobedience, for it is crucial in them that political and moral conceptions be extended or applied, in a substantial way, to non-humans and to other parts of nature or the environment.

Let me turn to a slightly different case of environmental disobedience, one also based in a real situation, to evaluate Carl Cohen's analysis. Cohen's account, I shall argue, doesn't yield the same result as Rawls's account, but it does make some forms of ecological thinking problematic on other grounds.

Case #2: Ramming Drift-Net Boats on the Pacific

An environmental group decides to outfit an ocean vessel in a campaign to ram drift-netting ships in the Pacific Ocean before any international regulations or laws of nation-states have made drift-netting fishing methods illegal or a violation of international policy. The environmental group believes that drift-netters are catching a large number of sea birds and mammals in their nets, not to mention an inordinate number of fish and squid, and that this is not in any way necessary, given alternative methods of catching fish, nor justified given the destruction it wreaks on sea birds and on marine mammals such as dolphins, seals, sea lions and sea turtles. The netting technique does not permit trapped sea animals to be readily freed from its deadly grasp, and most of them are traumatized by strangulation and suffocation, as they die in the nets. The environmental group is worried about a sudden and dramatic drop in the populations of some key mammals and sea birds and believes that the ecological system of the ocean is being turned into a biological wasteland by these methods.

The group waits several years for nation-states and the United Nations to take action to prevent or regulate drift-netting, but nothing is done. It thus announces its intention ahead of time to go after the drift-netters and makes very clear what it will do once it locates offending ships: it will ram them in such a way that their drift-nets will be disabled. After sailing to mid-ocean and finding a small fleet of drift-net boats, it spends considerable time following them to document the serious effects that their use of drift-nets is having on sea mammals supposedly 'incidental' to their real catch. It films the nets as they are retrieved and sea mammals are being hauled aboard. Finally, it believes that it has seen more than enough and decides to take direct action: it repeatedly warns one of the drift-net vessels to stop, but it continues anyway, fending off the warnings by ignoring them. The environmental vessel is more swift than the other vessel, and its skill is such that it can deftly ram it at just the right place along the side of the hull where the net-retrieval gear is attached, damaging the gear and cleanly severing the net. It proceeds to do so and subsequently retrieves the net and disposes of it so that it can never be used again, by weighing it down and sinking it below. It then pursues several other drift-net boats in the fleet and succeeds in doing the same, eventually chasing the whole fleet out of the fishing grounds. Once it is finished with this 'mission', the environmental ship heads for port with its evidence where it holds a press conference to reveal what the drift-netters are doing. The drift-netting fleet is composed of boats from only one nation so the captain of the protesting boat also contacts officials of that nation, tells them what his vessel has done, and invites them to press legal charges. He states that he and his crew are ready to contest any charges at either an international court or a court in the nation itself. But no charges are forthcoming.[4]

Cohen on Higher Law Justifications of Civil Disobedience

Like Rawls, Cohen provides a theory about the way justifications of disobedience should be understood.[5] He argues that although there are as many possible defences of civil disobedience as there are acts of this sort, there are basically only two general paths that can justify these actions, the utilitarian and higher law approaches, and that the higher law approach cannot succeed. He also implies that the civil disobedient is likely to place reliance on one or the other of these routes (Cohen, 1971, p. 104). If Cohen is correct, higher law justifications of environmental disobedience would be destined to fail and any higher law reasoning in Case #2 would not work.

How does Cohen define civil disobedience? Cohen offers a much more 'loose' definition of civil disobedience than Rawls

[4] This case is modelled after actions of Paul Watson's Sea Shepherd Society in the North Pacific, in the summer of 1990, and is excerpted in List, 1993, pp. 169–171 and 177–184. Watson's appeal to ecological laws is reported in his book *Sea Shepherd* (1982) and in a talk he gave on 'environmental advocacy and civil disobedience' at the Public Interest Law Conference, University of Oregon Law School, Eugene, Oregon, March 1990.

[5] Michael Martin has shown that philosophical theories of civil disobedience can provide insights into less civil forms of environmental disobedience, such as ecosabotage, and has fruitfully utilized Cohen's analysis of civil disobedience with this idea in mind (Martin, 1990, p. 298).

does, one that is more likely to capture the variety of real cases. He says, simply, that it is 'an act of protest, deliberately unlawful, conscientiously and publicly performed' which has as its target a law, policy or practice of a government or private party (Cohen, 1971, p. 39). On the face of it, Case #2 may not appear to coincide completely with this definition because both boats are far out in the ocean, away from the reach or applicability of the laws of political states, and at the time no government has assumed any jurisdiction over drift-netting. Nevertheless, even if the drift-netters are not breaking laws, very likely some rules of nautical navigation are violated by the protesting ship, and this would be enough to bring the case under Cohen's criteria. But to make it a case where higher law is invoked, the environmental group must supply additional reasoning for its actions.

Suppose, then, that the captain of the environmental ship argues that several higher ecological laws are being violated by the use of these drift-netting methods; specifically, he cites three such 'laws'. First, he says, is the law that all forms of life are interdependent, which means that predator-prey relationships are important for maintaining population control in natural ecosystems. In this case the actions of the drift-netters are violating predator-prey relationships between the various marine species through excessive human predation. Second, he appeals to the law of diversity, that diversity promotes stability, and concludes that actions of the drift-netters are seriously reducing the diversity of ocean species and the stability of the ocean ecosystem. The system may be heading for ecological collapse. Third, he argues that all resources are finite and that this applies to marine resources in the oceans. Using drift-netting methods violates this law by decimating populations of sea mammals, birds and fish. Thus, he implies, any maritime rule about interference with the sea-going activities of another vessel is superseded by the higher authority of ecological principles. The actions of ramming the drift-netting boats may be violations of these lesser rules of passage, but the actions of the drift-netters are more serious crimes against nature. When the rules of states conflict with these higher laws, one has no obligation to obey them. The protesting boat, he concludes, has taken a form of 'direct action' to block the fishing fleet from continuing to violate these laws and commit further crimes. Moreover, the captain points out that his ship has certain ethical rules about disobedience like this that prohibit him from doing anything to jeopardize or harm any form of life. He points out that, in this action, no one is injured, nothing more than some damage to machines is done, and he and his crew have succeeded in doing what they set out to do: to at least temporarily disable the drift-netting capacity of the offending boats, to save a good many sea mammals and birds, to thwart drift-netting in that part of the ocean, and to educate both the drift-netters and the international community about the ecological evils of drift-netting.

Cohen's Criticism of Higher Law Justifications

Why does Cohen argue that higher law justifications will not work in this kind of case? According to him, these justifications supposedly function by appealing either to divine laws that have a theological base or to natural laws that are grounded in the universe. In either situation their authority is supposedly supreme over the laws of states and can be validated either by some religious authority, revelation or belief, or by individual human conscience, reason or moral sense (Cohen, 1971, p. 111). The idea is that if the positive laws of a nation-state conflict with or violate these more supreme laws, even if they are legitimate enactments of legitimate states, one has no obligation to follow them and in fact has a right to disobey them (Cohen, 1971, p. 105). The higher laws have a very special character and a status different from the laws of states, on this theory. They provide a 'purely moral justification' of acts that are deliberate violations of positive laws. Clearly, then, an important part of the reasoning in Case #2 follows this line of thinking.

In Cohen's estimation, this is a 'venerable' form of argument that has deep roots in western philosophy and 'uncountable manifestations' in the political and religious documents of our cultural history. But the appeal is not intellectually satisfactory because of at least two difficulties: (1) the impossibility of reaching an 'objective and reliable judgment' about what the higher laws command or forbid; (2) the impossibility of reaching any such judgment about how the laws apply to concrete cases, without appealing to some judicial authority (Cohen, 1971, p. 114).[6]

With regard to the first difficulty, Cohen does not give any clear criteria for determining what an 'objective and reliable' judgment would be like, but he does raise some of the standard objections that, at one time, were typically made about such appeals. Thus he indicates that this has something to do with the difficulty of supplying 'publicly verifiable proof' that the laws are what the disobe-

[6] Cohen adds a third difficulty that I will not consider, the problem that these laws could at best justify direct civil disobedience rather than indirect.

dients claim that they are. Moreover the disobedients must be pre-
pared to defend the authority and reliability of the faculties they
use to verify these laws, which to Cohen includes such methods as
appealing to personal conscience, moral intuition, and self-evi-
dence. They need some technique that is intersubjectively available, verifiable, and produces similar results. Unfortunately, he
suggests, it is these special faculties and the results they supposedly yield that sceptics question. The demands of higher law are only
convincing to those who already believe in them, and many people
neither accept these laws nor believe that one can find 'satisfactory
rational grounds' for acknowledging the authority of these faculties (Cohen, 1971, pp. 115–116).

With respect to the second difficulty, the applications of higher
laws to concrete situations produce uncertainties and conflicts.
Even if the laws are agreed upon, it is 'notoriously difficult' in any
complicated situation to apply them, especially without some
established and respected judicial system. One reason for this is
the very generality of the laws, and thus their situational vagueness. This produces different and conflicting interpretations that
would normally be settled by a system of legal institutions and
actors. But no such system is available to the disobedients. Thus
they must fall back on their own partial and biased judgments and
decide these matters in their own cases, a situation that is distorted
at the outset by their involvement in the disobedience. In the end,
then, this kind of appeal rests on purely personal convictions, and
what begins with the promise of universality and certainty ends in
'a morass of idiosyncrasy and subjectivity' (Cohen, 1971, p. 118).
On the other hand, such appeals cannot be wholly disproven
either. They elude 'public falsification', and the ardent disobedient
may stick to higher laws even in the face of punishment, censure,
and objections from opponents. Cohen concludes from all of this
that the burden of proof lies with the protesters; they must convince sceptics that their appeals are objective.[7]

A Response to Cohen on Higher Laws

Cohen's critique is obviously designed to be a thorough one; it
raises several thorny philosophical questions and makes some general assumptions about moral reasoning that hold it to a rather
strict, even impossible, standard. With regard to ecological laws,

[7] Martin is so convinced that this critique is correct that he thinks it
applies to any use of higher laws to justify ecosabotage. See Martin, 1990,
p. 299, note 29.

his account challenges the environmentalist reasoner to clearly identify those laws and explain how they are to be justified and applied in a non-controversial way. Cohen thus gives environmental disobedients and moralists a heavy philosophical burden to bear. Because the issues he raises are many, I can address only several of them. I want to consider first what the status of ecological laws is in ecology and then determine whether there is not some reasonable way of understanding how ecological principles could serve to justify environmental disobedience. In the process I will consider the question of whether ecological morality must ultimately fail to be convincing in justifying the reasoning in Case #2 if it cannot rest on precise laws in ecology.

The Status of Ecological Laws

Robert McIntosh, the historian of ecology, makes admirably clear that there has long been considerable disagreement amongst ecologists about the nature of ecology as a science, and that this applies to ecologists' beliefs about ecological laws as well. Ecologists have raised questions about what the laws are and, in some cases, whether they even exist.

McIntosh argues that the meaning that ecologists typically ascribe to the idea of a 'law' is that of a universal descriptive generalization about regularities or patterns in such things as species or communities. But the problem is that they have never arrived at a set of generally accepted descriptions or constants of this kind and have been unable to transform the generalizations they have proposed into quantifiable laws as one finds in the physical sciences. McIntosh carefully shows that there are many different ideas that have been represented as significant candidates for ecological law in the history of this discipline. The lists of candidates have ranged in number from one to over thirty, and there is no consensus on what counts. Moreover, ecologists have not agreed upon the dimensions of ecology theory, the special context in which these laws would make sense for the purposes of prediction and explanation (McIntosh, 1985, pp. 272–273).

Another difficulty he points to is that the laws that are cited are mostly unhelpful in revealing anything about the dimensions of human behaviour. The relevance of non-human ecology for deciphering human ecology has never been very clear, and disputes about this continue to this day. Ecological scientists do not typically study human populations and communities but non-human ones, and thus it is uncertain precisely how their conclusions could

195

apply to humans or even to human interactions with non-human nature. At the same time, they are convinced that ecology has something important to say about these matters, and few dispute the obvious fact that these interactions are significant or that humans have serious impacts on non-human natural systems.

What this means in part is that any 'normative' appeal to a precise scientific ecology must remain in doubt. Though Cohen does not say as much, at this point in scientific history, environmentalists' appeals to ecology to verify 'higher' ecological laws are infected by the difficulties of knowing exactly what those laws are and of confirming their truth. However, this is a problem that scientists must resolve, and not ecological moralists, and it is at least possible that it will be resolved in the future. There is a communal system in place, in science, for accomplishing this. In addition, the laws of ecology are subject to the methods of validation and proof that exist in the biological sciences. This means that, if there is a theoretical difficulty in ecology in determining how to verify its laws, it is certainly a vastly different problem from that of justifying supernatural religious laws. The first difficulty Cohen mentions, then, is not quite as serious as he implies that it is.

Ecological Principles for Environmental Disobedience

Does this lack of historical precision and agreement mean that the appeal to ecological principles does not make any sense in justifying environmental civil disobedience? I would suggest that it does only if one takes personal and social moral principles to be scientific laws that require the validation of ecology. If one attributes a more modest role to ecology, this discipline can serve more modest functions. It does after all help us understand various lesser regularities and facts about specific ecosystems and non-human communities, and it can provide valuable information about human impacts on those natural systems. It can thus have another sort of utility in ecological moral reasoning. As Kristin Shrader-Frechette has ably argued, ecological science has a 'heuristic' power even if it has very little predictive power (Shrader-Frechette, 1993, p. 221).[8] Some of its pronouncements, even its most general ones, such as those about homeostasis or stability, may be questionable as precise truths, but ecological morality need not rest on such a strict

[8] Recently, Kristin Shrader-Frechette has nicely outlined the reasons why ecologists have difficulty understanding basic ecological processes. See Shrader-Frechette, 1993.

scientific basis, if that makes sense at all. Ethical justifications of environmental activism can be reasonable if they realize the limits of ecological generalizations and utilize these more specific ecological data in their premises. Ecology is a discipline that does not directly delineate the dimensions of ecological ethics anyway, but provides it with empirical understanding.

As one can see in Case #2, the arguments of the protesters do appeal to the certainty of higher ecological laws, as they understand them, and appear to borrow from the authority of ecological science. Insofar as they do, Cohen's criticisms have merit. There are yet no agreed-upon laws in ecology, thus the authority of ecological science cannot be invoked to conclusively undergird some of the reasoning in this case. However, ecological moralists need not take these 'truths' to be scientific laws alone; they can also be understood as general ethical principles that are verified by common sense and ecological observation in particular instances. In Case #2, these general principles could function as 'first-order ethical principles' that humans violate at their peril and at the risk of damage to non-human life and natural systems.

In any event, it takes little imagination to understand that these kinds of appeals can make sense in circumstances like those cited in Case #2. Devastation of large numbers of marine mammals through massively efficient technological devices such as drift-nets can obviously destroy significant populations of marine mammals, birds, and fish, seriously disturb ocean food-chains, and upset the stability of marine ecosystems, even if marine ecology cannot produce all of the relevant data that would back up these beliefs. The special and particular observations of marine scientists and other competent persons familiar with ocean ecosystems can contribute to an understanding of these facts and provide a rational enough basis for acting on them. The application of these principles need not be so biased and conflict-ridden that it leads inevitably to a morass of subjectivity and special pleading.

If one also believes that ecological morality consists of other important principles, such as the intrinsic or inherent worth of non-human species and systems, and the human responsibility not to cause harm to these parts of non-human nature; if one is convinced that sea creatures do have the capacity to suffer needlessly at human hands, and that ocean systems do provide crucial benefits to other animals, including humans, the search for an 'objective' foundation for ecological morality in this case is beside the point. The important question is not: Is there some completely objective way to verify higher ecological laws and thus infuse environmental arguments with absolute certainty? but: What ethical principles and ecological data are needed to effectively criticize drift-netting practices in these kinds of cases?

Conclusion

In the end, actions like those in Cases #1 and #2 should be assessed against standards of ecological and personal morality rather than strict ecological science or those philosophical theories of disobedience and political obligation discussed above. Ecological moralities can make rough sense of the factual circumstances and the ethical considerations that are important in these cases, and they can be connected to developing ecocentric political thinking that is slowly emerging in the world. Environmental disobedience is strongly ecological in orientation but need not be fastidiously scientific. It can be supported by ethical principles of an ecological and non-ecological sort and by specific ecological data, but it can also exhibit a personal morality of deep commitment to do something about the injustices that human societies, organizations, and individuals are perpetrating against non-human nature. Many environmental disobedients are concerned with the failure of governments to respond to ecological injustice and with their personal responsibilities to eliminate ecological evils. They would find unintelligible the demand that they tie their reasoning to anthropocentric political theories or to objective moral criteria that cannot be satisfied by human moral reasoning.[9]

[9] I am indebted to Professor Shrader-Frechette's work for clarifying some of my own thoughts about the functions of ecological principles in ethical reasoning.

Global Environmental Justice

DALE JAMIESON

Philosophers, like generals, tend to fight the last war. While activists and policy-makers are in the trenches fighting the problems of today, intellectuals are typically studying the problems of yesterday.

There are some good reasons for this. It is more difficult to assess and interpret present events than those which are behind us. Time is needed for reflection and to gather reliable information about what has occurred. The desire to understand leads to a style of life that is primarily contemplative and retrospective.

But there are also bad reasons for the relative neglect of contemporary problems. Philosophers typically write about what other philosophers write about, and if no-one has written about a problem it is difficult to get anyone to write about it. Philosophy is also a deeply historical subject and for the most part the tradition either has been silent about environmental problems or what it has said is itself part of the problem. Moreover, philosophers have a toolbox of theories, methods and concepts and like most people they want to work on problems that their tools can help to solve. And as I shall try to show, the results of applying philosophical theories of justice to problems of the global environment are disappointing.

One old philosophical wrangle which appears quaint in the context of today is the debate over whether and why there are duties and obligations that transcend national boundaries. It is easy to see why this was a problem in the past. Famines and other extreme events have occurred throughout history, but in many cases it was not known outside the affected regions that people were dying. Even when it was known and people were willing to help, little could be done to help those in need. When people are not culpably ignorant and they are not in a position to be efficacious there is little point in ascribing duties to them. Today things are very different with respect to information and causal efficacy. We live in an age in which national boundaries are porous with respect to almost everything of importance: people, power, money and information, to name a few. These help to make obligations possible. If people, power, money and information are so transnational in their movements, it is hard to believe that duties and obligations are confined by borders.

Dale Jamieson

A turning point in popular consciousness about transnational duties was the Ethiopian famine of 1978. The fact that people in Africa were dying on a massive scale from the lack of what people in the North have in excess could not be denied. Since then images of dying children have regularly been brought into the living rooms of the industrialized world. With images so stark and ubiquitous the old tactics of psychological evasion have begun to wither. We can no longer claim ignorance about the conditions of extreme poverty in which more than a billion people live. With the advent of jumbo jets and new technologies it can no longer be maintained that nothing can be done to help those in need who live beyond our national boundaries.

For present purposes I will assume that this old philosophical dispute has been resolved and that there are transnational duties and obligations.[1] I will assume further that it is meaningful to discuss whether some of these duties and obligations are related to ideals of global justice.

I will ignore many complications. I will use the terms 'duty' and 'obligation' more or less interchangeably, and will do the same with the terms 'global' and 'international'. I will be vague about the conditions under which a transnational duty is a duty of justice. I will simply assume that people have transnational duties and that it is an open question whether or not some of these are duties of justice. Some may deny that rich countries have duties of justice to intervene in Bosnia or Somalia (for example), but few people (I hope) would assert that it is meaningless or futile to even discuss whether or not they have such duties.

Our present topic arises because of the juxtaposition of the idea of global justice with that of environmental justice. In recent years the term 'environmental' has been used to modify all sorts of traditional harms and wrongs: racism, elitism, fascism, terrorism, blackmail and so on. In the domestic American context discussions of environmental justice are typically about the fact that the poor suffer disproportionately from the environmental pollution produced by society at large. Dramatic examples of this include the white working-class neighbourhood in Love Canal, New York, that was built on top of a toxic waste dump; the ongoing problem of uranium tailings negligently disposed of on Indian reservations in New Mexico and Arizona; and the continuing attempts to locate toxic waste dumps in poor black communities in the South. (For discussion of some of these issues see Bryant and Mohai, 1992.) In

[1] Of course there are still those who would deny that there are such duties. For discussion and references see Beitz, 1979, pp. 15–27.

the international context there are similar examples. Questions about global environmental justice are raised when rich countries export toxic wastes to poor countries, sell pesticides to them that have been banned domestically or make preservationist demands that would affect their prospects for development.

During the UNCED negotiations in Rio de Janeiro the Bush administration grumbled that calls for global environmental justice were just attempts to resurrect the 1970s idea of a new international economic order. Those who advocated the creation of a new international economic order wanted to redistribute wealth and power from North to South.[2] Many people viewed the Bush administration's own international environmental policy as similarly anachronistic—the 1980s idea of Reaganomics writ large. If developing countries would privatize their economies and open their markets, then they would become rich enough to protect their share of the global environment. On this view there is no role for transfers or concessions from the rich countries to the poor.

Taken together, these views suggest that the rhetoric of global environmental justice is just the latest wrapping for the old struggle between the world's rich and poor. If both the Bush administration and its critics are right, the only green that world leaders are interested in is money. The main function of the word 'environmental' in 'global environmental justice' is to signal this year's model of last year's concerns, and perhaps to seduce some unwitting environmentalists into aligning with one side or another.

I believe that there is more than this to the idea of global environmental justice. But once the concept is analyzed it does seem to break apart. It does not lend itself naturally to the application of 'big-picture' theories of justice of the sort given to us by Rawls (1971) and Nozick (1974). Indeed, in my view, although the idea of global environmental justice has many elements, in the end it leads us away from concerns about justice between nations and towards notions of individual responsibility and of moral obligations that are mediated by various non-governmental forms of association. I will begin by distinguishing several elements of the idea of global environmental justice.

[2] See 'Declaration on the Establishment of a New International Economic Order', Resolution 3201 (S-VI), 1 May 1974, United Nations General Assembly, *Official Records: Sixth Special Session*, Supplement No. 1 (A/9559) (New York, 1974), p. 3. For discussion see Beitz, 1979, pp. 127–176.

Dale Jamieson

Global Environmental Justice: Expanding the Beneficiaries

Part of what is keyed by the phrase 'global environmental justice' is the idea that we may owe duties of justice to entities that traditionally have been regarded as beyond the pale. These may include wild animals, plants, species, populations, ecosystems, forests, canyons and so on. On this view global environmental justice involves obligations to the global environment.

I agree that we have such obligations, at least to most animals. (My most recent defence of this idea is Jamieson, 1993.) The endangerment and extinction of many animals has been a global project in which many people and countries have been involved directly or indirectly. It makes sense to suppose that people and countries owe duties to creatures who have survived or not yet succumbed to our onslaught.

However plausible this may be, this is not what has been foremost in the minds of those who have been most vociferous in promoting the idea of global environmental justice. They believe that global environmental justice centrally concerns relations among humans rather than relations between humans and non-humans. If we want to understand what many people mean by 'global environmental justice' we will have to look elsewhere.

Global Environmental Justice: A Condition on the Pursuit of Justice

On the previous account the occurrence of the word 'environmental' signalled the expansion of the class of those who are the beneficiaries of justice. On the present account the word 'environmental' refers to a condition on the pursuit of justice.

This element of global environmental justice is an important one but it is probably the least discussed of the three that I will distinguish. Global environmental justice, on this view, is the idea that global justice can only permissibly be pursued in ways that are environment-preserving.

The thought can be explained by an analogy. 'Environmental' can be understood as modifying 'justice' in much the same way as 'sustainable' can be understood as modifying 'development'.[3] On this view, the only permissible paths to development are those which are sustainable. If a pathway is unsustainable then it fails

[3] However, it should be noted that the expression 'sustainable development' is itself an ambiguous and difficult one. A good introduction to the literature is Pezzey, 1992.

this condition. While there is a lot of controversy about which pathways satisfy this condition, there are some clear cases of those that do not. For example, an approach to development which involves destroying the natural resource base of a country in order to produce commodities for export would clearly seem to fail this condition and thus be ruled out by the idea of sustainable development. Similarly, an approach to global justice that was not environment-preserving would be ruled out by this conception of global environmental justice. As in the case of sustainable development it is not completely clear what this constraint comes to, but it is easy to imagine some cases in which it might be violated. For example, suppose that a rich country intends to transfer resources to a poor country in an attempt to rectify an existing injustice. But suppose that the poor country plans to use these resources to create a huge hydro-project that will destroy ecosystems, kill many animals and force many people from their homes. This would appear to violate the canons of global environmental justice, understood in this way.

So, one element of global environmental justice conditions the way justice can permissibly be pursued. In this respect it is like a 'side-constraint' on the pursuit of justice (for the notion of a 'side-constraint' see Nozick, 1974). This may be an important element of global environmental justice, but it is not the most important one to those who use this language.

Global Environmental Justice: Distributing the Benefits and Burdens of Environmental Commodities

Perhaps the most important idea of global environmental justice views the environment as a commodity whose distribution should be governed by principles of justice. Since many aspects of the environment cannot physically be transferred from one country to another, this view is more precisely thought of as advocating the distribution of the benefits and costs of environmental commodities according to principles of justice. It is an open question how environmental commodities are defined, how benefits and costs are assessed, and what theory of justice is appropriate.

Even without further characterization some elements of this view are clear. Those who promote this idea of global environmental justice argue that in the course of becoming rich the countries of the North incurred an environmental debt which they now owe to the countries of the South. The rich countries polluted the air, depleted the ozone, reduced biodiversity, and threatened the stability of the global climate. Indeed many would say that these environmental debts are the necessary costs of development and not just its inadvertent by-products. The countries of the North became rich by exploiting the environment. Now that they are rich these same countries place a very high value on environmental protection. Environmental commodities are more precious and vulnerable than ever because of the insults that the environment has already suffered. However, instead of acknowledging their environmental debt and arranging a payment plan, the countries of the North are demanding further sacrifices from the countries of the South. In order to help stabilize the climate Brazil is not supposed to develop Amazonia; India is expected to forgo the benefits of refrigeration rather than release ozone-depleting chemicals into the atmosphere; and Indonesia is supposed to devote some of its scarce land to habitat for the Javan Rhino rather than using it in productive activities for the benefit of its burgeoning human population. From the perspective of the developing world it looks like those who had the party expect those who didn't to pick up the tab. Indeed, it is even worse than this. The party is still going on in the rich countries of the North. Poor people are expected to forgo necessities while the consumerism of the rich continues to increase.

This picture of global environmental justice seems generally to cohere with our overall picture of global justice. The parties who are the subjects and beneficiaries of the obligations are nations.[4] The case for transfers from the North to the South seems very strong from the perspective of most major theories of justice. A Rawlsian might see the Difference Principle as warranting such transfers; an entitlement theorist might base them on the need to rectify past injustices; a utilitarian may view such transfers as utility-maximizing; and a communitarian might see them as required by the social bonds of the emerging global community. On this conception of global environmental justice, the big-picture theories of justice function as they ordinarily do. The environment is seen as a commodity to be distributed in accordance with principles of justice. In principle it is not different from money, food, or health care.

However, there are problems with thinking of the environment in this way. The first difficulty, unlikely to move many philosophers, is practical. Even if there were widespread agreement that

[4] Beitz, 1979, and Pogge, 1989, have recently rejected what Beitz calls 'the morality of states'. I agree with them on this point, but neither addresses questions of the environment, and our positive views regarding duties across national boundaries are quite distinct.

the rich countries have incurred an environmental debt that they must now begin to repay, it is far from clear what is required. There are questions about the size of the debt, its distribution across various societies and the pace at which the recession-racked economies of the North should be expected to pay it down. Even if there were agreement about all of this, the required steps would be politically impossible. 'Foreign aid', as it is generally called, is unpopular in most countries. While still a senator, now Vice-President Gore advocated a global 'Marshall Plan' (Gore, 1992, pp. 295-360). It is a testament to the political incompetence of his opponents that he could have been elected after advocating such a thing. (For an analysis of the role of environmental values in the 1992 American presidential election see Jamieson, 1992b.)

The case for this kind of environmental justice also runs into theoretical problems on close inspection. Northern countries, especially the USA, have been unwilling to transfer resources to poor countries without 'conditionality'. Conditionality requires beneficiaries to allocate resources in a particular way or to permit donors to play a role in the allocation process. Rich countries argue that without conditionality there is no guarantee that transfer payments will go towards preserving the environment. They point out that the governments of some developing countries assault and imprison their own environmentalists (e.g., Wangari Maathai in Kenya) or wink at those who kill them (e.g., the killers of Chico Mendez in Brazil). Moreover it is not just the rich countries who have abused the environment. Many poor countries have serious environmental problems caused by their own greed, short-sightedness and corruption.

The governments of most poor countries are hostile to conditionality. They see it as infringing their national sovereignty and expressing a lack of respect for their political institutions. Furthermore, poor countries point out that there is nothing conditional about the rich countries' exploitation of the global environment.

This clash between conditionality and sovereignty is part of the explanation for the anthropocentric and nationalist tones of the Declaration of Rio. After twenty years of a developing global environmental consciousness, the Declaration of Rio marked no real advance on the Stockholm Declaration of 1972. (Both are reprinted in Gruen and Jamieson, 1994.) The rich countries wanted conditionality and the poor countries wanted money; neither got much of what they wanted. Instead they agreed on a document that declared that there is a 'right to development', that 'human beings are at the centre of concerns for sustainable development', and that 'states have . . . the sovereign right to exploit their own resources pursuant to their own environmental and developmental policies'.

I believe that part of what this clash between conditionality and sovereignty illustrates is the difficulties involved in treating the environment as a commodity the benefits and burdens of which can be distributed on a global basis according to principles of justice. While this model may work for some kinds of environmental commodities (e.g., toxic wastes, pesticides, etc.) it will not work for all.[5] Many environmental goods are not transferable or are highly diffuse, or their value is non-compensatable.[6]

Consider the problem of biodiversity loss. One argument that has been made is that the entire world benefits from biodiversity, so countries that have a great deal of biological diversity within their borders should be compensated for their preservation efforts. Additional funds may also be owed to them because of biodiversity reductions caused by other parties. While this is a good idea in theory and probably should be supported even in practice, it bumps into problems of conditionality and sovereignty. The recipient of the compensation may not have the inclination or competence to use the transferred resources to preserve biological diversity. Or the government may simply decide that there are more urgent uses for the resources in eliminating poverty, homelessness and so on. To this donors may reasonably object that the recipients are supposed to be the guardians of a public good in which everyone has an interest; if they fail to discharge their duties the donors have a permission to intervene. But recipients may reasonably argue that these payments are in part compensation for the rich countries disadvantaging the poor countries by their past and present plundering of a public good for private gain; the recipients therefore have no obligation to use these resources in the ways which the donors demand. Even if there is agreement in principle about the purpose for which these resources should be used, there may be no way to ensure that they are used efficiently in practice without serious breaches of the national sovereignty of the recipi-

[5] One might reasonably object to this model even in some apparently clear cases. For example, it is not obvious that it is morally permissible to transfer toxic wastes from a rich country to a poor one, even if the benefits of receiving the waste appear to make people better off than they otherwise would be.

[6] Sovereignty intuitions are weak with respect to some other commodities as well as environmental ones. Few people believe that ownership entitles someone to destroy a great work of art. The analogy between artworks and environmental commodities is worth exploring in detail, but I cannot explore it here.

ent countries. In so far as these breaches occur, the relationship looks more like one of environmental imperialism than environmental justice. But in so far as interventions do not occur, the global environment may continue to suffer.[7]

It is difficult to take one side or the other in this dispute. I find it implausible to suppose that donors always have permission to impose conditions, or that they never have such permission. It seems to me that some forms of conditionality in some circumstances are justified. This belief is widely enough shared to warrant a brief investigation into its roots.

One reason for such a belief may be that unconditional transfers are not in the interests of the donors. This may be either because of a fear that the recipients will use these resources in ways that are directly counter to the interests of the donors, for example by supporting a military build-up, or because the donors will not obtain as much environmental protection as they desire.

A second reason for such a belief may be that unconditional transfers are not in the interests of the recipients. The thought may be that paternalistic conditionality will help recipients spend these resources more wisely, and thus further their own interests more effectively than would be the case if the transfers were unconditional.

A third source of the belief may be that unconditional government-to-goverment transfers do not ensure that the resources aid those who are entitled to the aid. This belief may involve a return to the idea that environmental justice involves obligations to non-human entities. The concern may be that recipient governments will not devote the resources to improving the forests and protecting the animal populations which are the real objects of concern. However, a second grounding for this belief involves seeing the citizens and residents of the recipient nations as those who are entitled to the benefits of the transfers. The fear is that the bene-

[7] In commenting on an earlier draft of this paper, Stephen M. Gardiner pointed out that the apparent clash between sovereignty and conditionality intuitions could be accounted for by a theory that distinguished duties to rectify past injustices from other duties that we may have. On this view the countries of the North may have duties unconditionally to transfer resources to the countries of the South in order to compensate them for past injustices associated with industrialization of the North. However, the countries of the South may also have duties not to pursue unsustainable development paths. On this view the clash between the sovereignty and conditionality intuitions flows from confusing distinct duties rather than from treating the environment as a commodity. I cannot pursue this interesting suggestion here.

fits will not 'trickle down' from the recipient governments to those who have the entitlements.

It may be that under various conditions all or most of these concerns could be made consistent with the idea that there are duties of justice to engage in government-to-government transfers of environmental benefits and burdens. But taken together they appear to erode the plausibility of this view. In the ordinary case a person or nation is permitted to be foolish with resources that are theirs as a matter of justice. Similarly they can frustrate the interests of those who owed them the resources, and even distribute them unjustly among their own people, without affecting their national claim to the resources. In my view the strength and depth of the conditionality intuition in this case counts against the plausibility of the view that the environment is a commodity which can be distributed among governments in accordance with principles of international justice.[8]

A second kind of environmental commodity that is difficult to deal with on the basis of this model is one which is not located within the boundaries of any country. The ozone shield and a stable climate are two such commodities. The share of the benefits associated with these commodities that any country obtains may not be proportional to its contribution to preserving them. In order to protect the ozone layer, the USA, for example, was willing to absorb additional costs (by banning spray cans) years before the Europeans were willing to contribute. Currently the Netherlands appears willing to absorb more costs than other nations in order to promote climate stability. The willingness to absorb these costs may have no clear relation to the amount of harm that a nation suffers from the occurrence of the problem. The costs can be distributed according to some formula that is acknowledged to be just, but the benefits cannot be distributed at all. The benefits will be a function of the particular effects of the maintenance of the climate and the ozone shield in particular regions. Given the complexity and unpredictability of the atmospheric system and its social effects, it makes little sense to treat these goods as producing distributable benefits. (I discuss these matters further in a series of papers, the most recent of which is Jamieson, 1992a.) For this reason it would be very difficult to treat

[8] The human rights movement brought the topic of conditionality into play. It is plausible to think of international guarantees of human rights as infringements of national sovereignty. It should be noted that although governments in the developing world typically oppose conditionality, often their citizens do not. See, for example, Glantz, 1990, pp. 43–44.

these problems according to the model of justice currently under discussion.

A third problem with treating the environment as a commodity, the benefits and costs of which can be distributed in accordance with principles of justice, is that many environmental goods are irreplaceable and irreversible. When species are lost or climate changes they will never return. Nature's path has been irrevocably affected by the development of western science and technology. It is hard to conceive what the alternatives might have been, much more how to compensate those whose preferences and ways of life have been frustrated or destroyed.

Global Environmental Justice versus a Global Environmental Ethics

Thus far I have been explaining some of the complications that arise with respect to the idea of global environmental justice, and the difficulty in squaring this idea with at least some of our intuitions about global environmental protection. This does not amount to the claim that there is no such thing as global environmental justice or that it ought not to be taken seriously. However, the notion is sufficiently problematic that we should try to examine alternatives that may be available in our moral traditions.

One problem that has haunted this discussion is the question of who the subjects and recipients of the duties are. As I have suggested, often in discussions of international justice it is assumed that it is governments which have duties and that typically they are owed to other governments. The costs and benefits 'trickle down' to the citizens or residents of each country. This assumption is problematic in the case of global environmental justice.

The global environmental movement has brought with it a new pattern of alliances and relationships. The environmental interests of the indigenous peoples of Brazil or the women of Kenya are often violated by their own governments, yet they may make common cause with women, indigenous people or non-governmental organizations in other countries. Non-governmental organizations, scientists and grassroots organizations have been profoundly important in affecting the future of the global environment. They have brought issues to light and pressured governments to take action, and often their own projects have been very effective. What this structure of relationships suggests to me is that rather than thinking about the problem of the global environment as one that involves duties of justice that obtain between states, we should instead think of it as one that involves actions and responsibilities among individuals and institutions who are related in a variety of different ways. Scientists may have duties to educate and train people who have little opportunity to develop the relevant skills and expertise on their own. Individuals in Europe or Japan may have duties to contribute to non-governmental organizations in Africa or Asia. Americans may have duties to limit their consumption or even to close down the local lumber yard that specializes in tropical woods.

What I am suggesting is not that the various ideas of global environmental justice that I have explored be abandoned, but rather that they be supplemented by a more inclusive ecological picture of duties and obligations—one that sees people all over the world in their roles as producers, consumers, knowledge-users and so on, connected to each other in complex webs of relationships that are generally not mediated by governments. This picture of the moral world better represents the reality of our time in which people are no longer insulated from each other by space and time. Patterns of international trade, technology and economic development have bound us into a single community, and our moral thinking needs to change to reflect these new realities.

There is another reason why this model is a good one for thinking about duties that involve the environment. One reason why it is awkward to think of the environment as the object of our concern, a condition on our actions or a commodity to be distributed, has to do with our peculiar relationship to the environment. While we can model various aspects of our relationship to the environment in these various ways, these models neglect the fact that we are situated in the environment. The environment conditions and affects everything that each of us does. The environment called us into existence and continues to sustain us. In part it constitutes our identities. To view the environment solely as a good to be distributed seriously misconceives our relationship to the Earth.[9]

[9] Although I have not been able to take all of them into account, I especially thank Stephen M. Gardiner and James W. Nickel for their comments on an earlier draft of this paper.

Environmental and Medical Bioethics in Late Modernity: Anthony Giddens, Genetic Engineering and the Post-Modern State

RUTH McNALLY AND PETER WHEALE

Introduction: Modernity or Post-Modernity?

A controversial question among contemporary scholars is whether advanced industrial societies are still in modernity, or whether they are on the threshold of, or even have entered, a new post-modern order (see, for example, Bell, 1973; Lyotard, 1986, p. 14; Lash and Urry, 1987). In *The Consequences of Modernity* Anthony Giddens writes: 'Beyond modernity, we can perceive a new and different order, which is "post-modern", but this is quite distinct from what is at the moment called by many "post-modernity"' (Giddens, 1990, p. 3). However, he does recognize that there is something perceptibly different about the present, which he characterizes as 'late modernity' (or 'high modernity'), an era in which the consequences of modernity are more radicalized and globalized than before (Giddens, 1990, pp. 3, 51).

For Giddens, the essence of modernity is its dynamism—a dynamism of such pace and scope as to be discontinuous with traditional social orders. One of the images Giddens uses to describe the dynamic experience of living in modernity is that of riding a juggernaut—'a runaway engine of enormous power which, collectively as human beings, we can drive to some extent but which also threatens to rush out of our control and which could rend itself asunder' (Giddens, 1990, p. 139).

The rapid global change which is characteristic of modernity derives from the dynamism which is inherent in four key modern institutions, which are (a) capitalism, (b) industrialism, (c) surveillance and (d) military power. The conception of the first three is substantially informed by the works of respectively Marx, Durkheim and Weber. Military power, the fourth characteristic institution of modernity, is an institution which, as Giddens observes, was comparatively neglected by these founding fathers of sociology. In addition to the dynamism deriving from the institutional dimensions of modernity and their inter-relations,

Giddens characterizes three other dynamic sources, or 'facilitating conditions', which are 'time-space distanciation', 'disembedding mechanisms' and 'reflexivity' (Giddens, 1990, p. 63).

In this study we attempt to give content to some of the schematic metaphors and abstractions Giddens has written about in *The Consequences of Modernity,* by applying his typological characterization of late modernity to genetic engineering. In so doing we hope not only to test Giddens's theory of modernity, but also to elucidate a hermeneutics of the social relations of modern genetic engineering. We describe the contribution of genetic engineering to the dynamism which defines modernity, both as a major component of modern institutions and as an embodiment of each of the types of facilitating conditions which Giddens characterizes. Finally, we conclude that the process of continuous reflexivity between the proponents and opponents of modern genetic engineering is radicalizing environmental and medical bioethics. Our thesis is that this interactive socio-technical process is playing a leading role in transforming late modernity along the contours of a realizable post-modern order.

Trust and Disembedding Mechanisms

Symbolic Tokens: Nucleic Acid Sequence Data

'Disembedding mechanisms are abstract systems which prise social relations free from the hold of specific locales, recombining them across wide time-space distances' (Giddens, 1991, p. 2). Giddens distinguishes two types of disembedding mechanisms— the creation of 'symbolic tokens' and the establishment of 'expert systems'. In this section we describe the creation of a symbolic token, namely, the transformation of nucleic acid molecules into dimensionless, timeless information, and the establishment of the 'bio-industrial complex' as an expert system.

Symbolic tokens are media of interchange which can be 'passed around' without regard to the specific characteristics of individuals or groups which handle them at any particular juncture, an example of which is money (Giddens, 1990, p. 22).

Since the elucidation of the Watson and Crick double-helix structure of DNA and the deciphering of the genetic code, the gene has been atomized and deconstructed. No longer the fundamental unit of heredity, it is now common for genes to be characterized and denoted in terms of the sequence of their nucleic acid bases. Thus rendered as pure information, the three-dimensional molecules of DNA and RNA are reduced to two-dimensional linear symbols, and transformed into 'symbolic tokens', a semiotics which constitutes the international *lingua franca* of molecular biology. Genetics as 'bioinformatics' is the information technology *par excellence*.

Nucleic acid sequence data constitute an international information system about our past, present and future, both as individuals and as a species. Illnesses, handicaps, behaviours and other qualities which, in modernity, are associated with genes are characterized as resulting from the presence or absence of genetic information (or misinformation). The various genome sequencing projects are founded upon faith that a species can be abstracted and reduced to 'pure' information.

Symbolic tokens are inherently 'globalizing'. A DNA sequence deposited in a computerized databank has the same meaning wherever and whenever it is read using the genetic code. The semiotics of genetics is a language—a social system in Luhmann's sense (Luhmann, 1986; 1989). It is a language system outside space and time, whose meaning is independent of subjectivity.

Expert Systems: The Bio-Industrial Complex

Giddens defines expert systems as 'systems of technical accomplishment or professional expertise that organize large areas of the material and social environments in which we live today' (Giddens, 1990, p. 27). The science of genetics is a powerful belief system in modernity which underpins a new 'expert system' which we have called the 'bio-industrial complex' (see Wheale and McNally, 1988a, Part II). The bio-industrial complex comprises new techniques, new knowledge, new systems of classification, new vocabularies, new professions and professional specializations, and new organizational structures whose systems of technical accomplishment and professional expertise are involved in, as well as conditioned by, the institutional dimensions of modernity. It is a world-wide complex of scientific expertise, technological capabilities and transnational capital accumulation operating in international markets. It interfaces with all industrial sectors including chemicals, food, agriculture, energy, resource-recovery, environmental control, healthcare and pharmaceuticals, and these in turn interface with the military and with numerous bureaucratic agencies. This new 'technological system' (see Clark *et al.*, 1984) is having profound effects upon our social and physical environment.

Given that no one can become an expert in more than a few

small sectors of the immensely complicated knowledge systems which now exist (Giddens, 1990, p. 144), in a similar way to other expert systems, the products and services of the bio-industrial complex are commissioned by consumers who lack full information and who therefore must place trust in the expertise of the system. It is only because the bio-industrial complex is trusted to meet expectations that it is able to disembed social relations. Trust in the bio-industrial complex is an expression of faith in genetics as a science and technology. Thus the maintenance of the bio-industrial complex as a disembedding mechanism is dependent upon continued faith in the abstract principles of genetics.

Time-Space Distanciation and the Four Modern Institutions

Time Space Distanciation through Recombinant DNA Technology

Giddens defines 'time-space distanciation' as 'the separation of time from space and their recombination in forms which permit the precise time-space "zoning" of social life' (Giddens, 1990, pp. 16-17). Critics of Giddens's use of 'space-time' metaphors argue that these concepts are merely notional abstractions without substance and therefore do not constitute a testable theory (Gregory, 1989; Saunders, 1989; McLennan, 1990; Urry, 1991). In this section we use recombinant DNA technology as a case study in an attempt to give content to these metaphors.

Recombinant DNA technology is a new set of *micro*genetic engineering techniques which manipulate heredity at the *molecular* level rather than at the level of whole animals and plants (see Wheale and McNally, 1988a, ch. 2). It derives its name from the fact that it recombines genetic material, thereby altering the time-space relationships of nucleic acids, mobile genetic elements, genetically engineered organisms, genomic ecosystems and ecosystems in general. *Spatial* dislocation is brought about by the manipulation of nucleic acids outside of living cells and their reinsertion into foreign cells. Genetically recombinant organisms are also *temporally* dislocated from their own genesis through somatic cell manipulation, and from their own heredity through germ-line manipulation.

Below we describe how the alteration of time-space relations in biological systems through recombinant DNA technology is involved in, as well as conditioned by, the four institutional dimensions of modernity.

Environmental and Medical Bioethics in Late Modernity

(a) Capitalism

Giddens defines 'capitalism' as a system of commodity production, centred upon relations between private ownership of capital and propertyless wage labour (Giddens, 1990, p. 55). Proponents of recombinant DNA technology claim this new technology has the potential to satisfy world markets at competitive prices. They argue that major savings will accrue to consumers through improved efficiency and reduced prices, and from entirely new products and services. Optimistic market predictions for the products and services of the genetic engineering industry have engendered a cluster of enabling technological innovations for genetic engineering research (see Wheale and McNally, 1986). The patentability of recombinant products and processes has proved to be as powerful an economic incentive to substantial corporate investment in molecular biology as the claimed technical merit of the technology (see Wheale and McNally, 1990a, Part I).

(b) Industrialism

'Industrialism' is the use of economic resources and mechanization to produce goods (Giddens, 1990, p. 56). It is the transformation of nature, and the development of the 'created environment'.

Genetic engineering aims to transform nature by exploiting nature. The potential claimed for this new technology is that it can take genetic resources, tailor them and then use them to design and construct molecules, microbes, cells and organisms to meet human demands and needs. A new industry—the genetic engineering industry—is developing for the manufacture and sale of genetically manipulated organisms, cells, enzymes, vectors and genes which produce goods and perform services in scientific research, health care, the chemicals industry, the food industry, agriculture, energy, environmental control, resource recovery and for military purposes (see Wheale and McNally, 1986; 1988a).

(c) Surveillance

Surveillance is fundamental to all the types of organization associated with the rise of modernity as it is the unavoidable consequence of the attempt to attain rationalized control of information through the use of technology and the bureaucratic organization of human activities (see Giddens, 1990, pp. 12, 59).

The knowledge constructed from research on the human genome is biometric. It comprises new measurements of population norms and deviations, information which constitutes a new system of classification, new definitions of normal and abnormal, and new ways of distinguishing them from each other. Nucleic

215

acid sequences are credited with providing information about our past, present and future, both as individuals and as a species. Nucleic acid sequence data lend themselves to applications which require the classification of people into groups for the purpose of institutional decision-making. Parents, police, health, education and immigration authorities, insurance firms, finance institutions and employers are each anxious to avail themselves of the new 'DNA fingerprinting', genetic screening and diagnostic technologies. Indeed, bioinformatics—computerized nucleic acid sequence information—is a burgeoning industry in its own right.

(d) Military power

'Military power' is the control of the means of violence by the nation-state and the 'industrialization of war'. The agents of biological warfare are bacteria, viruses, fungi and toxins which can be targeted at people, livestock or crops (see Wheale and McNally, 1988a, ch. 8). The rhetoric of the technological capability of recombinant DNA technology—that it is precise and controlled—has engendered the belief that it can be used to make biological weapons which are more efficacious, reliable and predictable than previously, and which potentially have a limited survival time in the environment. It is also considered to be a technology whereby one can develop vaccines against one's own biological agents. Because each of these features increases the utility of biological agents as strategic agents, recombinant DNA technology has reinstated biological weapons as a potential threat to national security, as a result of which a large amount of biological research, both classified and unclassified, funded by the military is undertaken in universities and other non-military public and private research institutions in the USA and the UK.

Reflexivity, the Double Hermeneutic and Self-Identity

Reflexivity is the 'reflexive ordering and re-ordering of social relations in the light of continual inputs of knowledge affecting the expectations and actions of individuals and groups' (Giddens, 1990, p. 17). Giddens describes the relation between sociology and its subject matter as the 'double hermeneutic': 'sociological knowledge spirals in and out of the universe of social life, reconstructing both itself and that universe as an integral part of that process' (Giddens, 1990, pp. 15–16).

There are some correspondences between the Giddensian conception of sociology and the Foucauldian notion of the 'human sciences' (Foucault, 1973; 1975). Human genetics is a 'human science' in the Foucauldian sense (see McNally, 1993). In recent years illnesses, handicaps and other traits considered to be 'undesirable' and which are considered to have a genetic basis have been constructed as a 'social problem' (the 'genetic problem') for individuals, for their families and carers, and for society.

One suggested 'solution' to the 'genetic problem' is to map and sequence the human genome in order to identify the loci which confer genetic susceptibility and develop diagnostic tests with which susceptible individuals may be identified; another is the expansion of the clinical and community genetics services which serve the reproductive population. If the human genome research 'solution' seems ambitious, the second is no less so: the Royal College of Physicians, for example, advocates the routine screening of the entire pregnant population (Royal College of Physicians, 1989).

The discourse on the 'genetic problem' and its 'solutions' not only transforms modern institutions, it alters both the objective statuses and the subjective states of individuals. As a human science, human genetics and its subject matter display the 'double hermeneutic' described by Giddens, characterized by the reflexive appropriation by lay people of expert knowledge, and their resistances to it. The double hermeneutic constitutes a further source of dynamism in modernity.

Risk and Dystopian Realism

The Risks of Recombinant DNA Technology

Modernity is perceived by many thinkers to be by nature a risk culture (see, for example, Giddens, 1990; 1991; Beck, 1992). This of course does not mean that social life is *de facto* inherently more risky than it used to be. For Giddens it is the *intensity* of risk which has changed and which is the basic element in the 'menacing appearance' of the circumstances in which we live today (Giddens, 1990, p. 125; 1991, p.3). Recombinant DNA technology engenders a new array of risks, awareness of which also transforms modern institutions.

In respect of capitalism, the perceived profitability of recombinant DNA technology in conjunction with the patentability of its products and processes has enticed transnational corporations into plant breeding, thus creating conditions conducive to economic concentration of the world's genetic resources. European Union (formerly Community) policy intended to improve the competitiveness of the biotechnology industry tends towards a form of corporatism (see Wheale and McNally, 1993), and the patentability of biotechnological inventions could result in reduced worldwide trade and increased transaction costs, the high risk consequence of which could be the collapse of economic growth mechanisms.

In respect of industrialism, as a result of recombinant DNA technology, more organisms of novel genetic composition are being produced and introduced—accidentally and deliberately—into the environment than would ever have been possible in an equivalent period of time using conventional breeding practices. Recombinant organisms can reproduce, migrate and mutate and could become 'biogenetic pollution'—a growing, moving, changing form of pollution. Recombinant DNA technology is also considered to be harmful to animal welfare. The potential of recombinant DNA technology is also considered to constitute a moral risk because of the choices and responsibilities it creates (see McNally and Wheale, 1986; Wheale and McNally, 1988a; 1988b; 1990a; 1990b; National Anti-Vivisection Society, 1987).

In respect of surveillance, there is the risk that genetic data will be detrimental to the interests of specific individuals and groups. The existence of genetic data on populations and individuals may lead to discrimination against those judged by genetic standards to be less desirable for the purposes of employment, borrowing money, immigration, reproduction, and even, in the case of prenatal diagnosis, unfit for life itself.

In respect of military power, the advent of recombinant DNA technology resurrected the military threat of biological weapons and consequently stimulated large-scale military investment on research into defences against them, and, it is alleged, on the development of offensive biological agents (Wheale and McNally, 1988a). Confidence in the ability to immunize one's own troops and civilians against biological weapons could precipitate biological warfare. The high-consequence risks of a biological war could be even more terrible than those of a nuclear war because biological weapons may replicate uncontrollably and can go on killing indefinitely.

Post-Modernity 1: Dystopian Realism

'If we are moving into a phase of post-modernity, this means that the trajectory of social development is taking us away from the institutions of modernity towards a new and distinctive social order' (Giddens, 1990, p. 46).

At this point, we shall develop a 'trajectory of social development' from the above account in order to derive a glimpse of what might lie on the other side of modernity. Driven by faith in the science and technology of genetics, the four characteristic institutions of modernity are undergoing rapid transformation. Such transformation is underpinned by the expectation of social benefits—profitable products and processes, unique ways of transforming nature to meet human needs and demands, improved knowledge for the efficient bureaucratic organization of human activities, and effective methods of defence against biological weapons. However, it also engenders a new array of high-consequence risks which threaten the very existence of the four modern institutions. These high-consequence risks could result in the end of capitalism through the collapse of economic growth mechanisms; the end of industrialism through ecological decay or disaster; the end of surveillance through the growth of totalitarian power; and the end of military power as a result of large-scale warfare. Each of these would mean, in Giddens's terms, the end of modernity, and the start of a dystopian post-modern order. 'On the other side of modernity . . . there could be nothing but a "republic of insects and grass", or a cluster of damaged and traumatized human social communities . . . . Apocalypse has become trite, so familiar of day-to-day life; yet like all parameters of risk, it can become real' (Giddens, 1990, p. 173).

Thus 'dystopian realism' predicts a post-modern order in which the characteristic dynamism of modernity is ended through the realization of the high-consequence risks of modernity. However, the above characterization of modernity, which largely identifies faith in science and technology as the source of modern dynamism, is incomplete. In the remaining sections we shall undertake a further consideration of 'reflexivity' as a source of dynamism and consider its potential, through 'utopian realism', to generate an alternative 'trajectory of social development' which could lead to a utopian, rather than dystopian, post-modern order.

Reflexivity and Utopian Realism

Reflexivity, Trust and Risk-Assessment

Modern genetic engineers are often surprised by the lack of public trust in the safety and morality of their endeavours, and, in general, are dismayed by the extent to which they are called upon to justify their experiments and innovations (see Krimsky, 1982;

Gershon, 1983). In this section, we attempt to explain how the loss of trust is a consequence of a combination of the perception of risk and reflexivity.

While acknowledging that reflexivity is a defining characteristic of all human action (Giddens, 1990, p. 36), Giddens argues that it has taken on a different character in modernity. In modernity, intellectuals have become increasingly cognisant of the ungrounded nature of scientific epistemology and the contingency of scientific knowledge (Lakatos and Musgrave, 1970; Mulkay, 1979; Barnes and Edge, 1982). This is having the effect of reducing the status of scientific communications. If faith in the epistemology used by the expert system declines, then the public's trust in it cannot be sustained and the future of the expert system itself is jeopardized.

Let us take, for example, risk-assessment. Alongside the expectation that abstract systems will provide certain social benefits, there is an awareness that they engender risks. Trust in abstract systems includes trust that they are able to assess such risks. Risk-assessment is a future-oriented activity which requires the calculation of 'harm' and the calculation of the 'probability' that such harm will arise (see McNally and Wheale, 1991; Wheale and McNally, 1993). When there is a loss of faith in the epistemology which underpins *all* science-based knowledge claims, the public no longer trusts expert systems to apprise it of the risks of technology because it knows that the theory underpinning the identification and measurement of harm and the likelihood of its occurrence is under-determined, and therefore, unknowable. 'Widespread lay knowledge of modern risk environments and awareness of the limits of expertise accurately to assess risk constitutes one of the "public relations" problems that has to be faced by those who seek to sustain lay trust in expert systems' (Giddens, 1990, p. 130).

Social Movements: The Bioethics Expert System

According to Giddens, social movements have an important role in the process of representative democracy. Social movements can be superimposed on the four institutional dimensions of modernity. Labour movements are associated with the development of unionism as a defence against the controlling power of capitalism. Free speech and democratic movements champion political participation and attempt to counter the surveillance of individuals and the bureaucratic operations of the modern state. Peace movements struggle against state control of the means of violence by both the military and the police, while ecological movements have as their site of struggle the 'created environment' (Giddens, 1990, pp. 159–161).

Modern genetic engineering occupies a pivotal position in the institutions of late modernity as it is implicated in virtually every major debate preoccupying modern society, including control of reproduction, law and order, worker health and safety, discrimination, consumer safety, environmental pollution, and warfare.

Since its advent, recombinant DNA technology has stimulated the proliferation of social movements which articulate what they consider to be the unacceptable risks of this new technology. Their formation is a consequence of the inherent reflexivity of modernity which generates a loss of faith in the science and technology of genetics, which in turn undermines trust that the bio-industrial complex will produce expected benefits and will accurately assess risk.

In modernity it is recognized that scientific truth-claims are contingent and do not, of themselves, provide a method for discriminating between competing values. Consequently, sectional interests which rely on the traditional authority of science can now be challenged with greater conviction by alternative knowledge claims such as 'alternative medicine', 'alternative food' and 'green consumerism'. Reflexivity also manifests itself in the appropriation of technical expertise by lay agents as part of their routine dealings with abstract systems (Giddens, 1990, p. 144). Consequently, rather than being lay recipients, the various counter-culture movements also wield technical expertise and constitute a new set of expert systems which define themselves as defenders of the public interest from the risks of capitalism, industrialism, surveillance and military power. In respect of genetic engineering, we have called this set of expert systems the 'bioethical expert system'. Clustered around the four institutional dimensions of modernity, the social movements of the bioethics expert system argue for the protection of workers, consumers, the environment and animal welfare, the safeguarding of civil liberties, freedom from the threat of biological weaponry, equitable distribution of the world's genetic resources, and sustainable development as proposed by the Brundtland Report (World Commission on Environment and Development, 1987).

At the same time as technical expertise is being appropriated by ethical expert systems, the converse is also happening: sectional interest groups which have traditionally relied on the legitimacy of science are attempting to regain the moral high ground from their critics by transparently appropriating their value-based arguments, and using them to support (and shape) their enterprises.

221

The result is that the conflict of different knowledge claims and the reflexive appropriation and re-appropriation of knowledge between technical and ethical expert systems are salient features of late modernity (Lyotard, 1986; Giddens, 1990). The creation of a 'counter-culture' has produced a dialectic, reflexive rather than materialist, in late modernity.

In the next section we describe how the reflexive dialectic of the bio-industrial complex and the bioethics expert system is generating the contours of a realizable utopian post-modern order.

Post-Modernity 2: Utopian Realism

If dynamism is constitutive of modernity, then, paradoxically, the end of modernity is the end of dynamism. As we described above, one realizable end to modernity is dystopia following the collapse of economic growth mechanisms, ecological disaster, the growth of totalitarian power or large-scale warfare.

An alternative end to modernity would be if the dynamism of the institutional dimensions of modernity were to be limited through utopian transformations which replaced capitalism with a post-scarcity system, industrialism with humanized technology, surveillance with multi-layered democratic participation, and military power with demilitarization.

The question then is how to 'harness the juggernaut, or at least direct it in such a way as to minimize the dangers and maximize the opportunities which modernity offers to us?' (Giddens, 1990, p. 151). 'What is needed', suggests Giddens, 'is the creation of models of *utopian realism*' (Giddens, 1990, p. 154). The argument is that the alternative futures envisaged through utopian realism can transform the future because their very propagation might help them to be realized.

Key players in the creation of models of utopian realism are the social movements, which, Giddens claims, are able to provide us with glimpses of possible futures and are in some part vehicles for their realization (Giddens, 1990, p. 161). It is they who criticize what they perceive to be unacceptable risks and lobby for alternative institutional formations. And in the reflexive dialectic, as this discourse is appropriated and re-appropriated by other expert systems, the pace and scope of the dynamism of modern institutions in the present is directed towards more utopian futures. This process can be illustrated using examples of how the radical bioethics dialectic is limiting the scope of the 'facilitating conditions' discussed above:

- The potential for time-space distanciation has been curtailed by regulations which prohibit certain forms of genetic recombination which are considered to present 'unacceptable' risks.
- Expert systems which embody bioethical values are being established by the State, for example, recombinant DNA advisory committees, animal experimentation and farm animal welfare committees, and environmental risk-assessment committees. Such expert systems are often formally empowered to restrict the activities of other expert systems, for example, the activities of the bio-industrial complex.
- The dynamic potential of nucleic acid sequence data as symbolic tokens has been reduced by a successful challenge to their reliability as forensic evidence.

The imposition of limits on the dynamic potential of facilitating conditions has the effect of reducing the dynamism of modern institutions. In addition to altering the pace of change, such limits also alter the scope of future transformations, by guiding them away from high risk contours. One example would be the 'greening of biotechnology' whereby, as a result of the appropriation of the aims of the bioethical expert system, the enterprises of the bio-industrial complex are being redefined as solutions to the high-consequence environmental risks of modernity (see, for example, Bishop, 1990). While the motivation for this reflexive appropriation is regarded with some cynicism, this new discourse on biotechnology as sustainable development generates different expectations of the bio-industrial complex, which in turn transform modern institutions, guiding them towards a more utopian future.

In summary, Giddens's idealized typology of modernity and its consequences takes us to the point where social movements are making guidelines for the future transformation of modern institutions, guidelines which define the contours of a post-modern order. Our application of this typology to modern genetic engineering indicates that it is at the heart of an interactive socio-technical process which could transform the four institutions of modernity along the contours of a realizable utopian post-modern order.

Genetic Engineering in the Post-Modern Order

In *The Consequences of Modernity* Giddens provides a persuasive ideal typology of the nature of late modernity together with an explanation of how the 'juggernaut-like' experience of living through it is a consequence of the dynamic processes which are intrinsic to modernity. In this study our purpose has been to undertake a substantive test of Giddens's schematic metaphors and to use his descriptive and explanatory framework as a heuristic device with which to conceptualize the social relations of genetics and genetic engineering. For the purposes of this analysis we have accepted Giddens's definition of the distinction between modernity and post-modernity, that is, modernity is characterized by an unprecedented scope and pace of change, while the post-modern order would be defined by an end to modernity's dynamic character.

Two explanatory variables emerge from this exploration of Giddens's account of dynamism in modernity. Firstly, the importance of conceptualizations of science and technology to modern dynamism. For example, the construction of nucleic acid sequence data as symbolic tokens, the establishment of the bio-industrial complex as an expert system, and the maintenance of the expectation that recombinant DNA technology alters the time-space relationships of living agents in socially beneficial ways, are each based on faith in genetics as a science and a technology. The diffusion of recombinant DNA technology into the four key institutions of modernity both transforms them and engenders risks, the ultimate outcome of which could be the realization of a dystopian post-modern order.

The second major source of explanation of the dynamism of modernity in Giddens's analysis derives from 'reflexivity'. In one sense, reflexivity is used to explain the dynamic nature of both the social and self-identity in modernity as ideas about the self and knowledge of social norms reflexively constitute and reconstitute each other in the 'double hermeneutic'. In another sense, reflexivity is linked to the loss of faith in genetics as a science and a technology, a loss of faith which undermines trust in the bio-industrial complex to deliver social benefits and accurately to assess risks, and which stimulates the formation of social movements—the bioethics expert system—which can successfully challenge the legitimacy of the bio-industrial complex.

The above duality—dynamism deriving from science and technology on the one hand, and from reflexivity on the other—is congruent with Giddens's 'structuration theory' in which he attempts to synthesize deterministic theories, which see human agency as being shaped by structural forms, with voluntaristic theories, which see reality as the product of human agency (Giddens, 1979; see also Clegg, 1989, pp. 138–148; Bryant and Jary, 1991). Overall, we are inclined to conclude that the balance of Giddens's analysis of late modernity is voluntaristic: technology derives its dynamism from the *expectations* that it will produce benefits, and that dynamism is constrained when loss of *faith* in scientific epistemology undermines *trust* in expert systems and symbolic tokens. In other words, it is the perception of the human agent which confers or constrains the dynamic potential of science and technology. That said, in the final event science and technology may be the ultimate shaping power: the high-consequence risks of genetic engineering can be realized and, as Giddens states, Apocalypse can become real (Giddens, 1990, p. 173).

To conclude on a more optimistic note. Openly embracing the idea of utopias as necessary to the constitution of preferable post-modern futures, Giddens argues that given the counterfactual character of modernity, 'a rigid division between "realistic" and utopian thought is uncalled for' (Giddens, 1990, p. 155; see also Smart, 1993, p. 106). The utopian prescriptions or anticipations which restrict modernity's endlessly open character and which could lead to a utopian post-modern order are the result of human agency. As Heller and Feher argue: 'The association of Utopia with unfeasibility is completely unjustifiable' (Heller and Feher, 1988, p. 35). The reflexive dialectic between the bioethics expert system and the bio-industrial complex could result in the imposition of limits on the pace and scope of the dynamism of modern institutions, resulting in their transformation along the contours of a future realizable utopian (rather than dystopian) post-modern order.

Highlights and Connections

FREDERICK FERRÉ

Given this chance to express my general reflections on our collection of papers, I shall highlight the themes that are of greatest importance to me and make connections between my own views and the views of the other authors (about half the total) who have chosen to address the same themes. This exercise in triangulation on the logical map created by the collection has been illuminating for me; I hope the following may serve to make some of the major features of our common terrain come into focus more clearly, thus underscoring which important issues concern many of us at present, despite our specific differences.

From such a vantage point I realize that my principal paper, defending Personalistic Organicism, is at heart a plea for environmental philosophers to get beyond modes of premature binary thinking that have long obsessed (and paralysed) modern thought. 'All-or-nothing', 'either-or', 'on-off' reflexes are ubiquitous and strong, going back at least to Descartes, but equally strongly expressed in Kant and the British Empiricists as well. Of course disjunction is finally necessary if our concepts are going to mean something rather than something else. I am not calling for the overthrow of the Law of Excluded Middle. But when it is too quickly appealed to, the resulting 'either-or' syndrome needs to be struggled against in our epistemological norms, our metaphysical assumptions, and our ethical judgements. I shall highlight my views and connect them to issues in this collection of papers under those three heads.

Epistemology

First, my aim is to support a form of epistemological holism that is too holistic even to reject analysis! Among philosophers with my analytical background and training, 'holism' often has a bad name: a flabby sort of emotive blather with no bones or muscles to give it internal strength. But I believe this is not a necessary, and certainly not a normative characterization of what I mean by the term. Perhaps we need a new term, if the word has been irretrievably ruined by its association with New Age enthusiasms and questionable medical claims.

Frederick Ferré

Still, until a new term is coined, I insist that a normative epistemic holism should *in*clude, not *ex*clude. This means to me that the standards of rigorous thinking, including the use of all the toughest, clearest methods we possess, and of course including quantitative measures and the breaking up of murky concepts, is a proper part of what I mean by a holistic epistemology. In addition, holistic epistemology recognizes contexts and relations as essential to understanding. It will tend to put these first in order of priority, subordinating analysis to a less sacrosanct status than modern thinkers have tended to give it. Epistemological holism will recognize that the epistemic norms that were attributed to modern science, such as 'crucial' experiments and 'conclusive' verification, are impossible ideals which, when foolishly insisted on, distort the character of genuine human reason.

In this connection I was delighted with the conclusion of Peter List's paper, in which he clearly rejects Cohen's exaggerated calls for rigour in ethical justification as an 'impossible standard' (List, pp. 194–5). The binary syndrome suggests that we must choose between 'rigorous' thinking (verificationism, in short) and mere emotivism. But we need not choose. Values, commitments, hunches, and postulates enter into the most rigorous thinking of which human beings are capable. I would merely nudge List to add, further, that the 'impossible standard' inappropriate for careful ethical thinking is also 'impossible' on its own home turf of natural science. The subject matter is more easily quantifiable in those domains, of course; and when quantifiable parameters are available, they should be attended to within appropriate wider contexts of understanding; yet recent revolutions in the philosophy of science should warn us against tying our ideals of rigorous thinking to excessively abstract and unreachable epistemic norms.

Metaphysics

I was pleased to see the explicit calls for attention to metaphysics in the papers of our two organizers, Robin Attfield and Andrew Belsey. Both clearly see the need for environmental philosophers to return to ontological foundations and to what Attfield calls 'robust metaphysics' (Attfield, p. 57). I share this sense of need. And again I want to urge that in our metaphysics as well as in our epistemology, we lean away from the bias toward binary thinking.

Let me touch on only two important topics out of many to illustrate my point. The first is the metaphysics of 'nature'. It may seem 'merely' a matter of conceptual analysis how the words 'natural' and 'artificial' are used, but in fact we are dealing with a theory of reality when we make our definitions and follow them to their conclusions. The 'either-or' binary bias is ever ready to lead us toward constructing theories in which nature is wholly 'spoiled' or 'contaminated' by the intrusion of artifice, purpose, or human intelligence. This, frankly, is one of my pet peeves. This position takes 'natural' and 'artificial' as though they were incompatible opposites instead of poles on a spectrum allowing for many degrees.

Consider: human purpose and intelligence are markedly responsible for an urban complex, for example, and that makes a city street a paradigm of artificiality. But for all that, the street is still made of mainly nature's materials and manifests nature's laws. A rural landscape—a farm, perhaps—is to a greater degree natural than the city street because there is a lesser degree of human intelligence ingredient in its causal history; still, the animals, the plants, even the topography, are to some quite significant extent artificial. They would not be as they are without the intervention of intelligence guided by purpose. This does not make them 'completely' artificial, however, whatever that would mean. There may be spots of wilderness left on earth that are almost entirely as they are without a whiff of human causal intervention. They stand then as at the opposite end of the spectrum from the city street. The important thing to notice is that they are on a spectrum. Assuming intelligence was evolved through nature, nature is in intelligence; and, vice versa, on earth at least, what nature has become shows almost everywhere, to some degree, that intelligence is in nature. I am glad that I could find remarks of Robin Attfield, Nigel Dower and Robert Elliot supporting what I would call a 'holistic theory of nature' in which culture and nonculture, though clearly distinguishable, are kept within an inclusive framework that avoids the tendency to all-or-nothing assumptions.

The second metaphysical issue, which will launch us soon toward ethics, is the question: 'What is an entity?' Here I part company with Holmes Rolston, who thinks that species and ecosystems are entities. I do not agree. Just as ecosystems are not, as Rolston acknowledges, literally 'irritable' (Rolston, p. 23), so species do not literally 'do' the things that Rolston's language attributes to them; e.g., they do not 'use' individuals, 'defend' a form of life, or 'resist' extinction (Rolston, p. 21). Particular organisms defend their lives, and in so doing enhance the possibility that future organisms like them will continue enjoying the good of their kind. Species, however, do not defend themselves. To say they do commits what A.N. Whitehead called the 'fallacy of misplaced concreteness'.

Frederick Ferré

When we work to save an endangered species, we labour to protect actual exemplars of a kind so that more of that kind will continue to grace the earth. We want more exemplars, concretely enriching the *kinds of good* that are actually enjoyed in this world and indefinitely perpetuating the *goods of this kind*.

Talking about species is useful. It points to significant regularities in nature. A species, *pace* Rolston (Rolston, p. 21), is not *a* process. Instead, naming a species points importantly to a large *set* of vital processes actually going on in nature. In that way species-talk is like natural-law-talk. Neither kind is entity-talk. That philosophical path leads to the ballooning of ontology beyond necessity. Why, then, should some, like Rolston, engage in it? I suggest that misplaced concreteness is tolerated so that species and ecosystems can be presented as independent value-loci. Thus the metaphysical issue about the status of entities quickly draws us into axiology and ethics.

Ethics

Axiology, as theory of value, occupies the border between metaphysics and ethics. Here, too, the binary bias is easy to find. In our papers it has been presented as a choice between *either* 'subjectivism' *or* 'objectivism' with regard to loci of fundamental (vs. derivative) value. Robert Elliot tries to get around the choice by affirming subjectivism, and human-centred subjectivism at that, in his theory of value; but attempts to avoid objectionable human chauvinism by allowing for normative (human) 'attribution' of intrinsic value to nonhuman loci (Elliot, p. 33). This fails, however, because for him the only *real* ground of values in the universe remains human subjects. Take away the human race, and there are no more normative 'attributed' intrinsic values left in the world. We are left with *either* human subjectivities *or* no values at all.

Holmes Rolston embraces the dichotomy and argues for an 'objectivism' in which values float free from any valuers at all. He realizes that this will seem as unintelligible as talking about 'thoughts without a thinker', or 'percepts without a perceiver', or 'deeds without a doer' (Rolston, p. 29); but he sees no acceptable alternative to grasping this nettle, unintelligible or not, since the only alternative he sees is anthropogenic subjectivism of Elliot's sort. For Rolston it comes down to *either* 'values without a valuer' (whatever that may mean) *or* 'valuing is felt preferring by *human* choosers' (Rolston, p. 29, emphasis added).

The problem, from my viewpoint, is unwarranted bullying by

the binary bias. I believe, with Elliot but against Rolston, that there is no logically intelligible alternative to sticking to the 'old paradigm'. There are indeed no values without a valuer. In that I am an unembarrassed subjectivist. But I believe, with Rolston and against Elliot, that the world is made up of entities with real intrinsic value, not only throughout the biotic realm but also, with Keekok Lee, even the abiotic world. In this I am an unrepentant objectivist. I feel myself close to Attfield at this point, at least through the biotic realm, where he says: 'I maintain that intrinsic value of this [objectivist] kind attaches to the flourishing of living creatures' (Attfield, p. 57); however, I lose him when he adds, astonishingly, 'even in the absence of all valuers both actual and possible'. On my view the 'flourishing creatures' *are* actual valuers.

We need not grant final incompatibility between what is importantly right in subjectivism (that values entail a valuer) and what is essential in objectivism (that the realm of nonderivative values extends vastly far beyond *human* subjects). There is no need for an either-or because, to some degree, there is an interiority, a 'for-itselfness', to every actual entity. Unlike Lee, however, who seems to think that mere 'in-itselfness' establishes value (Lee, p. 96), I would rest my case for nonderivative value in nature on homologues of human 'for-itselfness', in many attenuated degrees (measured by neurological and behavioural evidence) through the biotic world, and in greatly attenuated degree in the tiny nonliving organisms that cluster and recluster, constantly reaffirming their energetic patterning, through the abiotic world. A 'nonliving organism', on my understanding of organism (following Whitehead), is no contradiction in terms.

This brings me to the last topic on which I shall touch. If there is no need to be bullied into choosing between subjectivism *or* objectivism in value-theory, there is equally no need to make an 'either-or' normative choice between anthropocentrism *or* biocentrism, i.e., in the language of my paper, between Personalism *or* Organicism. With Robert Elliot, I find it impossibly 'grotesque' to think of humanity as 'just another species' (Elliot, p. 42). And with Mary Midgley, I argue that what I called 'perspectival anthropocentrism' is inevitable and perfectly licit (Midgley, p. 103; Ferré, p. 72). Moreover, although we are right to be anguished and outraged about what humans have done to harm our earth, there is no point in feigning that we are not distinctly human (Ferré, p. 72); indeed, as Midgley says, 'people do right, not wrong, to have a particular regard for their own kin and their own species' (Midgley, p. 111).

Frederick Ferré

Nevertheless we are organisms, too, and properly in solidarity with all that that means. One thing it means is that we do wrong to continue our magisterial alienation from the rest of the organic world. We need to learn in new modes of ethical holism what organic interconnectedness means for human persons. That way we avoid the negative implications of the 'individualism' that Rolston rightly warns against, without at the same time becoming 'careless' (Rolston, p. 22) with individual persons. But if the world is made of entities in real, internal relation to one another, 'individualism' of this negative, destructive sort is an aberration caused by the abstraction of our valuable personal selves from real connection with other valuable personal selves and from other non-personal centres of real value in the ever-widening environment, without which we would not be what or who we are.

I end where Mary Midgley also ends: with an appeal for less egoism, chauvinism, narrowness of sympathy, and for greater effort by philosophers to forge 'the ways of thinking' that will help us to do something about this (Midgley, p. 112). A good heuristic in this enterprise, I believe, would be to face and fight the binary bias, the instant all-or-nothing fallacy, the reflex either-or syndrome, wherever these rise to tempt us into premature disjunction.

Bibliography

Almond, Brenda 1990. 'Alasdair MacIntyre: the virtue of tradition', *Journal of Applied Philosophy* 7, 99–103

Aristotle 1985. *Nicomachean Ethics*, trans. Terence Irwin. Indianapolis: Hackett

Attfield, Robin 1981. 'The good of trees', *Journal of Value Inquiry* 15, 35–54

Attfield, Robin 1983. 'Western traditions and environmental ethics', in Robert Elliot and Arran Gare (eds.), *Environmental Philosophy*. Milton Keynes: Open University Press, 201–230

Attfield, Robin 1987. *A Theory of Value and Obligation*. London: Croom Helm

Attfield, Robin 1991. *The Ethics of Environmental Concern* (2nd ed.). Athens, GA and London: University of Georgia Press

Attfield, Robin 1992. 'Claims, interests and environmental concern', in C.C.W. Taylor (ed.), *Ethics and the Environment*. Oxford: Corpus Christi College, 84–89

Attfield, Robin 1993. 'Sylvan, Fox and deep ecology: a view from the continental shelf', *Environmental Values* 2, 21–32

Attfield, Robin 1994a. 'Has the history of philosophy ruined the environment?', in Robin Attfield, *Environmental Philosophy: Principles and Prospects*. Aldershot: Avebury, 77–87

Attfield, Robin 1994b. 'The comprehensive ecology movement', in Robin Attfield, *Environmental Philosophy: Principles and Prospects*. Aldershot: Avebury, 203–220

Attfield, Robin and Dell, Katharine 1989. *Values, Conflict and the Environment*. Oxford: Ian Ramsey Centre, and Cardiff: Centre for Applied Ethics

Bahro, Rudolf 1986. *Building the Green Movement*. London: GMP

Barnaby, Frank (ed.) 1988. *Gaia Peace Atlas*. London: Pan Books

Barnes, Barry and Edge, David 1982. *Science in Context*. Milton Keynes: Open University Press

Barnes, Jonathan 1987. *Early Greek Philosophy*. London: Penguin

Barr, John (ed.) 1971. *The Environmental Handbook: Action Guide for the UK*. London: Ballantine/Friends of the Earth

Barr, John 1972. 'Man and nature: the ecological controversy and the Old Testament', *Bulletin of the John Rylands Library* 55, 9–32

Barrow, John D. and Tipler, Frank J. 1986. *The Anthropic Cosmological Principle*. Oxford: Oxford University Press

Beck, Ulrich 1992. *The Risk Society: Towards a New Modernity*. London: Sage

Beitz, Charles R. 1979. *Political Theory and International Relations*. Princeton, NJ: Princeton University Press

Bell, Daniel 1973. *The Coming of Post-Industrial Society: A Venture in Forecasting*. New York: Basic Books

Bibliography

Benton, Ted 1993. *Natural Relations: Ecology, Animal Rights and Social Justice*. London: Verso

Berry, Wendell 1990. *What are People For?* London: Rider Books

Birch, Charles and Cobb, John B. 1981. *The Liberation of Life*. Cambridge: Cambridge University Press

Bishop, David 1990. 'Genetically engineered insecticides: the development of environmentally acceptable alternatives to chemical insecticides', in Peter R. Wheale and Ruth McNally (eds.), *The Bio-Revolution: Cornucopia or Pandora's Box?* London: Pluto, 115–134

Blackstone, William T. (ed.) 1974. *Philosophy and Environmental Crisis*. Athens, GA: University of Georgia Press

Bookchin, Murray 1980. *Toward an Ecological Society*. Montreal: Black Rose Books

Boulding, Kenneth E. 1964. *Meaning of the Twentieth Century*. New York: Harper and Row

Bowers, John 1990. *Economics of the Environment*. Telford: British Association of Nature Conservationists

Bradley, F.H. 1876. *Ethical Studies*. Oxford: Clarendon Press

Brennan, Andrew 1988. *Thinking About Nature: An Investigation of Nature, Value and Ecology*. London: Routledge

Broadie, Alexander and Pybus, Elizabeth 1974. 'Kant's treatment of animals', *Philosophy* 49, 375–383

Bryant, Bunyan and Mohai, Paul (eds.) 1992. *Race and the Incidence of Environmental Hazards*. Boulder, CO: Westview Press

Bryant, Christopher G.A. and Jary, David (eds.) 1991. *Giddens' Theory of Structuration*. London: Routledge

Butler, Joseph 1969. *Butler's Sermons*, ed. W.R. Matthews. London: Bell

Callenbach, Ernest 1978. *Ecotopia*. London: Pluto Press

Callicott, J. Baird 1980. 'Animal liberation: a triangular affair', *Environmental Ethics* 2, 311–338

Callicott, J. Baird 1984. 'Non-anthropocentric value theory and environmental ethics', *American Philosophical Quarterly* 21, 299–309

Callicott, J. Baird 1986. 'On the intrinsic value of nonhuman species', in Bryan G. Norton (ed.), *The Preservation of Species*. Princeton, NJ: Princeton University Press, 138–172

Callicott, J. Baird 1989. *In Defense of the Land Ethic*. Albany: State University of New York Press

Callicott, J. Baird 1991. 'The wilderness idea revisited: the sustainable development alternative', *The Environmental Professional* 13, 235–247

Callicott, J. Baird 1992. 'La nature est morte, vive la nature!', *Hastings Centre Report* 22(5), 16–23

Callicott, J. Baird 1993. 'The search for an environmental ethic', in Tom Regan (ed.), *Matters of Life and Death* (3rd ed.). New York: McGraw-Hill, 322–382

Chesterton, G.K. 1917. *Short History of England*. London: Chatto and Windus

Chesterton, G.K. 1923. *St Francis of Assisi*. London: Hodder and Stoughton

Chesterton, G.K. 1933. *St Thomas Aquinas*. London: Hodder and Stoughton

Chisholm, Roderick M. 1986. *Brentano and Intrinsic Value*. Cambridge: Cambridge University Press

Clark, John *et al*. 1984. 'Long waves, inventions, and innovations', in Christopher Freeman (ed.), *Long Waves in the World Economy*. London: Frances Pinter, 63–77

Clark, Stephen R.L. 1989. *Civil Peace and Sacred Order*. Oxford: Clarendon Press

Clark, Stephen R.L. 1992a. 'Descartes' debt to Augustine', in Michael McGhee (ed.), *Philosophy, Religion and the Spiritual Life*. Cambridge: Cambridge University Press, 73–88

Clark, Stephen R.L. 1992b. 'Orwell and the anti-realists', *Philosophy* 67, 141–154

Clark, Stephen R.L. 1993. *How to Think about the Earth*. London: Mowbray

Clayton, Tony 1991. 'The reality of sustainability', *ECOS* 12(4), 8–14

Clegg, Stewart R. 1989. *Frameworks of Power*. London: Sage

Cobb, John B. 1982. *Process Theology as Political Theology*. Manchester: Manchester University Press

Cohen, Carl 1971. *Civil Disobedience: Conscience, Tactics, and the Law*. New York: Columbia University Press

Commoner, Barry 1972. *The Closing Circle: Nature, Man, and Technology*. New York: Bantam Books

Cooper, David E. 1992. 'The idea of environment', in David E. Cooper and Joy A. Palmer (eds.), *The Environment in Question*. London: Routledge, 163–180

Cooper, David E. and Palmer, Joy A. (eds.) 1992. *The Environment in Question*. London: Routledge

Cowell, C. Mark 1993. 'Ecological restoration and environmental ethics', *Environmental Ethics* 15, 19–32

Craig, Edward 1987. *The Mind of God and the Works of Man*. Oxford: Clarendon Press

Crisp, Roger 1994a. 'Aristotle's inclusivism', *Oxford Studies in Ancient Philosophy* 12 (forthcoming)

Crisp, Roger 1994b. 'Naturalism and non-naturalism in ethics', in Sabina Lovibond and Stephen Williams (eds.), *Substance, Values, Truth*. Oxford: Blackwell (forthcoming)

D'Agostino, Fred 1993. 'Transcendence and conversation: two conceptions of objectivity', *American Philosophical Quarterly* 30, 87–108

Daly, Herman E. 1991. 'Population and economics: a bioeconomic analysis', *Population and Environment* 12, 257–263

Davies, Paul and Gribbin, John 1992. *The Matter Myth: Beyond Chaos and Complexity*. London: Penguin

Descartes, René 1970. *Philosophical Letters*, ed. A.J.P. Kenny. Oxford: Clarendon Press

Devall, Bill and Sessions, George 1985. *Deep Ecology: Living as if Nature Mattered*. Salt Lake City: Gibbs M. Smith

Bibliography

Diamandopoulos, P. 1967. 'Chaos and cosmos', in Paul Edwards (ed.), *Encyclopaedia of Philosophy*, vol. 2, 80–81

Dobson, Andrew 1990. *Green Political Thought*. London: Unwin Hyman

Ehrlich, Paul R., Ehrlich, Anne H. and Holdren, John P. 1977. *Ecoscience: Population, Resources, Environment*. San Francisco: W.H. Freeman

Elliot, Robert 1978. 'Regan on the sorts of beings that can have rights', *Southern Journal of Philosophy* 16, 701–705

Elliot, Robert 1982. 'Faking nature', *Inquiry* 25, 81–93

Elliot, Robert 1983. 'The value of wild nature', *Inquiry* 26, 359–361

Elliot, Robert 1984. 'Rawlsian justice and non-human animals', *Journal of Applied Philosophy* 1, 95–106

Elliot, Robert 1985. 'Meta-ethics and environmental ethics', *Metaphilosophy* 16, 103–117

Elliot, Robert 1989. 'Environmental degradation, vandalism and the aesthetic object argument', *Australasian Journal of Philosophy* 67, 191–204

Elliot, Robert 1992. 'Intrinsic value, environmental obligation and naturalness', *Monist* 75, 138–160

Elliot, Robert 1994. 'Extinction, restoration, naturalness', *Environmental Ethics* 16 (forthcoming)

Feinberg, Joel 1973. *Social Philosophy*. Englewood Cliffs, NJ: Prentice-Hall

Ferré, Frederick 1976. *Shaping the Future: Resources for the Postmodern World*. New York: Harper and Row

Ferré, Frederick 1982. 'Religious world modelling and postmodern science', *Journal of Religion* 62, 261–271

Ferré, Frederick 1988. *Philosophy of Technology*. Englewood Cliffs, NJ: Prentice Hall

Ferré, Frederick 1989. 'Obstacles on the path to organismic ethics: some second thoughts', *Environmental Ethics* 11, 231–241

Ferré, Frederick 1993a. *Hellfire and Lightning Rods: Liberating Science, Technology, and Religion*. Maryknoll, NY: Orbis Books

Ferré, Frederick 1993b. 'Making waves: on the social power of ideas', presented at the Annual Meeting of the Tenth International Social Philosophy Conference, University of Helsinki, Finland (unpublished paper)

Foot, Philippa 1988. 'Utilitarianism and the virtues', in Samuel Scheffler (ed.), *Consequentialism and its Critics*. Oxford: Oxford University Press, 224–242

Foricy, R. 1982. *Wind and Sea Obey Him*. London: SCM

Foucault, Michel 1973. *The Order of Things: An Archaeology of the Human Sciences*. New York: Vintage

Foucault, Michel 1975. *The Birth of the Clinic*. New York: Vintage

Fox, Matthew 1991. *Creation Spirituality*. San Francisco: Harper

Fox, Warwick 1986. *Approaching Deep Ecology*. Hobart: University of Tasmania Press

Frankena, William K. 1973. *Ethics*. Englewood Cliffs, NJ: Prentice-Hall

Frankena, William K. 1979. 'Ethics and the environment', in Kenneth E. Goodpaster and Kenneth M. Sayre (eds.), *Ethics and Problems of the 21st Century*. Notre Dame and London: University of Notre Dame Press, 3–20

Freud, Sigmund 1985. *Civilization and its Discontents*, in *Civilization, Society and Religion* (Pelican Freud Library, vol. 12). London: Penguin

Gallant, Roy A. 1980. *Our Universe*. Washington, DC: National Geographic Society

Gershon, Elliot S. 1983. 'Should science be stopped? The case of recombinant DNA research', *Public Interest* 71, 3–16

Giddens, Anthony 1979. *Central Problems in Social Theory*. London: Macmillan

Giddens, Anthony 1990. *The Consequences of Modernity*. Cambridge: Polity Press

Giddens, Anthony 1991. *Modernity and Self-Identity*. Cambridge: Polity Press

Glacken, Clarence J. 1967. *Traces on the Rhodian Shore: Nature and Culture in Western Thought from Ancient Times to the End of the Eighteenth Century*. Berkeley and London: University of California Press

Glantz, Michael M. (ed.) 1990. *On Assessing Winners and Losers in the Context of Global Warming* (Report of a Workshop, 18–21 June 1990, St Julians, Malta). Boulder, CO: National Centre for Atmospheric Research, Environmental and Societal Impacts Group

Goodin, Robert E. 1992. *Green Political Theory*. Cambridge: Polity Press

Goodpaster, Kenneth E. 1978. 'On being morally considerable', *Journal of Philosophy* 75, 308–25

Goodpaster, Kenneth E. 1979. 'From egoism to environmentalism', in Kenneth E. Goodpaster and Kenneth M. Sayre (eds.), *Ethics and Problems of the 21st Century*. Notre Dame: University of Notre Dame Press

Goodpaster, Kenneth E. and Sayre, Kenneth M. (eds.) 1979. *Ethics and Problems of the 21st Century*. Notre Dame and London: University of Notre Dame Press

Gore, Al 1992. *Earth in the Balance: Ecology and the Human Spirit*. Boston: Houghton Mifflin

Gregory, David 1989. 'Presences and absences: time-space relations and structuration theory', in David Held and John B. Thompson (eds.), *Social Theory of Modern Societies: Anthony Giddens and his Critics*. Cambridge: Cambridge University Press, 185–214

Griffin, James 1986. *Well-Being*. Oxford: Clarendon Press

Gruen, Lori and Jamieson, Dale (eds.) 1994. *Reflecting on Nature: Readings in Environmental Philosophy*. New York: Oxford University Press

Gunn, Alastair S. 1991. 'The restoration of species and natural environments', *Environmental Ethics* 13, 291–310

Habermas, Jürgen 1982. 'A reply to my critics', in John B. Thompson and David Held (eds.), *Habermas: Critical Debates*. London: Macmillan

Hand, Seán (ed.) 1989. *The Levinas Reader*. Oxford: Blackwell

Hare, R.M. 1963. *Freedom and Reason*. Oxford: Oxford University Press

Hargrove, Eugene C. (ed.) 1986. *Beyond Spaceship Earth: Environmental Ethics and the Solar System*. San Francisco: Sierra Club Books

Hargrove, Eugene C. 1989. *Foundations of Environmental Ethics*. Englewood Cliffs, NJ: Prentice-Hall

Hargrove, Eugene C. 1992. 'Weak anthropocentric intrinsic value', *Monist* 75, 183–207

Harrison, Fraser 1982. *Strange Land*. London: Sidgwick and Jackson

Hart, H.L.A. 1973. 'Bentham on legal rights', in A.W.B. Simpson (ed.), *Oxford Essays in Jurisprudence* (2nd series). Oxford: Oxford University Press, 171–201

Hawkes, Nigel 1993. 'Greening the Red Planet', *Geographical Magazine*, February 1993, 20–23

Hayward, Tim 1992. 'Ecology and human emancipation', *Radical Philosophy* 62, 3–13

Heller, Agnes and Feher, Ferenc 1988. *The Postmodern Political Condition*. Cambridge: Polity Press

Hepburn, R.W. 1984. 'Contemporary aesthetics and the neglect of natural beauty', in R.W. Hepburn, *Wonder and Other Essays*. Edinburgh: Edinburgh University Press

Hobbes, Thomas 1651. *Leviathan*, ed. Richard Tuck. Cambridge: Cambridge University Press, 1992

Hoff, Christina 1983. 'Kant's invidious humanism', *Environmental Ethics* 5, 63–70

Hohfeld, Wesley N. 1919. *Fundamental Legal Conceptions as Applied in Judicial Reasoning*. New Haven and London: Yale University Press

Hume, David 1962. *Enquiries Concerning Human Understanding and Concerning the Principles of Morals*, ed. L.A. Selby-Bigge. Oxford: Clarendon Press

Hurka, Thomas 1987a. '"Good" and "good for"', *Mind* 96, 71–73

Hurka, Thomas 1987b. 'The well-rounded life', *Journal of Philosophy* 84, 727–746

Jacobs, Michael 1990. *The Green Economy*. London: Pluto

James, William 1925. *The Varieties of Religious Experience*. New York: Longmans, Green

Jamieson, Dale 1992a. 'Ethics, public policy and global warming', *Science, Technology and Human Values* 17, 139–153; reprinted in Earl Winkler and Jerrold R. Coombes (eds.), *Applied Ethics: A Reader*. Oxford: Blackwell, 1993

Jamieson, Dale 1992b. 'From Baghdad to Rio: reflections on environmental values and behavior' (unpublished paper)

Jamieson, Dale 1993. 'Ethics and animals: a brief review', *Journal of Agricultural and Environmental Ethics* 6, Special Supplement 1, 15–20

Johnson, Lawrence E. 1991. *A Morally Deep World*. Cambridge: Cambridge University Press

Kant, Immanuel 1928. *Critique of Teleological Judgment*, trans. J.C. Meredith. Oxford: Clarendon Press

Kant, Immanuel 1948. *The Moral Law: Kant's Groundwork of the Metaphysics of Morals*, trans. H.J. Paton. London: Hutchinson

Kant, Immanuel 1949. *The Philosophy of Kant: Immanuel Kant's Moral and Political Writings*, ed. Carl J. Friedrich. New York: Random House

Kant, Immanuel 1963. *Lectures on Ethics*, trans. Louis Infield. New York: Harper and Row.

Kant, Immanuel 1964. *The Doctrine of Virtue*, trans. Mary J. Gregor. New York: Harper and Row

Katz, Eric 1992a. 'The big lie: human restoration of nature', *Research in Philosophy and Technology* 12, 231–241

Katz, Eric 1992b. 'The call of the wild', *Environmental Ethics* 14, 265–273

Kelley, Kevin W. (ed.) 1988. *The Home Planet*. Reading, MA: Addison-Wesley

Khalid, Fazlun W. and O'Brien, Joanne (eds.) 1992. *Islam and Ecology*. London: Cassell

Kipling, Rudyard 1927. *Verse 1885–1926*. London: Hodder and Stoughton

Kirk, G.S., Raven, J.E. and Schofield, M. 1983. *The Presocratic Philosophers*. Cambridge: Cambridge University Press

Koestler, Arthur 1978. *Janus*. London: Hutchinson

Kohák, Erazim 1984. *The Embers and the Stars*. Chicago: University of Chicago Press

Korsgaard, Christine 1983. 'Two distinctions in goodness', *Philosophical Review* 92, 169–195

Krimsky, Sheldon 1982. *Genetic Alchemy: The Social History of the Recombinant DNA Controversy*. Cambridge, MA: MIT Press

Lakatos, Imre and Musgrave, Alan (eds.) 1970. *Criticism and the Growth of Knowledge*. Cambridge: Cambridge University Press

Lash, Scott and Urry, John 1987. *The End of Organised Capitalism*. Cambridge: Polity Press

Leopold, Aldo 1966. *A Sand County Almanac*. New York: Oxford University Press

Lessing, Doris 1981. *The Sirian Experiments*. London: Cape

Lewis, David 1989. 'Dispositional theories of value', *Proceedings of the Aristotelian Society, Supplementary Volume* 63, 113–137

List, Peter (ed.) 1993. *Radical Environmentalism: Philosophy and Tactics*. Belmont, CA: Wadsworth

Llewellyn, O. 1992. 'Desert reclamation and conservation in Islamic law', in Fazlun W. Khalid and Joanne O'Brien (eds.), *Islam and Ecology*. London: Cassell, 87–97

Locke, John 1963. *Two Treatises of Government*, ed. Peter Laslett. Cambridge: Cambridge University Press

Lovelock, James 1988. *The Ages of Gaia*. Oxford: Oxford University Press

Luhmann, Niklas 1986. 'The autopoiesis of social systems', in R. Felix Geyer and Johannes van der Zouen (eds.), *Sociocybernetic Paradoxes:*

Bibliography

Observation, Control and Evolution of Self-Steering Systems. London: Sage, 171–192

Luhmann, Niklas 1989. 'Law as a social system', *Northwestern University Law Review* 83, 136–150

Lyotard, Jean-François 1986. *The Post-Modern Condition: A Report on Knowledge*. Manchester: Manchester University Press

Mackie, J.L. 1977. *Ethics: Inventing Right and Wrong*. London: Penguin

Macmurray, John 1961. *Persons in Relation*. New York: Harper

Mannison, Don, McRobbie, Michael and Routley, Richard (eds.) 1980. *Environmental Philosophy*. Canberra: Research School of Social Sciences, Australian National University

Marshall, Alan 1993. 'Ethics and the extraterrestrial environment', *Journal of Applied Philosophy* 10, 227–236

Marshall, Peter 1992. *Nature's Web: An Exploration of Ecological Thinking*. London: Simon and Schuster

Martin, Michael 1990. 'Ecosabotage and civil disobedience', *Environmental Ethics* 12, 291–310

Marx, Karl 1971. *Marx's Grundrisse*, ed. David McLellan. London: Macmillan

Mayr, Ernst 1988. *Towards A New Philosophy of Biology*. Cambridge, MA: Harvard University Press

Mazri, Al-Hafiz B.A. 1992. 'Islam and ecology', in Fazlun W. Khalid and Joanne O'Brien (eds.), *Islam and Ecology*. London: Cassell, 1–23

McCloskey, H.J. 1983. *Ecological Ethics and Politics*. Totowa, NJ: Rowman and Littlefield

McIntosh, Robert 1985. *The Background of Ecology: Concept and Theory*. Cambridge: Cambridge University Press

McLennan, Gregor 1990. 'The temporal and the temporizing in structuration theory', in Jon Clark, Celia Modgil and Sohan Modgil (eds.), *Anthony Giddens: Consensus and Controversy*. London: Falmer Press, 131–139

McNally, Ruth 1993. *A Foucauldian Analysis of Abortion for Foetal Handicap* (unpublished MA Dissertation, Brunel University)

McNally, Ruth and Wheale, Peter R. 1986. 'Recombinant DNA technology: re-assessing the risks', *Science, Technology and Society Association Newsletter* 25, 56–69

McNally, Ruth and Wheale, Peter R. 1991. *The Environmental Consequences of Genetically Engineered Viral Vaccines*. Brussels: Commission of the European Communities, DG XI, Contract No. B6614/89/91

Merchant, Carolyn 1982. *The Death of Nature*. London: Wildwood House

Merchant, Carolyn 1990. 'Environmental ethics and political conflict: a view from California', *Environmental Ethics* 12, 45–68

Midgley, Mary 1978. *Beast and Man: The Roots of Human Nature*. Ithaca, NY: Cornell University Press

Midgley, Mary 1983. *Animals and Why they Matter*. Athens, GA: University of Georgia Press

Midgley, Mary 1992. *Science as Salvation*. London: Routledge

Mill, John Stuart 1874. 'Nature', in J.S. Mill, *Three Essays on Religion*. New York: Greenwood Press, 1969, 3–65

Monod, Jacques 1972. *Chance and Necessity: An Essay on the Natural Philosophy of Modern Biology*. New York: Vintage

Moore, G.E. 1903. *Principia Ethica*. Cambridge: Cambridge University Press

Moore, G.E. 1922. 'The conception of intrinsic value', in G.E. Moore, *Philosophical Studies*. London: Routledge and Kegan Paul, 253–275

Morrison, Darrel 1987. 'Landscape restoration in response to previous disturbances', in Monica G. Turner (ed.), *Landscape Heterogeneity and Disturbance*. New York: Springer

Mulkay, Michael J. 1979. *Science and the Sociology of Knowledge*. London: Allen and Unwin

Murdoch, Iris 1970. *The Sovereignty of Good*. London: Routledge

Naess, Arne 1973. 'The shallow and the deep, long-range ecology movement. A summary', *Inquiry* 16, 95–100

Naess, Arne 1989. *Ecology, Community and Lifestyle: Outline of an Ecosophy*, trans. and ed. David Rothenberg. Cambridge: Cambridge University Press

Nagel, Thomas 1986. *The View From Nowhere*. Oxford: Oxford University Press

National Anti-Vivisection Society 1987. *Bio-Hazard*. London: National Anti-Vivisection Society

Nature Conservancy Council 1989. *Guidelines for Selection of Biological SSSIs*. Peterborough: Belmont

Norton, Bryan G. (ed.) 1986. *The Preservation of Species*. Princeton, NJ: Princeton University Press

Norton, Bryan G. 1991. *Toward Unity Among Environmentalists*. New York: Oxford University Press

Norton, Bryan G. 1992. 'Sustainability, human welfare and ecosystem health', *Environmental Values* 2, 97–111

Nozick, Robert 1974. *Anarchy, State and Utopia*. New York: Basic Books

O'Neill, John 1992. 'The varieties of intrinsic value', *Monist* 75, 119–137

O'Neill, Onora 1989. *Constructions of Reason: Explorations of Kant's Practical Philosophy*. Cambridge: Cambridge University Press

Pagden, Anthony 1982. *The Fall of Natural Man*. Cambridge: Cambridge University Press

Passmore, John 1980. *Man's Responsibility for Nature* (2nd ed.). London: Duckworth

Pearce, David (ed.) 1991. *Blueprint 2*. London: Earthscan

Pearce, David, Markandya, Anil and Barbier, Edward B. 1989. *Blueprint for a Green Economy* [*Blueprint 1*]. London: Earthscan

Pezzey, John 1992. 'Sustainability: an interdisciplinary guide', *Environmental Values* 1, 321–362

Pogge, Thomas W. 1989. *Realizing Rawls*. Ithaca, NY: Cornell University Press

Bibliography

Porter, Roy 1981. 'Environment', in W.F. Bynum, E.J. Brown and Roy Porter (eds.), *Dictionary of the History of Science*. London: Macmillan, 124–125

Prall, David 1921. *A Study in the Theory of Value*. Berkeley, CA: University of California Press

Price, H.H. 1962. *Thinking and Experience*. Cambridge, MA: Harvard University Press

Putnam, Hilary 1987. *The Many Faces of Realism*. La Salle, IL: Open Court

Rawls, John 1971. *A Theory of Justice*. Cambridge, MA: Harvard University Press

Read, Herbert 1940. *The Philosophy of Anarchism*. London: Freedom Press

Regan, Tom 1983. *The Case for Animal Rights*. Berkeley: University of California Press

Regan, Tom 1990. 'Christianity and animal rights: the challenge and promise', in Charles Birch, William Eakin, and Jay B. McDaniel (eds.), *Liberating Life: Contemporary Approaches to Ecological Theology*. Maryknoll, NY: Orbis Books, 73–87

Regan, Tom and Singer, Peter (eds.) 1976. *Animal Rights and Human Obligations*. Englewood Cliffs, NJ: Prentice-Hall

Richards, Graham 1989. *On Psychological Language*. London: Routledge

Rolston, Holmes, III 1975. 'Is there an ecological ethic?', *Ethics* 85, 93–109

Rolston, Holmes, III 1986a. *Philosophy Gone Wild*. Buffalo: Prometheus Books

Rolston, Holmes, III 1986b. 'The preservation of natural value in the solar system', in Eugene C. Hargrove (ed.), *Beyond Spaceship Earth: Environmental Ethics and the Solar System*. San Francisco: Sierra Club Books

Rolston, Holmes, III 1988. *Environmental Ethics: Duties to and Values in the Natural World*. Philadelphia: Temple University Press

Rolston, Holmes, III 1991. 'The wilderness idea reaffirmed', *The Environmental Professional* 13, 370–377

Routley [now Sylvan], Richard and Routley [now Plumwood], Val 1980. 'Human chauvinism and environmental ethics', in Don Mannison, Michael McRobbie and Richard Routley (eds.), *Environmental Philosophy*. Canberra: Research School of Social Sciences, Australian National University, 96–189

Royal College of Physicians 1989. *Prenatal Diagnosis and Genetic Screening: Community and Service Implications*. London: Royal College of Physicians

Ryder, Richard D. 1989. *Animal Revolution: Changing Attitudes Towards Speciesism*. Oxford: Blackwell

Ryder, Richard D. 1992. *Painism: Ethics, Animal Rights and Environmentalism*. Cardiff: Centre for Applied Ethics

Saunders, Paul 1989. 'Space, urbanism and the created environment', in David Held and John B. Thompson (eds.), *Social Theory of Modern*

Societies: Anthony Giddens and his Critics. Cambridge: Cambridge University Press, 215–234

Scarce, Rik 1990. *Eco-Warriors: Understanding the Radical Environmental Movement*. Chicago: The Noble Press

Schelling, Thomas 1983. 'Climatic change: implications for welfare and policy', in *Changing Climate: Report of the Carbon Dioxide Assessment Committee*. Washington: National Academy Press

Seed, J., Fleming, P., Macy, J. and Naess, A. 1988. *Thinking Like a Mountain: Towards a Council of All Beings*. London: Heretic Books

Sen, Amartya 1979. 'Utilitarianism and welfarism', *Journal of Philosophy* 75, 463–489

Sessions, George 1979. 'Spinoza, perennial philosophy and deep ecology' (unpublished paper)

Shrader-Frechette, Kristin 1993. 'Problems with ecosystemic criteria for land policy', in Lynton Caldwell and Kristin Shrader-Frechette, *Policy for Land Law and Ethics*. Lanham, MD: Rowman and Littlefield

Sidgwick, Henry 1907. *The Methods of Ethics*. London: Macmillan

Singer, Peter 1976. 'All animals are equal', in Tom Regan and Peter Singer (eds.), *Animal Rights and Human Obligations*. Englewood Cliffs, NJ: Prentice-Hall

Singer, Peter 1979. *Practical Ethics*. Cambridge: Cambridge University Press

Singer, Peter 1986. *Animal Liberation: A New Ethics for Our Treatment of Animals*. London: Jonathan Cape

Smart, Barry 1993. *Postmodernity*. London: Routledge

Sober, Elliott 1986. 'Philosophical problems for environmentalism', in Bryan G. Norton (ed.), *The Preservation of Species*. Princeton, NJ: Princeton University Press, 173–194

Soskice, Janet Martin 1985. *Metaphor and Religious Language*. Oxford: Clarendon Press

Starhawk 1984. *The Spiral Dance*. New York: Harper and Row

Stewart, Ian 1990. *Does God Play Dice? The New Mathematics of Chaos*. London: Penguin

Sylvan, Richard 1988. 'Mucking with nature' (unpublished paper, c. 1988)

Sylvan, Richard 1990. *Universal Purpose, Terrestrial Greenhouse and Biological Evolution*. Canberra: Research School of Social Sciences, Australian National University

Sylvan, Richard 1992. 'Mucking with nature' (unpublished paper, c. 1992)

Taylor, Paul W. 1981. 'The ethics of respect for nature', *Environmental Ethics* 3, 197–218

Taylor, Paul W. 1986. *Respect for Nature*. Princeton, NJ: Princeton University Press

Thompson, Janna 1990. 'A refutation of environmental ethics', *Environmental Ethics* 12, 147–60

Thomson, Judith Jarvis 1990. *The Realm of Rights*. Cambridge, MA: Harvard University Press

Bibliography

Toynbee, Arnold and Ikeda, Daisaku 1976. *Choose Life*. London: Oxford University Press

Turner, Kerry and Pearce, David 1993. 'Sustainable economic development: economic and ethical principles', in Edward B. Barbier (ed.), *Economics and Ecology: New Frontiers and Sustainable Development*. London: Chapman and Hall, 177–194

Turner, Monica G. (ed.) 1987. *Landscape Heterogeneity and Disturbance*. New York: Springer

Urry, John 1991. 'Time and space in Giddens' social theory', in Christopher G.A. Bryant and David Jary (eds.), *Giddens' Theory of Structuration*. London: Routledge, 160–175

Vlastos, Gregory 1975. *Plato's Universe*. Oxford: Clarendon Press

Watson, Paul 1982. *Sea Shepherd: My Fight for Whales and Seals*. New York: Norton

Watson, Richard A. 1983. 'A critique of anti-anthropocentric biocentrism', *Environmental Ethics* 5, 245–256

Wheale, Peter R. and McNally, Ruth 1986. 'Patent trend analysis: the case of microgenetic engineering', *Futures* 18, 638–657

Wheale, Peter R. and McNally, Ruth 1988a. *Genetic Engineering: Catastrophe or Utopia?* London: Wheatsheaf

Wheale, Peter R. and McNally, Ruth 1988b. 'Technology assessment of a gene therapy', *Project Appraisal* 3, 199–204

Wheale, Peter R. and McNally, Ruth (eds.) 1990a. *The Bio-Revolution: Cornucopia or Pandora's Box?* London: Pluto

Wheale, Peter R. and McNally, Ruth 1990b. 'Genetic engineering and environmental protection: a framework for regulatory evaluation', *Project Appraisal* 5, 23–37

Wheale, Peter R. and McNally, Ruth 1993. 'Biotechnology policy in Europe: a critical evaluation', *Science and Public Policy* 20, 261–279

Wheeler, John A. 1983. 'Law without law', in John A. Wheeler and W.H. Zurek (eds.), *Quantum Theory and Measurement*. Princeton, NJ: Princeton University Press

White, Lynn 1967. 'The historical roots of our ecologic crisis', *Science* 155, 1203–1207

White, Morton 1978. *The Philosophy of the American Revolution*. New York: Oxford University Press

Whitehead, Alfred North 1929. *The Function of Reason*. Boston, MA: Beacon Press

Whitehouse, David 1993. 'Warm glow for the Red Planet', *The Guardian*, 4 February 1993

Whittaker, R. 1972. 'Evolution and measurement of species diversity', *Taxon* 21, 213–251

Williams, Bernard 1981a. 'Persons, character and morality', in Bernard Williams, *Moral Luck*. Cambridge: Cambridge University Press, 1–19

Williams, Bernard 1981b. 'Internal and external reasons', in Bernard Williams, *Moral Luck*. Cambridge: Cambridge University Press, 101–113

Williams, Bernard 1985. *Ethics and the Limits of Philosophy*. London: Fontana.

Williams, Bernard 1992. 'Must a concern for the environment be centred on human beings?', in C.C.W. Taylor (ed.), *Ethics and the Environment*. Oxford: Corpus Christi College, 60–68

Williams, Raymond 1983. 'Ecology', in Raymond Williams, *Keywords*. London: Flamingo, 110–111

Windelband, Wilhelm 1921. *An Introduction to Philosophy*. London: T. Fisher Unwin

Wittbecker, Alan E. 1986. 'Deep anthropology: ecology and human order', *Environmental Ethics* 8, 261–270

Woodcock, George (ed.) 1977. *The Anarchist Reader*. London: Fontana

World Bank 1992. *World Development Report 1992*. Oxford: Oxford University Press

World Commission on Environment and Development 1987. *Our Common Future* (The Brundtland Report). Oxford: Oxford University Press

Index

Index

Index

WITHDRAWN FROM STOCK QMUL LIBRARY

QMW LIBRARY
(MILE END)

250